ROUTLEDGE LIBRARY EDITIONS: EMPLOYEE OWNERSHIP AND ECONOMIC DEMOCRACY

Volume 1

PEOPLE'S CAPITALISM?

PEOPLE'S CAPITALISM?

A Critical Analysis of Profit-sharing and
Employee Share Ownership

LESLEY BADDON, LAURIE HUNTER,
JEFF HYMAN, JOHN LEOPOLD AND
HARVIE RAMSAY

Routledge
Taylor & Francis Group
LONDON AND NEW YORK

First published in 1989 by Routledge

This edition first published in 2018
by Routledge
2 Park Square, Milton Park, Abingdon, Oxon OX14 4RN

and by Routledge
711 Third Avenue, New York, NY 10017

Routledge is an imprint of the Taylor & Francis Group, an informa business

British Library Cataloguing in Publication Data
A catalogue record for this book is available from the British Library

ISBN: 978-1-138-29962-7 (Set)
ISBN: 978-1-315-12163-5 (Set) (ebk)
ISBN: 978-1-138-56021-5 (Volume 1) (hbk)
ISBN: 978-1-138-56023-9 (Volume 1) (pbk)
ISBN: 978-0-203-71189-7 (Volume 1) (ebk)

Publisher's Note
The publisher has gone to great lengths to ensure the quality of this reprint but points out that some imperfections in the original copies may be apparent.

Disclaimer
The publisher has made every effort to trace copyright holders and would welcome correspondence from those they have been unable to trace.

PEOPLE'S CAPITALISM?

A Critical Analysis of Profit-sharing and Employee
Share Ownership

Lesley Baddon
Laurie Hunter
Jeff Hyman
John Leopold
Harvie Ramsay

Routledge
London and New York

First published 1989
by Routledge
11 New Fetter Lane, London EC4 4EE
29 West 35th Street, New York, NY 10001

Typeset by LaserScript Limited, Mitcham, Surrey.
Printed and bound in Great Britain by
Mackays of Chatham PLC, Chatham, Kent

British Library Cataloguing in Publication Data

Baddon, Lesley
    People's capitalism: a critical analysis of profit-sharing and
    Employee   Share Ownership.
    1. Great Britain. Companies. Personnel. Remuneration.
    Determination. Use of company performance assessment 2. Great
    Britain.
    Shareholding by personnel
    I. Title
    331.2'15
    ISBN 0-415-01357-0

Library of Congress Cataloging in Publication Data

People's capitalism?

    Bibliography: p.
    Includes indexes.
    1. Profit-sharing—Great Britain. 2. Employee ownership—Great
Britain. 3. Industrial relations—Great Britain. I. Baddon, Lesley.
HD3025.A4P46 1989 331.2'164 88-32339
ISBN 0-415-03157-0

Contents

List of tables

vi

List of figures

Foreword

One of the aims of the Conservative government, since it came to office in 1979, has been to expand the base of share ownership as part of a more general philosophy which sets great store on the values of a 'home-owning, share-owning democracy'. An important element in the expansion of share ownership generally has been the advocacy of employees owning shares in the capital of the company that employs them, and this expansion has been aided by a continuation and development of legislation initiated by the last Labour government. Closely associated with the employee share ownership schemes has been a growth of profit-sharing arrangements which may in their own way serve to encourage close links between employees and their employer, and the merits of such an approach have also been a focus of Conservative policy, culminating in legislation granting taxation benefits for approved forms of Profit-related Pay (PRP) schemes.

It was against this emerging and developing background that the project on which this book is based was devised and carried out with the aid of a generous grant from the Leverhulme Trust. The main purposes of the project were threefold: to provide some dimensions on the take-up of profit-sharing and employee share ownership schemes and on the characteristics of companies engaging in these forms of financial participation; to develop, through a case-study approach, a better understanding of the motivation of employers in adopting schemes of financial participation; and to gauge the response of employees to the schemes made available to them by their employers. As explained in the book, the programme of research involved a fairly large-scale postal survey of companies, both with and without financial participation schemes, a second stage in which a number of respondents were interviewed to obtain a better understanding of the motivation for and operation of different kinds of scheme, and a case-study stage which required more in-depth work by interview and survey among management and employees in five selected companies. A postal survey of trade unions was also undertaken.

The research was carried out by a team of academic researchers based in the Centre for Research in Industrial Democracy and Participation in the University of Glasgow, but it involved staff from Stirling and Strathclyde universities also. Team research is, in the best of circumstances, a demanding activity, and in this case the (even limited) geographical and institutional separation inevitably added to the problems of co-ordination and timing. The production of the book, in addition to a series of other papers and publications reporting on specific aspects of the research, reflects strong commitment to the project not only on behalf of the researchers themselves, but on the part of the secretarial and technical staff who contributed throughout. Particular mention in this regard is due to Maureen Robb, for her assistance at all stages of the survey work and the analysis of the data generated; and to Ann Adamson and Janette Schofield (Department of Social and Economic Research, University of Glasgow); Dorothy Anderson and Rachel Haigh (University of Stirling) and Ann Cottrell (Sunderland Polytechnic) for secretarial assistance throughout.

Our thanks also extend to those who participated in responding to our company survey and to the attitude surveys carried out in the case study organizations. We are greatly indebted to those companies who agreed to participate in the case studies and particularly to management staff who patiently answered a great many questions and made arrangements for employee interviews and surveys to be carried out.

Finally, we acknowledge with thanks the contribution made by a number of trade unions who helped us to fill in a necessary part of the picture, the response and reactions of the trade union movement to developments which would seem to pose important questions of tactics and strategy for their organizations.

The very considerable degree of co-operation which we received from so many individuals and organizations would, however, have been to no avail had it not been for the grant from the Leverhulme Trust, and it is to the trustees that the team owes its greatest debt.

Lesley Baddon
Laurie Hunter
Jeff Hyman
John Leopold
Harvie Ramsay

January 1989

Part 1

The profit-sharing debate

1

Introduction to the debate

BACKGROUND

Though the surge of activity in debate and practice over employee participation in organizational decision-making which peaked in the 1970s has subsided to more sober levels, continued interest in the subject has been maintained, but with a somewhat altered focus, reflecting changed political and economic priorities raised during a period of prolonged economic recession and trade union weakness. A significant expression of this change has been the shift in emphasis from representative forms of involvement, typified by the Bullock proposals for the appointment of worker directors, to participative strategies which aim at more direct contact between management and individual employees. A reflection of this approach can be seen in recent pronouncements by the Conservative government encouraging direct communication between organization and individual, linking the development of a shared culture of enterprise and initiative with the rewards which may be anticipated in consequence:

> The Government is completely committed to the principle of employees being informed and consulted about matters which affect them. Our future industrial competitiveness and prosperity depend on both employers and employees having the same belief and commitment to make employee involvement work ... [Gummer, 1984, quoted in Cressey *et al.*, 1985: 7]

Employee involvement can take many forms. In the research reported in this study we are mainly concerned with *financial participation*, which can be divided for our purposes into two broad

3

categories: *profit-sharing*, in which employees are given the opportunity to take some of their income from employment in a form related to the profits of their employer; and *share ownership*, in which employees are enabled to acquire some degree of ownership over the assets of the employer. For reasons that will emerge, this distinction is one that has to be quite firmly drawn from the outset, since the two forms generally have rather different implications for motivation and behaviour within the participative framework.

Though profit-based remuneration has a long history, the take-up of schemes involving a measure of financial participation has historically been low in the United Kingdom, both absolutely and in comparison with some of its industrial competitors. The first identifiable phase of profit-sharing occurred in the middle years of the nineteenth century, when the experience of the Henry Briggs company generated considerable enthusiasm among sympathetic employers. There is little doubt that this initial phase of profit-sharing and its less common share ownership offshoot were introduced primarily as a means to prevent or inhibit union activity: indeed, the Briggs company only turned to its new profit-sharing 'tactic' following the failure of more traditional aggressive tactics in combating union recruitment and activity (Church, 1971: 5). Other schemes launched during this period often masked similar intent: some prohibited 'workmen' from union membership and most restricted bonus entitlements to employees whose individual and collective behaviour was deemed to be satisfactory. A prime consideration for implementing these early schemes was to contain collectivist pressures and for this reason schemes were often withdrawn when profits declined and with them, the threat of union influence.

The late 1880s saw a resurgence of profit-sharing and co-partnership in the form of share allocations with the introduction of eighty-eight schemes between 1889–92, compared with just forty in the previous fifteen years (Bristow, 1974: 274). As with the earlier phase of profit-sharing this revival could be directly associated with the effects of a buoyant economy on employment and consequent labour unrest (Church, 1971: 10), though Bristow also describes how companies would consider financial participation in order to increase productivity and help 'overcome resistance' to new processes of work (Bristow, 1974: p. 279). Discussing the renowned profit-sharing scheme introduced by the Taylor family in 1892 (which continued until 1966) Pollard and

4

Turner (1976) ascribe three main motives to the use of share ownership. Two of these are based on the charitable exercise of moral philanthropy based upon the emotional satisfaction of giving, coupled with empathy towards recipients. The third is the more pragmatic and level-headed concern of its being 'good for business' through promoting 'peace and goodwill' and, in so doing, maintaining control over employees, which in the final analysis, is 'at the core of every profit-sharing scheme' (pp. 10–12). There were further surges of employer enthusiasm for profit-sharing in 1908–9 and in the period immediately prior to the First World War, again, in Church's view, to be considered 'as a method of combating labour unrest' and having 'little to do with philanthropic motive. It was a method of management' (1971: 10).

The inter-war period saw a re-emergence of interest followed by unsteady expansion until 1929 and then slow decline throughout the depression years until the outbreak of war in 1939. In 1938, 399 establishments, covering approximately a quarter of a million participants, had schemes in operation, little more than ten years earlier.

Similar fluctuating patterns typify the post-war period, with a number of profit-sharing and share ownership schemes introduced in the early 1950s apparently being abandoned a few years later.[1] A Ministry of Labour survey indicated that in 1954, 310 schemes were in operation in 297 companies, involving about 350,000 participants. No further surveys were conducted after this time, owing to the small number of schemes continuing to operate. The mean supplement to earnings provided by these schemes was estimated at 6.3 per cent, equivalent to about three weeks' earnings, compared with an average profit-related bonus of 5.3 per cent between 1910 and 1938 (Hanson, 1965: 333). Following the mid-1950s decline, little further interest was shown in this approach to financial participation until the early 1970s (Brannen, 1983: 130), when first Conservative and, later, Liberal policies helped to stimulate the present renaissance.

The fluctuating history of employee profit-share arrangements suggests that such schemes have been implemented for two main purposes; as an act of faith by employers towards their employees, or as a means of securing employee compliance, often through inhibiting collective aspirations and activity. However, even during earlier peaks of employer interest, the number of schemes actually in operation at any one time was never more than a few hundred, confined largely to a limited range of industries such as gas,

5

engineering and chemicals.[2] Indeed, between 1865, the time of the first significant experiment, and the peak year of 1919 a total of only 635 plans had been implemented (Bristow, 1974: 262). A second important feature identified by the various Ministry of Labour reports was the high rate of discontinuation, with financial success probably being the key factor in determining scheme progress (Church, 1971: 13).

Nevertheless, other factors can account for the comparatively low rates of employer endorsement of profit-sharing and share ownership. In recent years, two reasons in particular may be advanced for low take-up: first, that the tax laws provided insufficient incentive for any but the most committed of employers to introduce profit-sharing; second, that political differences between the major parties offered insufficient legislative stability to induce companies to embark upon a possibly costly and probably temporary enterprise where tax incentives introduced by one government might be removed through a change in administration. This happened, for example, in 1974 when the incoming Labour government removed tax advantages from both executive share schemes and all-employee share-option schemes introduced by the Conservatives in the preceding two years.

By the mid-1980s this position had changed considerably, with legislation currently operating in the United Kingdom being described by one group of advocates as:

> the finest employee share scheme legislation in the world ... As a combination set [the main advantages] are unique ... All together there are now no less than eight types of employee share schemes, all of them with some form of tax relief or advantage ... [Copeman *et al.* 1984: 170]

Furthermore, the major political parties have all demonstrated some degree of commitment to employee share ownership: the 1978 Finance Act, which heralded the start of the new participative initiatives, was introduced by the Labour government, albeit with support from the Liberal Party and under pressure from them. Subsequent amendments and further legislation by the Conservative government have confirmed their support, whilst Liberals have traditionally been strongly in favour of profit-sharing, an enthusiasm subsequently shared by their SDP partners.[3]

These changes in political opinion, coupled with tax incentives, have induced significant growth in three major types of share ownership scheme. First there are schemes in which *all* eligible employees in an enterprise receive share allocations based on company profitability. Second, there are option schemes in which employees are invited to purchase shares in their company through a recognized savings scheme. When the savings period terminates, participating employees have the choice of taking up their shares or their savings plus interest earned during the period. The third type of scheme which receives government tax concession support is the so-called discretionary share option scheme, in which specified individuals or groups of employees are invited to purchase shares. Further details of the government- approved schemes may be found in Appendix 1.

In addition to these types of Inland Revenue-approved schemes, there is evidence of many cash-based profit-sharing schemes which do not involve employee participation or scheme ownership but are characterized by some form of bonus to employees based on profit or some other financial measure of performance at plant or company level.

We are therefore faced by a potentially rich assortment of financial participation arrangements, particularly if the range is broadened to include co-operative and co-partnership arrangements for production. These diverse channels of financial involvement tend to be associated with a similarly broad spectrum of motive and objective. A valuable attempt to draw these strands together within an economic context has been made by James Meade (1986), who provided an analysis of the main types of labour involvement in profit-sharing and asset ownership. A dichotomy is drawn between the need for labour to be involved in ownership of capital assets and the extent to which, under any scheme, labour achieves partial or complete control over assets. Four main types of scheme are identified:

1 *Employee share ownership schemes* (ESOS), in which employees are allocated or are able to acquire shares in the capital of their employing organization.
2 *Profit-sharing or revenue-sharing schemes* (PS/RS), in which there is no necessary ownership of capital but employees are able to incorporate into their income from employment some share in profit or net revenue.
3 *Labour-managed organizations or co-operatives* (LMC), in which employees themselves provide the management of the

7

enterprise or organization, and the equity is fully owned by employees.

4 *Labour–capital partnerships* (LCP), in which employees share in the firm's revenue and exercise some role in controlling the firm's operations, but without any requirement for ownership of capital.

Meade (1986:15) shows that these schemes differ in their approach to the key issues of ownership of assets and control, as follows:

		Is labour required to own all or part of the capital invested in business?	
		Yes	No
Does labour control or participate	No	ESOS	PS/RS
in control of the business?	Yes	LMC	LCP

Our main concern in this book is with the ESOS and PS/RS types of scheme, and the differences between them are clearly revealed. In neither case is there a necessary exercise of control over the business such as would exist in a fully fledged co-operative or partnership, so that the issues associated with these latter forms as a result of participative labour management do not arise. The ESOS and PS/RS approaches differ, however, in that only the former involves asset or equity ownership, and this is likely to carry different implications for the *behavioural* responses under different structural forms.

The *economic* motivation for the adoption of ESOS or PS/RS types of approach cannot lie in philosophies which seek to change the balance of social control over business, but rather with a more partial sharing by workers in the equity or the net proceeds of the business. The PS/RS schemes seek simply to relate pay to business performance by holding out to employees the prospect of sharing in profits which can be enhanced by greater work effort on their part. The ESOS type of approach goes further in providing for partial ownership of equity, thus committing employees to an investment in the affairs of their employer. A further understanding of the differences requires separate examination of these two varieties of scheme.

THE ECONOMICS OF FINANCIAL PARTICIPATION

Profit-sharing or revenue sharing

The economics of profit-sharing can be examined at either the micro- or the macro-economic level. The *micro-economic* concern is for the implications of profit-related remuneration in the individual enterprise. Two characteristics are important here. First, there is the potential incentive effect of a payment system which links workers' productive performance and their remuneration. This link has much in common with output-related incentive payment systems, which seek to encourage higher productivity per employee, to the advantage of the employer through improved unit costs and of the worker through extra earnings. Similarly, profit-sharing may be seen as offering an incentive to employees to increase profitability, but operating as a group rather than an individual stimulus. A disadvantage of profit-sharing, like other forms of group incentive payment systems, is that it loses the directness of the effort–pay relation typical of most individual schemes; and, in large organizations particularly, the link between individual effort and profitability may be hard to discern, with adverse consequences for the intended productivity effect. Nevertheless, profit-sharing may be thought more effective than individual incentives in eroding the 'them and us' divide between owner and employees: the fact of employees sharing in the net proceeds of production could, in principle, increase commitment to enterprise goals and raise efficiency and profitability. Thus the 'sharing' aspect of profit-sharing schemes, even if not entirely successful in relating output performance to profitability, may *indirectly* raise productivity by an 'X-efficiency' effect (i.e. one which improves the performance of the enterprise not by improving internal resource allocation but by some more amorphous change which releases untapped productivity – for example, by greater employee co-operation, less resistance to change, greater loyalty leading to reduced labour turnover, etc.).

Secondly, profit-sharing may offer the employer the advantage of wage flexibility. The larger the share of worker remuneration that is not pre-set but directly variable with corporate profits the more readily will labour costs adjust to fluctuations in the enterprise product market. With a more flexible price of labour, there will be less need for quantitative adjustments in labour demand, so that employment fluctuations over the enterprise

9

business cycle will be more moderate than with rigid labour costs. The advantage to the employer is a reduction in the fixed or quasi-fixed costs of employment, while for the employee the reduction in pay levels during recession may be compensated by greater employment security. In general, however, trade unions regard this sort of variability with suspicion.

The second level of analysis, the *macro-economic*, has recently come into prominence as a result mainly of a series of writings by the American economist Martin Weitzman (e.g. 1983, 1984, 1985). If profit-sharing across enterprises is widespread, and if the predicted productivity enhancement and wage-flexibility/employment-stability effects are achieved in substantial measure, the consequences will be reflected in the aggregate performance and behaviour of the macro-economy. However, Weitzman's argument goes beyond this, and because of its apparent influence in recent government thinking a brief synopsis is in order. Weitzman's method is essentially one of comparative systems analysis, in which two model economies are compared, one with a conventional (fixed) wage system, the other characterized as a 'share economy' in which employers typically remunerate workers in a profit-sharing (more strictly, a revenue-sharing) basis for at least part of their payment. In the share economy Weitzman sees the prospect of an escape from the problems of stagflation which affect the wage economy. The differences in behaviour engendered by compensating employees according to a numeraire directly related to the firm's performance are predicted to drive employers to mop up all excess labour, so achieving full employment, but without generating the inflation which typically follows from the expansion of aggregate demand in the wage economy.

Weitzman's starting point is the realistic assumption of monopolistic competition in product markets. Prices are set by producers as a direct mark-up over wages independently of the state of aggregate demand and wages are a datum for employers. Three possible positions of an economy can be envisaged: excess labour demand, excess labour supply, or equilibrium, with demand and supply equalized. Equilibrium is a knife edge at which the capitalist wage economy cannot long remain because of less than perfect labour markets and downwardly inflexible wages, which will tend to push it into the Keynesian excess labour supply zone. But in the share economy every additional worker employed up to the point where marginal product equals the *base* wage will be worthwhile, since it increases revenue by more than cost, resulting in increased profit. It therefore pays the enterprise in the share economy to mop up unemployed labour because of the additional profit it brings. Thus the share economy will generally operate in the excess demand sector.

For this to come about, however, requires a preponderance of profit-sharing firms. If only a few firms are engaged in profit-sharing, there will continue to be an excess supply of workers available for hire after a recessionary shock, for whom the share-economy firms will be the employer of last resort at reducing levels of remuneration. In the share economy, where all firms use profit-sharing, there will be no labour unemployed and available for hire at decreased pay, hence compensation will not in fact be reduced in the short run. When the wage-economy firm is pushed off the knife edge equilibrium it falls into the excess supply zone, where a reduction in money wage costs is needed – which requires monetary or fiscal policies to depress employment and wage demands; and experience shows this can be a long, inefficient process. By contrast, the share economy, through potential if not actual wage flexibility, allows output and employment to be maintained. The on-going search by share- economy employers for extra labour to enhance profits ensures continued excess demand, with the (marginal) reduction in remuneration providing sufficient flexibility to leave the real aggregates unaffected.

The main problem with the Weitzman approach is 'getting there'. For his proposed solution to work a massive, simultaneous switch by employers to a profit-share contract would be necessary – a scenario which seems highly improbable. For only through large-scale conversion would the extra labour employed be sufficient to generate enough demand for goods and services to offset the downward pressure on wages that would otherwise result.[4] There are also other objections to the Weitzman approach. For example, the analysis is couched entirely in theoretical terms and has little empirical basis: perhaps because there is no economy, with the possible exception of Japan, where profit-sharing is sufficiently widespread to demonstrate empirical substantiation of the arguments.[5] Other problems include the depth to which the base wage might have to be depressed and the long-term adaptive processes which might evolve in a permanently excess demand economy.

Whatever the superficial attractiveness of the Weitzman scheme, it does not seem likely to be taken up as a major policy development in the foreseeable future, and the political interest in profit- sharing,

11

if it lies at all in the macro-economic sphere, is more restricted. Thus, for example, the Conservative government's consultative document on *Profit-related Pay* (1986) is concerned with both micro- and macro-effects, the interest at macro-level being focused on the potential for greater wage flexibility. The government's view is that wage rigidity in the face of recessionary pressures is a chronic ingredient in the British economy's difficulties: where wages do not adjust downward, falls in employment become more necessary, being reflected in high levels of redundancy. Here profit-related pay is seen not as a direct solution to the contemporary unemployment problem but as contributing to a more flexible labour market in the long term which would be more capable of sustaining stable levels of output and employment.

Employee share ownership schemes

The essence of employee share ownership schemes is that a capitalist 'wage' employer incorporates in the payment to labour ordinary shares of the company. Two main pairs of options exist: the shares may be newly issued or may be existing shares bought up at market prices for redistribution to the employees; and the shares, once acquired, may be held in a special trust fund for the workers collectively or allocated to individual workers to be held personally.[6]

In these circumstances, clearly, motivation for adoption of the scheme will not be *directly* in the increase of profits or productivity. Instead, the purpose is to allow employees to develop a sense of belonging to the company, and almost certainly to envisage share ownership as breaking down the 'them and us' dichotomy. If this latter objective is met it may *indirectly* contribute to greater efficiency (of the 'X- efficiency' type) and enhance profitability in which the employees may further share: this could arise in a number of ways, for example from greater company loyalty and reduced labour turnover, increased job experience and the acquisition of company-related specific skills, etc. And, of course, if the 'them and us' barrier is broken down by the development of more unitarist sentiments, it may lead to an improved industrial relations climate, with less time lost through strikes, absenteeism, and discontent reflected in efficiency loss, leaving more managerial and supervisory time to be devoted to productivity improvement.

The extent of other economic effects arising from share

ownership depends on how shares are held and how decisions are made. As Meade (1986) has pointed out, if the shares are held in trust, with the dividends being used either to build up the shares to be distributed to employees as a supplement to regular wages, there will be different implications for different generations of employees. If dividends are used to build up the trust, older workers will be asked to make a sacrifice for future generations of employees. Whether conflict of interest manifests itself depends on the mechanisms available to employees to influence decisions. This might be achieved through some form of consultative body involving employee representatives, or collective bargaining might seek to influence the strategy of dividend payment or trust expansion.

In the trust case, also, there may be a difference of interest between non-employee shareholders and worker shareholders with respect to decisions about increasing employment. Non-employee shareholders have an interest in expanding profits so long as (marginal) wage cost is covered, and will be willing to extend employment to new workers who satisfy that condition, helped by the wage subsidy available from the share ownership scheme. In contrast, worker shareholders will see that subsidy as reducing their share in the trust fund as employment is expanded. Again, therefore, the mechanism of employee influence in decision-making will be important in the trust case.

Where shares are distributed for personal ownership these problems do not arise, for the acquisition of new shares cannot be at the expense of shares already held by an employee, and it will be up to the individual to decide whether he wants to keep the shares (after whatever minimum interval is permitted under the scheme). Whether this scheme is successful in motivating company attachment will, in part, be reflected in the willingness of employee shareholders to go on holding their shares.

Although the individual ownership approach is free of the problems of the trust scheme, it has problems of its own, such as might occur when a 'bulge' occurs in retirement, with a greater number of shares being realized by those leaving the firm than are being acquired for new employees (who will often not be immediately eligible). This could have serious short-term implications for the firm's capitalization. Meade rightly argues that there is merit in having some part of this kind of scheme in the form of a trust to provide stability in the face of such occurrences.

ECONOMIC IMPLICATIONS OF FINANCIAL PARTICIPATION

There is clearly a complexity of possible motivations in the adoption of profit-sharing or share ownership schemes. Equally clearly, the variants of the main alternatives carry different implications, depending on specific design elements. Macro-economic changes of the type and scale envisaged by Weitzman seem unrealistic, and what limited evidence is available does not give strong support to what is, in the last resort, a theoretical proposition. Blanchflower and Oswald (1986) have summarized the empirical literature on profit-sharing and share ownership, and although there is a study by Estrin and Wilson (1986) which shows a positive relation between profit-sharing and employment, it is based on such a small and unrepresentative sample that it does nothing to negate the more general evidence from the UK that no significant relation exists. Nor, on an international basis, is there much to alter this conclusion. On the face of it Japan offers the best test of the Weitzman hypothesis, and Freeman and Weitzman (1986) report some suggestive evidence in favour (cf. Blanchflower and Oswald, 1986: 21). However, as discussed below, Wadhwani (1985) draws negative conclusions from his empirical work on Japan.

Apart from the macro-economic effects on employment, the evidence on increased profitability and productivity is mixed. Perhaps the stronger evidence in favour of a positive relation with these factors is that of Fitzroy and Kraft (1986, 1987) using a sample of West German metal working firms. But Cable (1987) has demonstrated that these results depend on the researchers' imposition of an arbitrary weighting structure, without any adequate theoretical underpinning, and the conclusions drawn must therefore be regarded as suspect.

Blanchflower and Oswald (1986) conclude their examination of the evidence as follows:

> there is little to be said for the view that, for employment reasons, the Government should do more to encourage employee share ownership schemes ... The argument for cash-based profit-sharing is less weak and more interesting. There is a little empirical evidence in its favour ... However, it is hard to believe that wider profit-sharing will make any significant difference to unemployment.[p. 22]

14

We do not pursue the macro-economic arguments further in our own empirical work. More realistically, on the micro-economic side, profit-sharing or share ownership schemes may be expected to bring some benefits to the companies which operate them, and we review below some of the evidence which relates to this aspect. Here the economic evidence is, at best, ambiguous, and it may well be that the likeliest source of benefits will be in the more general area of attitudinal change. Yet, as we have seen, for real benefits to accrue it would seem to be necessary that companies spell out their objectives clearly and select their schemes appropriately in relation to these aims. It will thus be an important concern in the following chapters to see how far these requirements are borne out.

Enough has also been said to indicate that differently designed schemes, under the headings of both profit-sharing and employee share ownership, may carry considerable implications for economic decision-taking with regard to employment and investment, as well as for productivity and profitability. Meade has pointed to the need for a careful analysis of the micro-economics of alternative schemes, particularly their implications for employment decisions, the balance of interests between new hires and existing employees, and between different generations of employees, and the mechanisms put in place to allow employees to have some voice in decision-taking in relation to these matters.

These aspects have carry-over effects to the realms of collective bargaining or other forms of joint decision-making, and it becomes an issue of some importance how far the employee benefits of profit-sharing and share ownership are determined by the discretion of the employer. We have indicated that the rationale behind profit-sharing is to offer employees a direct link between company performance and pay, whilst pointing to a more complex relationship between ownership, attitudes, and performance in schemes offering share allocations to employees, for, although employers and employees alike are potential beneficiaries of financial participation, there is surprisingly little hard evidence on what the benefits are, or to whom they accrue. A central aim of this study therefore is to progress beyond the occasionally emotive claims which surround (and sometimes obscure) formal participation in order to reveal more of the substance. We start by examining the potential benefits to employers.

BENEFITS TO EMPLOYERS?

The company generally takes the first step in introducing programmes for employee participation. For what reasons do management introduce a particular scheme? What benefits are expected? Why does it make the introduction at a particular time? From our analysis above one might anticipate that prior to its introduction appropriate objectives and strategies for financial participation would be formulated, along with suitable organizational structures to administer the scheme and monitor change. In some instances company aims might be specific and readily identifiable: in others, loose or rather generalized, but, whatever their location in the expectancy spectrum, we would expect consistency of objectives with recognized organizational culture and practice to be combined with assumptions about employee behaviour, discussed below. This implies that financial participation might be contemplated for many reasons, the anticipated value to the company depending upon prevailing organizational norms and relationships with employees. Similarly, management structures designed to establish and maintain these schemes may also vary with the purposes for which the schemes have been introduced.

Three principal management objectives have been identified with respect to employee participation and profit-based schemes (see Creigh *et al.*, 1981):

1 *Instrumental or economic:* to secure through involvement a greater productivity which will be reflected in enhanced profitability (which need not, of course, preclude employees from obtaining benefits). A variant of this approach would be the interest shown by the government in profit-related pay, in which a proportion of employees' pay would be flexible in line with levels of profit, the assumption being that companies with reduced profitability would reduce their pay bill through downward adjustment in levels of earnings rather than through shedding labour. Employees in successful companies would benefit through higher earnings tied to company profitability (Weitzman, 1984). The potential and implications of this approach are examined more fully in the following section.

2 *Developmental*: to improve the scope for personal development and fulfilment of employees through increased organizational commitment. Such paternalistic motivation, emphasizing

employee-centred factors, may of course be quite consistent with organizational gains in efficiency.

3 *Defensive*: to counter organization by trade unions or to limit extensions of joint control involving trade unions. This might focus particularly on the pre-emptive impact of share ownership or profit-sharing in seeking to reduce 'them and us' divisions which management might perceive as being exaggerated by an extension of union control.

The coherence with which managers pursue these, or other, objectives will be scrutinized through the case studies. In the meantime we reflect upon what the schemes can offer employees, for those benefits which accrue to employees, or are denied to them, are likely to run alongside and indeed derive from objectives set by management. This is most clearly the case in the negative outcome of employees who risk losing financial benefit if their work performance or behaviour fails to reach standards required by management. Though this is most visible in profit-sharing arrangements, managerial threats and ability to withhold share payments in return for unacceptable employee behaviour has been an inescapable feature of share ownership schemes throughout their long history.

Even under these 'deterrent' conditions, however, management needs to seek employee compliance to financial participation in order to gain reasonable levels of acceptance and support. More broadly, therefore, and located further towards managerial 'developmental' objectives, we find share ownership positively promoted as a means of serving the interests of both employee and employer. The purported benefits which employees (and indirectly employers) might expect from such an approach are reviewed below.

BENEFITS OF SHARE OWNERSHIP TO EMPLOYEES?

Ownership of private property provides the base upon which the network of potential employee benefits rests. Ownership occupies a central position in this approach for a number of reasons: first, it fits in neatly with an ideology based on the primacy of property ownership, whether productive or domestic. That property ownership conveys certain rights and responsibilities upon the owners introduces an important dynamic into thinking on employee

17

attitudes and behaviour. Hence rights of industrial ownership are held to induce a feeling of pride and responsibility akin to those 'natural' sentiments associated with home ownership, with which financial participation is frequently identified. 'On wider share ownership, it should be as natural for people to own shares as to own their own house or own a car' (Thatcher, 1986: 2).

Moreover, ownership rights provide the putative means to participate in decisions regarding the uses to which the property should be put:

> An employee should not only be working on the shop-floor or in the office. He should also be present at the Annual General Meeting as a shareholder. He should be wanting to satisfy himself that management is efficient and that profits are as good as they could be. [Thatcher, 1986: 2]

The potential to exercise these rights, allowing for a measure of management accountability to employees, is arguably an indispensable feature, and possibly a defining characteristic, of industrial democracy (see Cressey *et al.*, 1985, for an elaboration of this point). A further possible objective is to broaden the distribution of wealth among the population at large, and hence to reinforce the principle of a democracy in which individual freedom is assumed to rest upon access to property ownership: 'the more widely share ownership can be spread throughout the community, the more individual investors there are in the stock market and the more all our citizens own capital, the better it will be for general political reasons'.[7]

The extent to which attempts to broaden wealth distribution through wider share ownership and profit-sharing schemes have been successful, however, is open to considerable speculation. First, share allocations to employees typically comprise only a very small proportion of total distributed share holdings, and second, it has often been considered that employees' retention of their allocation is low, the large institutional investors being the ultimate beneficiaries of small shareholder disposals. A similar process appears to be taking place with shares issued as part of the government's privatization programme.[8]

Ownership is also seen as a key factor because of its association with responsibilities. At one level it may be argued that individuals who have an ownership stake in property, whether domestic or productive, are oriented more positively towards it than if they are

18

tenants or contracted labour. Copeman and his colleagues (1984: 15) argue that a prime weakness of the market economy has been its failure to develop employee share participation, thereby condemning employees to remain outsiders to their own places of work, possibly culminating in the 'growth of political philosophies aimed at destroying the free enterprise system'. The authors conclude that employee share distributions will popularize capitalism to unprecedented levels and, through accumulating share ownership, remove the 'them and us' dichotomy along with the political and industrial power struggles which derive from it (ibid.: 16).

How far attitudes and behaviour are influenced by financial participation remains something of a mystery, however: the restricted number of surveys which have been conducted do not lead to straightforward, unambiguous conclusions and require tentative interpretation of the findings. A recent major study of employee attitudes by Bell and Hanson (1984) illustrates the point neatly: the authors ascribe favourable employee perceptions to a range of profit-sharing variables through allocating what might otherwise be interpreted as 'non-committed' responses in a positive direction. Though empirically legitimate, the conclusion of 'significant' attitudinal change as a consequence of profit-sharing is open to some doubt (see Ramsay et al., 1986; IDS, 1986).

Behaviour changes directly and unambiguously attributable to transfer of ownership are similarly difficult to pin down. Wright and Coyne (1985) in a study of twenty companies bought out[9] by their managers concluded that the companies tended to perform 'better', according to a range of criteria, than under their previous owners. Performance in these companies had improved without the bulk of employees participating in the transfer of ownership. The authors found that companies which had undertaken *employee* buy-outs appeared to experience heightened motivation among those who participated.

Ambiguity is also reflected in recent American research reviewed by Klein and Rosen (1986: 387–406). A study by Tannenbaum et al. (1984) pointed to no significant differences in profitability or financial growth between samples of employee ownership and conventional companies, though survival rates were enhanced in the former. Marsh and MacAllister (1981) reported higher productivity increases for Employee Share Ownership Plan (ESOP) companies of a medium size, whilst in their analysis of forty-three companies with employee ownership Rosen and Klein

(1983) found higher employment growth in such concerns. Wagner (1984) analysed thirteen companies that were at least 10 per cent employee-owned, concluding that, on specified financial criteria, performance in these companies was higher than in traditional companies.

It is clear that many of the above studies found evidence of improved performance in employee-share companies, though the criteria for measuring performance varied considerably, ranging from variables such as longevity to key financial ratios. This variation raises the question whether such evidence can be generalized, an issue which has been taken up by Klein and Rosen:

> All of the studies are based on relatively small and possibly biased or unrepresentative samples of employee ownership firms. Further, it is difficult to interpret the results because the direction of causality is ambiguous. Are employee ownership companies more successful because employees work harder under employee ownership? Perhaps companies are very successful first and then they put in ownership plans, in order to share the wealth, reward employees, achieve tax savings, etc. A third possibility is that instead of employee ownership leading to financial success or vice versa, some third factor causes both employee ownership and financial success. For example, an active and aggressive management may bring a company to financial health and may also be sympathetic to employee ownership. [1986: 398]

Their own preliminary research of twenty-three employee ownership companies amplifies some of the ambiguities where a tendency by employee participants to concur with general positive statements such as 'I'm proud to own stock in this company' contrasts with signs of ambivalence about its impact upon work behaviour and attitudes, and even more with statements relating to their purported ownership position – employees tended not to feel like a 'real owner in this company'. Could, therefore, the generally favourable inclinations to profit-sharing perhaps be associated with more calculative instincts? Appreciation of the financial rewards associated with ESOPs was commonly expressed, leading the authors to comment that 'employees are *primarily* motivated and inspired by the potential financial rewards of ESOP employee ownership' (Klein and Rosen, 1986: 403; emphasis added).

One finding consistent with the financial reward thesis was that participant responses tended to be positively correlated with company contributions to the ESOP. The higher the contribution the greater satisfaction was expressed with the plan, with behaviour and employee intentions towards the company contentedly following in its wake: 'A large ESOP contribution makes employees, on the average, feel good about the ESOP, their jobs, and their companies' (ibid.). How a poorly perceived and operated scheme might affect employees in terms of these variables is open to question, but Bell and Hanson's finding that profit-sharing was popular among 93 per cent of respondents 'because people like to have a bonus', and the 42 per cent who agreed that share price fluctuations might cause disappointment or bitterness, certainly add strength to a possible instrumental orientation to share ownership (1984: 27). This in turn suggests that whilst financial participation may be formally distinct from the main sources of remuneration any potential for improvement may be sought by employees or, where available, by their representatives through collective representation to management.

FINANCIAL PARTICIPATION AND COLLECTIVE RELATIONSHIPS

Financial participation by employees does not in itself carry any particular implications for collective relationships between employer and employees or the unions or associations which represent their interests. In practice the reactions created by the development of one or other form of financial participation tend to be significantly influenced by the role of the trade unions in their introduction and regulation, or by the exclusion of unions from the participative relationships. Thus in Sweden, for example, the development of employee investment funds owed its origin to trade union initiatives, whereas in Britain and the United States the role of the unions is generally much less influential.

We have already seen that one of the motives for management in introducing profit-sharing or share ownership may be the defensive one of restraining the growth of union membership or the extension of union influence into new areas of joint regulation. We also observed that the operation of particular types of scheme could hinge on the ability of employees to participate in mechanisms associated with financial participation. Evidently much will depend

21

on the motives giving rise to any scheme and on the consequences of motivation for the design of the scheme and its interaction with existing collective relationships.

As we have seen, there is little doubt that, historically, financial participation schemes in Britain were contemplated by some managements in order to forestall collective employee activity, especially during periods of economic prosperity, low unemployment, and labour unrest (Bristow, 1974; Ramsay, 1977). Such opportunistic schemes tended to wither away when the perceived dangers presented by circumstances favourable to collective pressure had passed (Brannen, 1983: 2). With these antecedents it is perhaps not surprising that many unions, as well as the TUC, have traditionally been wary of profit-sharing and share ownership.

Reasons for union opposition to financial participation tend to vary. One obvious consideration is that unions believe that the schemes are introduced by management intent on preventing or inhibiting their influence by its appeal to employee loyalties and commitment through share issues. Second, although they add to the total remuneration package, financial participation schemes are typically introduced and controlled unilaterally by management, and are not regarded as negotiable. As such they comprise an element in the pay and conditions of employees located formally outside the boundaries of collective regulation which might represent an initial stage in a progressive diminution of influence within the one area where most observers would agree that collective participation is legitimate: in pay determination.

The unions see themselves further disadvantaged in that the conditions of employee eligibility and the extent of the profit or share allocation is usually at the discretion of the board of directors or calculated according to some predetermined formula devised by senior management and likely to be 'transparent' only to the more financially percipient. Similarly a decision to alter or wind the scheme up could also be made without reference to the union. Together these factors could serve to reduce the security of earnings which has traditionally comprised a main plank in union activity and ideology – often expressed in negotiations for 'consolidation' of variable pay elements. The higher the emphasis on 'profit-related' pay the lower one might expect union enthusiasm to be.

Third, financial participation schemes do not represent any meaningful thrust by unions into strategic areas of managerial

22

decision-making, which remain remote and independent of collective influence. At best they might provide limited opportunities for individual employees to participate as shareholders, though there is no shortage of references to studies which locate investor influence securely with financial institutions and their advisers and demonstrate that individual shareholders contribute little to organizational decision-making (Minns, 1980). More specific 'control' criticisms pertain to the lack of employee influence over the conditions in which the business operates, over decisions on the inclusion of items into the Profit and Loss Account which crucially bear upon the levels of profit to be allocated, and over the quality of management and the decisions made by this body (IDS, 1986). Whilst all these factors will exert vital influence over the level of profits, the employees themselves are powerless, through their own efforts, to affect share distributions made to them, a point recently emphasized by Smith (1986) in his reference to the lack of ability of shareholding British Aerospace employees to prevent the closure of one of the company's plants: 'In reality worker-shareholders, like the hundreds of thousands of small investors who own shares in British public companies, have virtually no power and rarely, if ever, can exert influence to change the affairs of the business.'

Nevertheless, it would surely be premature to anticipate that profit-sharing schemes will remain indefinitely independent of other social pressures and developments relating to remuneration which take place within the organization, or in the economy at large. And, once implemented, a scheme does offer additional opportunities for employees and their representatives to make observations, comment upon, and suggest alterations, which ultimately add up to some influence, however minimal and informal initially, in the scheme's operation and outcomes.

Perhaps because of the prospect of benefits there are signs that union resistance to profit-sharing is beginning to shift (IDS, 1986: 9–10), and a slow recognition of bargaining opportunities is beginning to emerge. A parallel might be drawn by the gradual evolution of collective bargaining over occupational pension schemes, an employee benefit once recognized (with equal 'bored hostility' by the union movement, one might add) as at the discretion of employer benevolence, but now seen in many organizations as a legitimate area for joint regulation by management as well as unions, and this despite the continuing formal existence of many union statements and policies deploring the need for reliance upon private occupational pensions as a source of retirement subsistence (Hyman and Schuller, 1984).

One important restriction on increased union involvement in negotiation of employee share ownership schemes in particular is that the tax advantages available to approved schemes tend to be tightly prescribed, leaving little room for discretion in the design of the scheme. This by no means rules out the scope for union contributions to design and implementation but it is undoubtedly an inhibiting factor in many cases.

In summary the British experience seems largely to have consisted of the development of financial participation schemes in which employees and their representative organizations have had little input through negotiation. Schemes in general appear to be very much creatures of the employer's initiative, design, and implementation, though subject increasingly to legal requirements where the schemes seek to take advantage of tax concessions. It will be one of our concerns in later chapters to see not only how trade unions have responded in practice to the growth of profit-sharing and share ownership schemes in general, but also how their role is perceived in the context of specific schemes.

FINANCIAL PARTICIPATION EXPERIENCE IN OTHER COUNTRIES

Though the British experience offers few insights into the consequences of share ownership for employers, developments abroad may offer additional information concerning the incidence, objectives, and effects of employee share ownership schemes. Unfortunately, experience in other countries also appears to be somewhat limited. In a summary of a study presented recently in the journal *Industrial Participation* (1985–6), of twenty-three countries examined by the survey, only in France and Spain was profit-sharing considered to be 'common', and though it is not a rarity in the United States most schemes there are of comparatively recent origin. It appears that employer interest in financial participation is stimulated by law-induced tax incentives, either on a voluntary basis, as in the UK and USA, where the law serves to encourage employers to introduce appropriate schemes, or as in France, where all companies above a minimum size have been required by legislation passed in 1967 to introduce profit-sharing, a facility which was also made available on a voluntary basis to smaller companies and employees in the public sector (Creigh *et al.*, 1982: 155).

In France the 1967 system operates on the basis of a collective fund, invested at enterprise level on behalf of individual employees. By 1975 it was estimated that more than 10,000 undertakings had entered into profit-sharing agreements, covering an employment population of 4.75 million, representing 22.5 per cent of the total labour force, a smaller proportion than expected, owing to the comparatively small number of French companies with more than the 100 employees required by the legislation to enter into profit-sharing agreements. Subsequently an additional scheme offering free allocations of shares to employees was legislated for in 1980 for use in publicly quoted companies. Creigh *et al.* estimate that about two-thirds of eligible companies are participating in this scheme. Additional schemes are also available in France, including a share option scheme introduced in 1970.

Though share ownership schemes are not as common in West Germany as in France, interest has been stimulated through tax incentives designed to promote share option schemes and employee savings plans. The option schemes have had varying degrees of success in terms of employee participation rates, which have been higher in smaller enterprises and amongst white-collar employees, where in both cases union numbers and activity are not high, a relevant consideration, as union opposition to share option schemes is believed to have restricted their coverage in larger, unionized concerns (Creigh *et al.*, 1982: 157).

A natural direction in which to turn for further information on share ownership schemes is the United States, but until recently developments there have been little different from the British scene in that share ownership practice has failed to keep pace with ideology: 'the idea of broad ownership of capital ... has remained a distant goal – good in theory, but relatively little practised' (Klein and Rosen, 1986: 387). By the 1970s the picture had ostensibly started to change under pressure from different directions: a particular impetus was presented by heightened foreign and domestic competition, spurring managements to pursue cost-effectiveness programmes in which prominence was given to enhanced employee motivation and satisfaction. This coincided with a resurgence of thought directed towards traditional principles of equitable ownership of property, these two strands being drawn together in a series of legislative changes promoting Employee Stock Ownership Plans in the mid-1970s.

ESOPs operate by establishing a trust to which the company contributes capital allocated to accounts provided for the benefit of eligible employees. Generally ESOPs are 'all- employee schemes', with allocations being proportional to pay. Shares are distributed to participants only when they leave the company or upon retirement. Full voting rights are confined to a minority of schemes. In recent studies it has variably been estimated that between 4,000 and 7,000 ESOPs are operating in the USA; one study concluded that at least 7 million participant employees and assets of $19 billion are currently involved in such plans (Blanchflower and Oswald, 1986: 15), whereas other estimates suggest that 4 per cent of the total work force are involved (Rosen, 1984: 250).

Though the ESOP approach was established in order to meet broad economic and ideological objectives, its attraction to employers appears rather more singular. Significantly, it has been suggested that the potential tax and financial advantages have been the prime attraction to many employers (Rosen, 1984: 250), who are able to extract considerable fiscal benefits, at little initial cost to themselves, from the schemes. Broadening 'share ownership' was seen as a secondary, and not necessarily desirable, feature even to those companies which had introduced schemes. The extent to which 'ownership' may serve as a *deterrent* to the vast majority of firms without ESOPs is an open question. However, expressions of concern that increased employee ownership might inhibit managerial authority or freedom of action appear to be misguided, for it seems that companies have little to fear; little impact has been made by employee inputs into corporate decision-making, either through shareholders' rights (Rosen, 1984) or through participation programmes established in companies which have introduced shareholder plans (see Blasi *et al.*, 1983). Indeed, it has been argued that schemes involving share ownership are not intended to create any such impact (Schuller, 1985: 61). Combined with our earlier examination of evidence from America concerning employee behaviour, attitude, and performance changes associated with share ownership, there are signs that benefits to employers which are directly attributable to employee share distribution have not yet been firmly established.

As we have seen, experience from other countries is considerably more limited, but is of interest in that share ownership schemes are not common in those countries in which government support offering employers tangible incentives is not forthcoming. The reasons for this lack of support are not immediately easy to understand if we accept the arguments put forward by advocates of employee shares; but it is possible that in those countries alternative means have been employed to promote the levels of employee commitment and integration identified as employers' most important objective in introducing profit-sharing (Smith, 1986: 382). When appropriate government support is forthcoming, as in France and more recently in the USA and UK, companies may turn to share ownership: in Smith's UK study, for example, changes in legislation provided the impetus for over one-third of companies to introduce share option or $ADST^{10}$ schemes (ibid.: 382). However, even under favourable conditions, as in France, employee ownership schemes remain confined to a minority of companies and employees.

One country in which share ownership has not been actively promoted by the government is Japan, which nevertheless enjoys a high level of industrial relations and production stability. Large companies also make extensive use of bonuses tied to profitability, and some commentators have indicated that the two phenomena are directly linked. Though it has not been a practice of Japanese management to encourage employees to purchase company shares, or to offer shares as part of remuneration, enterprise loyalty is encouraged through the pay structure and through a range of non-financial benefits provided for 'core' workers (George and Levie, 1984). In larger companies pay consists of a basic wage, influenced by age, seniority, and status, supplemented by management-controlled bonuses for good attendance and efficient performance.

A major element of basic pay consists of bonuses directly linked to enterprise profitability and paid on a twice-yearly basis. These profit-related bonuses have been estimated to account for as much as 25 per cent of earnings (Blanchflower and Oswald, 1986: 20) and, because of this and their relatively widespread coverage, have been likened to the type of 'share economy' model outlined earlier and proposed by Weitzman as superior to the wage economy in terms of macro-economic performance. Indeed, Freeman and Weitzman (1986) argue that Japan's low unemployment rate and level of wage inflation are attributable to this profit-related pay dimension. However, the evidence and conclusions for this proposition have been questioned by Wadhwani (1985), who comments that Japan's low unemployment rate (2.2 per cent between 1979 and 1982) may not be directly comparable with other developed countries', owing to differences in measurement and statistical techniques (p. 13). Weitzman's partial reliance upon longitudinal studies using pre- and post-war data is also unreliable, owing to restricted pre-war employment data. Moreover, using a ratio of post-war unemployment relative to pre-war indicates 'nothing "special" about Japan's improved performance' (Wadhwani, 1985: p. 20).

Finally Wadhwani questions Weitzman's claim of lower output variability through profit-based remuneration as inconclusive and develops an economic model which suggests that there is also no conclusive evidence of a direct relationship between profit-sharing and inflation rates. He considers that 'there is nothing in the empirical evidence discussed above to suggest that profit-sharing has desirable macro-economic effects for the reasons give by Weitzman' (1985: 38). These findings do not imply, however, that there are no beneficial effects to be gained from profit-sharing, either at enterprise level or within the economy as a whole. In the present study we have insufficient aggregate data to attempt macro-level analysis, but our case studies of companies, coupled with comprehensive survey data, will permit examination of the extent and nature of establishment-level initiatives and identification of any behavioural effects attributable to profit-sharing or to share ownership generally.

NOTES

1 I. Gordon-Brown, letter to *The Times*, 10 November 1975.

2 *Report on Profit-sharing and Labour Co-partnership in the United Kingdom*, Cmnd 544, 1920, pp. 13–15.

3 For further discussion of the political contribution to the development of employee share schemes see Chapter 2.

4 In a more recent paper Weitzman (1986) presents a defence of his arguments against some of the main criticisms which have been advanced. In so doing he may be interpreted as departing somewhat from rigorous theoretical analysis and moving to a position where increased profit-sharing is regarded as most unlikely to be harmful to the economy, and capable of yielding helpful outcomes, even if not applied throughout the economic system.

5 But see below, p. 14, and the final section of this chapter.

6 There is no necessary presumption of profit-sharing in share ownership, though if (as does happen) the shares are bought from the firm's profit there is clearly also an element of profit-sharing in this approach. In that event the discussion of the previous section would apply.

7 N. Ridley, Hansard, 11 December 1981.

8 H. Neuberger, letter to *The Times*, 19 December 1985.

9 A management buy-out occurs when a small team of (usually) senior managers in an enterprise arrange the finance necessary to purchase the company, or part of it, from its owners. An employee buy-out involves an appreciably higher proportion of employees who, in return for a shareholding, contribute finance to purchase the company.

10 See Chapter 2.

2

Political and legislative background

As our historical introduction has shown, interest in profit- sharing is not a new phenomenon. The current enthusiasm can be related very directly to legislative encouragement, beginning with the 1978 Finance Act under the Lib-Lab pact and accelerating under the Conservative governments since 1979. The Conservatives have eased some of the restrictive rules for ADST schemes, introduced tax incentives for SAYE share option schemes under the 1980 Finance Act, and encouraged the spread of discretionary schemes under the 1984 Finance Act. In view of the significance of the legislative underpinning of profit-sharing and the support it has attracted from all the major political parties at various stages, it is necessary to examine the underlying philosophy of each party. First we review briefly the legislation and its impact. Details of the schemes under consideration are to be found in Appendix 1.

PRESENT LEGISLATION AND SCHEMES

There are three types of profit-sharing and employee share ownership scheme which have been encouraged by current legislation:

1 *ADST (Approved Deferred Share Trust) schemes.* Under the 1978 Finance Act (as amended) these schemes are approved by the Inland Revenue and must be open to all full-time employees with five years' service. However, others may be invited to participate. The company allocates profits (usually once a trigger is released) to a trust fund which acquires shares in the company on behalf of employees. Individuals do not actually

30

receive the shares for two years, and have to hold them for a total of five years to avoid income tax completely.

2 *SAYE (Save as you earn) share option schemes.* These schemes operate under the 1980 Finance Act (as amended), with eligibility rules which are similar to ADST schemes. Employees contract to save for either five or seven years and are granted options over shares at the start of the savings period. At the end of the savings period they can exercise their option or withdraw their savings with interest. The savings are exempt from income tax and are therefore very attractive to higher-rate taxpayers. Capital gains above the exemption limit are subject to tax.

3 *Discretionary or executive share option schemes.* Under the 1984 Finance Act companies can select employees (usually senior executives) to participate and these participants receive generous tax advantages and stand to make substantial capital gains which are taxed through capital gains tax (30 per cent), not income tax (60 per cent). (1987/88 rates.)

A fourth tax-beneficial scheme – Profit-related Pay (PRP) – was introduced under the Finance (No. 2) Act, 1987. Under this scheme half of PRP is free of income tax, up to the point where it is 20 per cent of the employee's total pay, or £3,000 a year if lower. PRP must cover at least 5 per cent of pay, and at least 80 per cent of eligible employees must participate. The scheme can be calculated on the basis of any recognizable employment unit, not necessarily the company as a whole.

Companies can provide more than one of these schemes, and additionally may operate cash-based profit-sharing or share-based profit-sharing schemes which do not qualify for tax benefits under the various Acts. The legislation has had a marked impact on the creation of schemes, as can be seen in Table 1.

If the growth of ADST and SAYE schemes has been steady, then the upsurge in discretionary schemes since 1984 has been nothing short of spectacular. The rapid growth of these schemes has, however, been a cause of concern, not elation, on the part of some of the strongest advocates of profit-sharing schemes. The Wider Share Ownership Council believe that companies should not be permitted to operate discretionary schemes on their own and have urged the Chancellor to amend the legislation to this effect. They argue that the existence of executive-only schemes cuts across the objectives of integration and involvement, which employee share ownership is meant to generate.

31

Table 1 Inland Revenue-approved profit-sharing and employee share ownership schemes

Year	Finance Act, 1978, schemes	Finance Act, 1980, schemes	Finance Act, 1984, schemes
1979	78	n.a.	n.a.
1980	106	7	n.a.
1981	77	113	n.a.
1982	67	76	n.a.
1983	49	74	n.a.
1984	69	100	32
1985	64	129	1,178
1986	98	94	824
1987	103	100	733
1988 (end June)	45	49	407
Total	756	742	3,174

n.a.: not applicable, as legislation not in force at this date.
Note: Companies may operate more than one scheme. Therefore the total number of companies operating schemes is less than the total number of schemes.

THE POLITICS OF PROFIT-SHARING AND EMPLOYEE SHARE OWNERSHIP (PS/ESO)

With governmental encouragement a vital factor in the growth of these schemes (as evidenced also by overseas experience; see Chapter 1) it is clearly important to examine the objectives the political parties hope to achieve through their support of profit-sharing and employee share ownership. At first sight there appears to be a consensus of support for legislation to assist the spread of employee share schemes. However, underlying the apparent unanimity we can detect three distinct themes running through the policies of the parties, with areas of overlap and areas of distinct differences. The three themes are human relations, market forces, and social ownership.

Human relations and co-partnership

The focus here is on the view of the firm and how to motivate employees within it. The emphasis is on creating a common identity between employees and management, and schemes are judged by their ability to achieve this. Support for these objectives can be found in all the major political parties, but the one with the longest standing commitment to them is undoubtedly the Liberal Party. A clear statement of Liberal policy was made in 1928:

> The real purpose of profit-sharing, in conjunction with the system of organised consultation which is described in the following chapters, is to show that the worker is treated as a partner, and that the division of proceeds of industry is not a mystery concealed from him, but is based upon known and established rules to which he is party. [Liberal Party, 1928: 199]

Such views were reflected in various policy statements over the next fifty years, but it was not until the period of the Lib-Lab pact that Liberal policy was able to influence government decisions. Part of the deal for the continuation of the pact was the Labour government's adoption of Liberal proposals on profit-sharing. This was a reversal of Labour's previous position of opposition to such schemes.

The Liberals have welcomed the legislation in support of SAYE share option schemes and the loosening of the restrictions on the operation of ADST schemes. The Liberal-SDP Alliance was also responsible for an amendment to the 1982 Employment Act which required companies to include in their annual report a statement of action taken to develop employee participation. Financial participation such as employees' share schemes had to be commented on specifically.

The theme of co-partnership is at the forefront of present-day Liberal support for profit-sharing, which according to David Steel:

> can encourage greater involvement, better working conditions, greater job satisfaction, reduce the rift between management and employees, the 'us and them' attitudes, encourage co-operation, stimulate involvement, improve management competence, reduce waste, boost productivity, and provide a more equitable distribution of the wealth created.[1986: 42]

This is a substantial list of claims to be made for one policy strategy. Steel attempts to justify them by citing examples of worker co-operatives, cash-based profit-sharing, added-value schemes, and employee share ownership. The emphasis is on 'partnership' and breaking down 'us and them': through giving each employee a stake and a say in the business 'management performance, productivity, morale and job satisfaction could be transformed' (ibid.: 38). It is a view of the world which still has a place for trade unions; not organizing centralized, confrontational patterns of wage negotiation but 'permitting a more pluralistic and participative patchwork of partnership to blossom from the basic groundwork of minimum wages' (p. 32).

Liberals see their strategy of co-partnership as a 'third way' between the private enterprise of the Conservatives and the state ownership of Labour; a third way so that industry would 'become the joint responsibility of *both* employees and shareholders, working together towards an agreed end, in the successful achievement of which both will share' (Scottish Liberal Party, 1983: 16). To stress the link between profit-sharing and industrial relations, the Liberals what the strict rules of the current legislation replaced by simplified ground rules which would be specified and monitored by an Industrial Democracy Commission, not by the Inland Revenue (Steel, 1986: 42–3). The main fiscal incentive to encourage the spread of schemes would be exemption from National Insurance contributions. Schemes should be spread to the public sector via cash profit-sharing and output bonuses in the trading sector and performance bonuses in the service sector. For those workers unable to benefit from profit-sharing, Liberals propose tax relief for everybody willing to buy shares. Steel believes that the use of a supervisory body coupled with significant fiscal incentives would enable profit-sharing to develop voluntarily.

The co-partnership theme is also one strand of Conservative Party support for profit-sharing and employee share ownership. The traditional paternalism has now been joined, if not superceded, by arguments which stress the direct impact of the market on wage flexibility and employee motivation and the drive towards 'a property owning, share owning democracy' via policies such as privatization share flotations and Personal Equity Plans. These different approaches reflect wider divisions within the Conservative Party based on its 'wet' and 'dry' wings.

Kenneth Carlisle, MP, has outlined the Conservative case for profit-sharing, drawing on the paternalist tradition of the party (1980). He argues that it has an ability to generate wealth if businesses achieve a 'unity of purpose' through employees identifying with their company and knowing that the entire work force would benefit from the firm's success. Schemes would 'help to spread an understanding of the realities of the market-place, of the need to make profits and to earn an adequate return on capital employed'. These goals are designed to encourage production and provide work incentives, but the introduction of profit-sharing has a wider political objective for the Conservatives. Through spreading wealth, Carlisle hopes, the Marxist spectre would be expunged, and as many people would own shares as owned their own houses. The future of a popular capitalism would therefore be ensured. Thus Carlisle sums up the goals of profit-sharing schemes:

> They could play an important part in good human relations in industry and the creation of wealth. They could form a radical engine to achieve as wide a spread in share as in home ownership. They could give individual workers an opportunity to achieve a real measure of economic independence, and help us to break into the virtuous cycle of investment by employees in place of immediate consumption. [1980: 11]

The Conservatives have long supported encouragement of profit-sharing and employee share ownership through tax incentives. The 1970–4 Heath government introduced two measures to encourage share option schemes, one for executives, the second for all employees.

Proposals to introduce all-employee savings-related share option schemes were introduced in the 1973 Finance Act. These related directly to the paternalistic, co-partnership strand in Conservative thinking. As Patrick Jenkin, Chief Secretary to the Treasury, put it: 'What the schemes can do is establish a community of interest between company and employee and to break down the barriers that are part of the trouble that lies behind the difficulties in industrial relations'.[1] The schemes were, however, subject to incomes policy restrictions until December 1973, and few were introduced before the incoming Labour government abolished the favourable tax treatment. The Conservative Party Committee on Personal Capital Building and Wider Participation in the Creation of Wealth (the Howell Committee) later produced a green paper paralleling the proposals on profit-sharing introduced by the Lib-Lab pact in 1978. Conservative members were instrumental in amending that scheme in a number of significant ways, in particular by reducing the period during which shares could not be sold without a tax penalty from fifteen to ten years.

Profit-sharing and the market

In some of the Conservative government's recent policy developments we can detect a change in the basis of support for profit-sharing and employee share ownership, away from the paternalistic emphasis on co-partnership towards policies derived from the monetarist, market-oriented wing of the party.

An early example of policy derived from market thinking was the 1972 Finance Act, which introduced executive share options. This legislation was similar to that introduced later under the 1984 Finance Act and reflects the Conservatives' firm belief in the need to provide incentives to motivate senior executives and to help firms recruit and retain key managers. Significantly, ministers did not believe such arguments applied to all employees, on the grounds that the link between individual effort and company fortunes was 'inevitably diffuse and remote'.[2] Underlying the desire to create incentives is a belief in the managerialist thesis: that the objectives of owners and managers may not coincide. As Patrick Jenkin, Chief Secretary to the Treasury, put it in 1972:

> It has become increasingly necessary over recent decades to provide some means of reducing and, if possible, eliminating that divergence of interest between the owners and the managers of the business so as to inject into the business the dynamism and enterprise which has through the ages characterised the owner-managers.[3]

Hence the Conservatives' support for schemes for senior managers, which they have continued to champion despite the alternative view that such schemes are at best merely tax dodges and at worst undermine productivity by creating and emphasizing divisions within the firm. All other parties are opposed to executive schemes because of their elitist and potentially divisive nature.

The market-oriented side of Conservative policy has come to the fore in the proposals for profit-related pay. Market considerations were included earlier in the case for the 1980s share ownership legislation. Nicholas Ridley, when Financial Secretary to the Treasury, advanced the view that the government's profit-sharing measures were designed – along with other policies – to improve the supply-side performance of the economy by promoting an incentive for people to work more effectively, particularly by improving incentives and helping people to own property. The benefits of share ownership in the private sector were contrasted with the plight of workers in the nationalized industries, in such a way as to emphasize the link with the market and the need for privatization. 'When someone is employed by a large monopolistic nationalised organisation which is partly or wholly isolated from market forces, it is not possible to produce this incentive.'[4]

Thus the privatization of nationalized industries, usually with a large measure of preferential treatment for employees, the introduction of tax incentives to encourage profit-sharing and employee share ownership, combined with sales of council houses, are all part of a move towards the goal of a 'property-owning, share-owning democracy'. As Nicholas Ridley put it, 'Our aim is to build upon our property owning democracy and to establish a people's capital market, to bring capitalism to the place of work, to the high street and even to the home.'[5]

Profit-related pay, however, should not be seen as part of the paternalist co-partnership approach, nor of a drive to wider share ownership, but as a means of achieving wage flexibility and of motivating individual workers by linking their pay directly to the market.[6] It is seen in the context of Weitzman's vision of a share economy. Even here, as discussed in Chapter 1, a major doubt in travelling this route is that a substantial proportion of firms would have to travel it together, and it is unlikely that the tax incentives will be sufficient to enable this to occur.

As presented in the government's consultative document, profit-related pay is meant to help employees identify with their company in a similar way to the change in relationships which is claimed for employee share ownership schemes, but in a more direct way. The discussion on this point is linked to the expansion of tax-incentive-based share schemes whose success, it is claimed, has been 'amply demonstrated', although two paragraphs later it is conceded that 'it is early days yet, but the indications are that the benefits of increased commitment and identification are starting to come through'. PRP, it is claimed, could produce 'further benefits of this kind'.[7]

At the macro-level the objectives of PRP are to increase pay flexibility and to bring the market to bear more directly on pay negotiations instead of reference to 'the going rate'. It is acknowledged that the effects on unemployment of this change may take a long time to filter through.

The relationship between financial participation and the labour market is also a concern of the former Alliance parties. The Liberals link their support for profit-sharing to their policy on a comprehensive incomes strategy and would establish a Pay, Prices, and Employment Commission to monitor pay settlements in large companies, with the power to impose a counter-inflation tax and a price sanction if a pay settlement was excessive, but permission to pay above the norm via predetermined profit-sharing formulae.

From co-partnership to social ownership?

If we have detailed two strands of often contradictory thought underlying Conservative support for financial participation, we can discover also a degree of tension and contradiction in Labour policy on the subject. Until recently the Labour Party was, at best, neutral about profit-sharing and employee share ownership, but was more likely to be hostile. Bristow (1974: 288) reported that 'in 1927 the Labour Party still officially condemned profit-sharing as an insidious weapon in the employer's arsenal against trade unions'. The way forward for Labour was through nationalization of key sectors of industry, with rights for workers' representation through trade unions built into the legislation. Recently this Fabian inheritance has come under challenge from two quarters. On the one hand the party has had to respond to the apparent success of individual ownership of both shares and houses fostered by the Conservative government, as well as adjust to the latter's claimed success in managing the economy. On the other, while seeing some virtue in the commitment and loyalty that might be generated through financial participation, Labour has had to guard against the paternalism inherent in the human relations approach while remaining conscious of, and responsive to, its links with the trade unions and the need to support collective bargaining. We develop these points in the next chapter, but here we detail how the ambiguities and tensions present in the Labour Party's approach have resulted in contradictory responses to legislation on profit-sharing and employee share ownership.

The Labour Party opposed much of the early Conservative legislation, but largely because it was against favourable tax treatment rather than because of objections to share schemes in principle. As Dennis Healey put it in moving the repeal of the 1972 and 1973 provisions, 'We have no antipathy towards share schemes as such .... Any respectable share incentive scheme should be able to stand on its own feet without relying on crutches in the shape of tax privileges.'[8] Thus the Wilson government nullified an earlier House of Lords decision (Abbott *v*. Philbean, 1960) that the gain on share option schemes was not taxable. In 1974 the incoming Labour government abolished the favourable tax treatment introduced by the Tories in the 1972 and 1973 Finance Acts.

More specifically Labour had objected to the Conservatives' measures on the grounds that they were merely a device to reward the high-salaried executive at the cost of the Revenue rather than at the cost of shareholders.[9] This objection applied specifically to executive schemes, but Labour also objected to the fact that workers in non-quoted companies would be excluded, especially those in the public sector.

Given this background, it may seem rather odd that it was a Labour government which introduced the tax concessions for ADST-type schemes in 1978. As was pointed out in a *Financial Times* editorial, the proposals were 'a straight concession by the government to the Liberals'.[10] It must be remembered that these proposals came at the height of the debate around the Bullock Report, but apart from the Liberals there was little enthusiasm for such schemes. Even the Confederation of British Industry (CBI) were only mildly interested at that time. The Inland Revenue consultative document which preceded the legislation did, however, emphasize that profit-sharing was quite distinct from the issue of industrial democracy. In advancing the proposals in 1978, Labour were sensitive to the wider debate on industrial democracy, and Joel Barnett, Chief Secretary to the Treasury, did not see profit-sharing as a substitute for other forms of industrial participation. The objectives, for Labour, were limited:

> I have no wish to overstate the benefits that the scheme may achieve, but I hope that in the long run it will help to improve the efficiency and productivity and, therefore, the effectiveness of the corporate sector as a whole.[11]

The Labour Party, then, was bumped into legislating for the ADST-type scheme by the Liberal Party, and since 1979 the initiative in this area has lain firmly with the Tories. The debates on the various changes to the legislation introduced by the Tories indicate Labour's ambivalence in this policy area. Some Labour MPs thought the schemes beneficial, some opposed them in favour of collective-based schemes, others were opposed not on ideological grounds but on pragmatic considerations of the problems that arose with them, while others again felt simply that they were not working. Labour was particularly opposed to the 1984 executive schemes for reasons similar to their objections in 1972.

More recently, however, prominent figures in the Labour Party have advocated employee share ownership in the wider context of moves towards social ownership as presented to the 1986 conference (Labour Party, 1986). The social ownership strategy will be discussed fully in the next chapter, but at this stage it should be stressed that the image of co-partnership and co-operation in employee–employer relations is firmly to be found in Labour's future plans (Hattersley, 1985a, 1987).

CONCLUSION

Political party support for profit-sharing and employee share ownership has had a long history, but actual legislation has come to the fore only in the last fifteen years or so. This is not a uniquely British phenomenon; legislative encouragement of such schemes has been of significance in the USA, West Germany, and France, and the Swedish government's encouragement of employee investment funds demonstrates an alternative route. More recently the Irish government has introduced legislation paralleling the UK's 1978 and 1980 Acts (Meenan, 1986).

Within the UK we have detected three broad themes underlying politicians' support for schemes – human relations, market forces, and social ownership. All parties believe, almost without reservation, that profit-sharing and employee share ownership will lead to greater employee identification with the company they work for, and this in turn will lead to an increase in productivity, efficiency, and profits. As we shall see in Chapter 5, the human relations approach equates with one of the strands in management thinking on the subject. The objective of changing employee attitudes and through this changing employee motivation is accepted as a long-term goal. Neither management nor the politicians who believe in this objective have produced much evidence to demonstrate that the links actually exist. The case studies in this book allow us an opportunity to examine the claims in some detail.

The market-oriented strand in politicians' thinking is also echoed in management policy, which favours the short-run impact of financial participation on incentives and motivation. On this issue the politicians are not in agreement. The Conservatives have developed financial participation legislation designed to link individual workers to the market. Discretionary schemes are aimed at small numbers of senior executives, but the PRP proposals are much more wide-ranging.

However, there is evidence that on this issue the objectives of the government and of employers may not coincide. The stress on individual responses to market forces may cut across the stress on co-partnership and co-operation to be found in the arguments for employee share ownership. Thus the CBI, while accepting the case for employee involvement through financial participation, cannot bring itself fully to accept the government's model of flexible pay through PRP and reject the alleged employment effects of the scheme (CBI, 1986).

This is perhaps evidence that the government's thinking on these issues is muddled and that there is a need to disentangle the various objectives which may be pursued through profit-related pay, profit-sharing, and employee share ownership. As we shall see in Chapter 5, different objectives may best be pursued by different policies, and to conflate the range of policies with the entire range of objectives may only serve to obscure and confuse.

While all parties broadly agree on the human relations approach, there is a marked divergence on the other two themes. The market approach based on the individual stands in marked contrast to the social ownership approach of the Labour Party. Yet the progress the Conservatives have made through privatization, employee share ownership and wider share ownership has forced the other parties to respond to the situation and adapt their policies. The adjustment in the Labour Party has to take account of historical developments and the policies of the broader trade union and labour movement. It is to these that we now turn.

NOTES

1 Hansard, House of Commons Standing Committee H, col. 340, 9 May 1973.

2 ibid.

3 Hansard, House of Commons, vol. 837, col. 610, 17 May 1972.

4 Speech to *Glasgow Herald* seminar on employee share schemes, 13 April 1983.

5 Speech to Wider Share Ownership Council forum on employee share schemes, 3 October 1984.

6 *Profit-related Pay: a Consultative Document*, Cmnd 9835, 1986.

7 ibid., p. 4.

8 Hansard, House of Commons, vol. 873, col. 610, 9 May 1974.

9 John Gilbert, Hansard, House of Commons, vol. 837, col. 585, 17 May 1972.

10 *Financial Times*, 3 February 1978.

11 Hansard, House of Commons, vol. 948, col. 1657, 27 April 1978.

3

The labour movement and profit-sharing

In Chapter 1 we have seen that there is historical evidence that profit-sharing has been used by some managements as a counter to trade unionism in periods of labour unrest (Bristow, 1974; Ramsay, 1977). In Chapter 5 we examine the current evidence of the defensive/deterrence effect. Here we examine the policies of the broad labour and trade union movement towards profit-sharing and employee share ownership.

TUC POLICY

Given these antecedents, it is not surprising that the initial trade union position was one of extreme caution, if not outright opposition. The basis of current TUC policy was laid down in 1974. Three objections to company-based schemes of profit-sharing were raised.

> First, such schemes do not in reality provide any real control over the managerial decisions ... Second, there is no advantage to workpeople tying up their savings in the firm since this doubles the insecurity ... [third] they do little or nothing to reduce the inequality of wealth. [TUC, 1974]

The Trades Union Congress also expressed concern that such schemes excluded the public sector. Profit-sharing, however, was not a subject of report or debate at annual congress for well over a decade, until 1986, when the need to review the policy was recognized (TUC, 1986a: 278). Such a review (TUC, 1986b) was prompted by the Chancellor's proposals on profit-related pay rather than by the growth of schemes, which the TUC considered to be small. The TUC, however, was cognisant of the implications of PRP for collective bargaining, for industrial democracy, and for collective approaches to equity ownership, and for these reasons challenged the government's support for profit-related pay on the grounds of its alleged impact on employee commitment and on pay flexibility and employment. The arguments echoed the points made in the 1974 document.

The principal objection both to existing profit-sharing schemes and to the proposed PRP is their non-negotiable nature. This, the TUC believes, leads to a number of difficulties, including fluctuations in the level of profit-share outwith the influence of employee effort; the manipulation of profit figures, especially in multinational companies; and the manipulation of profits to influence mergers and take-over prospects. The non-negotiability of present schemes can and does lead to disputes, such as at Hotpoint in 1985 because of the company's decision to reduce the cost-of-living increase by discounting profit payments.

The TUC was also concerned that low-paid workers would receive a higher-than-average share of their total income in the form of profit-related pay, so that when profits fell and profit shares were cut, the low-paid would suffer more.

The TUC felt that the claim that profit-sharing improved employee commitment 'is open to doubt', but even if it could be proved the TUC wants a committed work force to be complemented by a management committed to the long-term interests of employees – job security, participation in decision-making, sharing the benefits of change, and working together towards a set of common goals. Nor does the TUC believe that improved company performance which might be associated with profit-sharing is due to pay flexibility. It is even more critical of the putative employment effects of wage flexibility, and is particularly critical of Weitzman's ideas, especially the way the government is trying to use them.

On top of these objections to profit-sharing in principle, the TUC is critical of the practical proposals for PRP. It finds the proposals convoluted and likely to be difficult to implement. It objects to the probability that existing cash-based profit- sharing schemes will be converted into Inland Revenue-approved one. Thus tax relief will be given without necessarily creating new schemes. Finally it is concerned that PRP will be based on calculations which are not readily available or can be interpreted in a number of different ways, which would 'undermine the integrity of any measure of profits'. The TUC therefore concludes that PRP will not have the beneficial effects claimed by the Chancellor and is very dubious whether tax relief to encourage PRP is either desirable or even likely to be effective.

While this response was prompted by the government-initiated debate on PRP and the TUC linked its earlier criticisms of profit-sharing to this new development, none the less it did indicate that the trade union movement may have to address the wider question of profit-sharing and employee share ownership and offer guidance to unions on how to approach the issue. None has yet been produced, and it is helpful to examine individual union responses to profit-sharing and employee share ownership and to determine the extent to which they too have been influenced by the government's initiative on PRP and employers' initiatives on financial participation schemes.

INDIVIDUAL UNION POLICIES

The thirty unions which mainly recruit in the private sector (where profit-sharing schemes are found) were asked whether or not they had an official policy on profit-sharing or employee share ownership, if either had been a subject of debate at policy-making conferences since 1978, whether the union had been party to a negotiated agreement on profit-sharing and, finally, whether they were aware of any profit-sharing arrangements introduced unilaterally by management. Union respondents were also asked to express an opinion on a number of statements about the influence and impact of profit-sharing.

Profit-sharing aroused neither union antagonism nor enthusiasm – a situation encapsulated by one commentator as 'bored hostility' (IDS, 1986). Very few of the unions surveyed had any formal policy on profit-sharing. Nor had the subject been discussed at recent conferences. The three unions operating in the banking and finance sector (the Banking, Insurance & Finance Union, BIFU; the Clearing Bank Union, CBU; the National Union of Insurance Workers, NUIW) did, however, have a recent policy on profit-sharing. It concerned the non-negotiable nature of schemes and pressure to extend schemes throughout the industry and to made the basis of the schemes more equitable.

This may well be a line unions take up in the future as they

45

reconcile themselves to schemes introduced unilaterally by management. While only a handful of unions reported any formal policy or discussion at conference, a dozen unions were aware of schemes introduced unilaterally by management and a further eight did not know the details of the local situation at head office. A number of unions, however, while not having a formal policy, operate an *ad hoc* policy of responding to scheme proposals on their merit. The Electrical Electronic Telecommunications & Plumbing Union (EETPU), for example, has described its approach as 'positive but cautious'. The principal objection is not to profit-sharing *per se* but to its non-negotiable status.

The evidence from our survey of companies is that all types of financial participation schemes are introduced unilaterally. Only twenty-three out of 373 schemes (5.8 per cent) had been bargained over, and this was more likely for traditional cash and incentive schemes than those based on the legislation. But even with cash schemes the incidence of bargaining was low, probably because such schemes are more prevalent in small companies and in the service sector, where trade union membership is at its lowest. Also, these bonuses often constitute a small, almost guaranteed, addition to wages, and as such their negotiation may not be considered a priority by the unions.

The overall absence of bargaining cannot be attributed to schemes being introduced primarily in non-union companies. In our company sample almost 70 per cent of the respondents who currently recognize a union employ at least one type of profit-sharing or employee share ownership scheme. Indeed, multiple regression analysis indicated that the relationship between share ownership schemes (not cash-based and incentive-bonus schemes) and trade union recognition was significant in itself and not just a product of company size (Baddon et al., 1987: 32).

Thus it would appear that in many unionized companies forms of financial participation are being introduced without reference to trade unions. This is understandable in the case of executive schemes, given that they apply only to a small number of senior managers. Union indifference over SAYE schemes might be explained by such schemes being optional, not directly affecting pay, and involving only a minority of the work force. Our overall survey evidence indicates that only 23 per cent of employees participate, but the figure falls to 8 per cent among manual employees, who are more likely to be unionized. In the case of ADST schemes, the rules laid down by the Inland Revenue leave little scope for negotiation between unions and employers, as the discretionary elements within these schemes become set after Revenue approval, and require shareholder approval, company approval, and Revenue reapproval of any change. This means that, as schemes tend not to be negotiated before this stage, the final form a scheme takes will almost always be entirely the product of management/Inland Revenue requirements. If unions are to influence the shape of schemes they will have to become involved at the earliest stage. This seems an unlikely prospect for SAYE, ADST, and executive schemes, but will be of greater significance if companies go down the PRP route as the government now hopes they will. The advent of PRP is forcing many unions to examine their policies on the whole area of financial participation.

Although our company survey indicated that financial participation schemes were not subject to negotiation, ten of our thirty unions claimed to have negotiated on the introduction of profit-sharing and employee share ownership schemes. Most of these cases related to cash-based schemes or incentive payments, but examples of negotiation on Finance Act-based schemes were cited. Whilst the initiative for such negotiations usually came from management, there were examples of unions representing higher-paid white-collar employees putting forward proposals to establish schemes. This has been done by the British Airline Pilots' Association (BALPA), the CBU, and the Engineers' & Managers' Association (EMA). One manual union, the Ceramic & Allied Trades' Union (CATU), claimed to have initiated a cash-based scheme.

The EETPU has been at the forefront of these developments, and in 1985 discussed the possibility of adding a form of financial involvement among employees as part of any proposed strike-free industrial relations package, with a view to creating an even greater sense of commitment by both work force and management to the enterprise.[1] Such human relations-derived sentiments lay behind the demand by the union's white-collar section for financial participation schemes in the Environmental Engineering Industry National Joint Council, which covers the electrical contracting, plumbing, and heating and ventilation industries. This is the first example of such a demand being raised on an industry-wide basis.[2]

The more typical union experience, however, is of schemes introduced unilaterally by management. A number of claims have been made by management about the virtues of schemes. Similarly unions have made a number of counter-claims about their defects.

Union respondents were asked to comment on a number of such claims.

A major plank in employer (and government) support for profit-sharing and employee share ownership is that they help to create a sense of loyalty and identity with the company. Unions were divided three ways on this proposition – equal numbers agreeing, disagreeing, and being indifferent to the claim. On the other hand union respondents were quite emphatic that financial participation schemes did not enable employees to have a say in the way their company was run. Union respondents took a more cynical view of profit-sharing, believing strongly that employees like it only for the money it brings them.

The general air of cynicism and apathy held by unions was transferred to their members. Unions felt that employees are apathetic about profit-sharing and indeed felt that it was not beneficial to them. Nor did they feel that profit-sharing was an effective incentive to make people work harder. While seeing little virtue in profit-sharing, they were divided on the view that it is an anti-trade union device. Only two unions disagreed with this proposition, but as many unions were indifferent to the point as agreed.

RESPONSES TO PRIVATIZATION

In the 1980s trade unions have had to respond to the Conservative government's privatization programme. A feature of the programme has been that a tranche of shares has been set aside for employees, usually at preferential rates. Trade unions opposed to privatization in principle have recommended that their members do not take up these offers, but the government has drawn great satisfaction from the extremely high response of employees to their allocation of shares. This has rarely been below 90 per cent and in the case of Cable & Wireless was as high as 99 per cent.

More recently, however, a more sophisticated response to the issue of shares to employees had been developed. This is particularly so at British Airways, where the joint trade union committee has encouraged employees to assign their proxy votes to the committee, so that a coherent block of employee votes could be used to apply pressure at the shareholders' AGM. The initiative for this came from BALPA, the airline pilots' union, and almost a fifth of employees had responded, giving the joint union committee control of some 2 per cent of BA equity. The success of the BA scheme inspired the union in the British Airports Authority to attempt a similar arrangement as part of the BAA flotation.

Many unions are finding that the policy of opposition to members holding shares in privatized companies is untenable, given the overwhelming response of members to the offers available to them. This discrepancy between union policy and membership response prompted the National Communications Union to review its policy at its 1987 conference. At the 1987 Congress the Union of Communication Workers called on the general council of the TUC to review the policy on social ownership with regard to, *inter alia*, the maintenance and improvement of employee share schemes.

The government may not relish the prospect of blocks of employees attempting to exercise control as shareholders, although the companies involved have adopted a co-operative stance. The government would, however, be expecting altered attitudes to industrial relations from employees by virtue of their being shareholders in their company. There are two cases to date, Jaguar and British Telecom, where that has proved not to be the case.

In Jaguar pay negotiations in 1986 profit-sharing and employee share ownership became a central part of the negotiations. While the company sought a second two-year pay deal, the white-collar unions wanted the profit-sharing scheme to be part of collective bargaining and indicated that they would be prepared to accept moderate pay rises in exchange for a greatly expanded shareholding in the company.[3] However, the two-year deal agreed for manual workers was at a much higher level than originally offered, following a two-day stoppage over the role of industrial engineers. This stoppage took both senior shop stewards and management by surprise, and demonstrated a clear desire by production workers to have more control over their working conditions as well as their pay, notwithstanding any benefits of employee share ownership or the company chairman's 'hearts and minds' programme'.[4] These events took place in a company where all but two workers took up the employee share offer on privatization, and where half the employees rejected a cash alternative to shares agreed in the 1984 pay negotiations.

The situation at British Telecom is of even greater significance. Following privatization, management have pursued a policy of decentralization to some thirty profit centres, the managers of which have authority to introduce changes in working practices and to negotiate them locally. Less emphasis was to be placed on national negotiations, which the company hopes to end in 1988. BT was meant to be able to pursue these policies because the main union, the National Communications Union (NCU), had a 'moderate' leadership, elected by individual ballots, and 96 per cent of its employees are shareholders. BT expected loyalty from its employee shareholders, but when the proposed flexibility changes threatened earnings, jobs, and working practices the result was a strike. Shareholding made no difference. As one picket said, 'It made no difference at all. It's just another kind of bonus'.[5]

The aftermath of the strike has been messy. In June 1987 BT decided that employees would receive nothing from the profit-sharing scheme because of the strike in January and February. This was despite an increase in pre-tax profits of 11.7 per cent. The decision affected all employees, as Inland Revenue regulations do not permit a differentiation between strikers and non-strikers. The decision was taken without reference to the unions, but John Golding, then General Secretary of the NCU, felt the decision would harm staff morale. BT still face the problem of introducing flexible working practices with a work force which remains hostile to change and whose dissatisfaction with the settlement to the strike was evident in the narrow defeat (77,372 to 74,604) of a motion at the NCU conference calling on John Golding to resign immediately. There can be no presumption that an overwhelming acceptance of shares in the company against union advice can be equated with commitment to the company if the company in turn does not show loyalty and commitment to its employees. As a newspaper editorial put it, at the time of the strike:

> BT is justified in pointing out that its profit after dividends is very much less, and it is right to insist that changes in working practices are necessary. More dubiously, though, it has implied that it expects loyalty because of the financial stake it has given employees in the company. But the lesson of the dispute would appear to be that a financial stake is worth little unless accompanied by a modicum of industrial democracy and a mechanism for consultation. A more participative managerial style might have reduced the atmosphere of resentment surrounding the dispute.[6]

There is, then, evidence of some change in trade unions' response to the growth in uptake of employee share ownership. There are

50

signs of movement away from the attitude of 'bored hostility' to attempts to turn the issue of shares to individual employees to the advantage of the collective interest of trade unions. The initial response urging members to reject the share offers has been found wanting, but so too has the belief that employees, by virtue of holding shares worth a few hundred pounds, will willingly agree to changes which may affect their earning capacity and work practices to a much greater degree.

COLLECTIVE OWNERSHIP

From the response of trade unions to the initiatives of employers and government, we turn now to an area where the initiative, however, limited, has come from the labour movement, namely moves towards forms of collective employee share ownership.

In rejecting profit-sharing in its 1974 policy statement the TUC did indicate its support for the development of a form of capital-sharing at national level, based on a national fund administered through the trade union movement. Through it the TUC hoped to address one of the perceived failings or company schemes, their failure to reduce the inequality of wealth. These sentiments were endorsed in a Labour Party Green Paper, *Capital and Equality*, which found company-based schemes to be 'offensive to both trade unions and socialism' (Labour Party, 1973: 15) and advanced instead the idea of a national capital-sharing scheme with a national workers' fund. Companies would be compelled to transfer 1 per cent of their equity shares to the fund each year. Such a fund would cover *all* workers on an *equal* basis, and was to be run by a governing council, with worker representatives nominated through TUC channels clearly in a majority.

Share schemes based on collective ownership, especially those in which unions exert some control over aggregate funds, present a more favourable proposition to labour movements in different countries. Labour's 1973 plans were based on ideas being developed in Denmark but, like other similar schemes, have met with considerable resistance from employers and their political allies, precisely because existing property and ownership rights might be compromised if such schemes were to be adopted. For this reason, progress toward financial participation through collective funds has made little headway in most European countries, and the

51

schemes which have been introduced tend to be diluted versions of these originally intended by their proponents.

Probably the best known of the collective schemes are the proposals associated with the Swedish economist Rudolf Meidner, whose committee submitted a far-reaching plan to the 1976 congress of the Swedish manual workers' union confederation, the LO (Meidner, 1978). The main proposal was that a percentage of profits earned by private companies should be transferred as shares to a wage- earner fund administered and controlled by the unions. Ownership and voting rights would reside with the fund, and not with individuals, in order to provide unions with substantive means to influence board-level decisions and to build up dividend income which would contribute towards the provision of educational and training services to members, which in turn would enable them to gain sufficient expertise to participate in board-level decision-making as anticipated by legislation passed in 1976.

The aims of the proposed system have been summarized by Martin (1984: 273):

1 To conform with union policies of wage solidarity but without redistributing income from labour to capital.
2 To counteract concentrations of wealth and power.
3 To provide workers with the means to influence industrial development.

The ultimate objective of the scheme would be to bring private industry under collective labour ownership and union control, a prospect not willingly contemplated by private industry, which made strong and persistent representations to the government during the succeeding years, leading subsequently to a much modified form of the proposals, with objectives more acceptable to employers. The present scheme legislation was enacted in 1983 and involves the establisment of separate investment funds, each permitting a maximum 8 per cent shareholding in any one company, and though the unions are allocated a role in the management of each fund this may also involve other employees as well as non-employee representation.

The Swedish experience demonstrates clearly that the choice of share ownership policies and the types of approach to be encouraged will depend crucially upon governmental inclinations and broader industrial stratagems as constrained or encouraged by political influences exercised by different groups who might expect to benefit, or otherwise. Indeed, Martin believes that the ambiguous position adopted by the Swedish Social Democrats to the Meidner plan contributed to their electoral defeat in the 1976 general election (1984: 286), and that their commitment in principle to wage-earner funds aided their victory in the 1982 election, though in both cases not by very much (p. 328).

The Swedish experience is, however, only one model which the British trade union and labour movement has turned to from time to time. The *Capital and Equality* report received only a lukewarm reception within the Labour Party and did not become a policy option of the 1974–9 government (Elliot, 1984: 189). Neither has the policy been pursued by the TUC. Prior to the 1987 general election the Labour Party adopted its 'social ownership' policy (Labour Party, 1986). This may be seen as a shift away from the traditional model of nationalization to a form of public ownership which is compatible with consumer and employee rights (Thomas, 1986). Specifically it was proposed to take British Telecom and British Gas back into public ownership, to create a new body, British Enterprise, to acquire stock in strategic sectors, and to establish a British Investment Bank and a British Savings Bank to establish 'a significant socially-owned presence in the financial sector'. But, although citing Swedish wage-earner funds, its proposals on financial participation drew more upon the American model of Employee Share Ownership Plans. These were to be encouraged, along with worker co-operatives, combined with wider statutory rights to information, consultation, and representation for all employees.

Although acknowledging the American origins of ESOPs, the social ownership document urges avoidance of three pitfalls in the American scheme. First, that benefits have, in some cases, been unfairly distributed. Second, that workers have not had voting rights with their shares: and third that pension funds have sometimes been used to set up funds.

Labour's proposals, however, although presented as a collective-based alternative form of ownership in contrast to the individual ownership of the Conservatives' plans, would not bring private industry under collective ownership and control at a national level. ESOPs may permit employee shareholders to have a greater say in the running of their firm, but the evidence from the United States, reviewed in Chapter 1, suggests that the impact has been limited. Moreover, Unity Trust, the main advocate and financer of ESOPs in the UK, believe that no more than around 14 per cent of a company's employees should participate in an ESOP, because of the risk of tying up limited assets in their work.[7]

The collective control arguments in favour of ESOPs in *Social Ownership* are, as in much Labour Party thinking, confused and conflated with human relations-derived arguments. Thus the authors of *Social Ownership* state that 'employee share ownership can be associated with significant benefits such as increased workforce motivation and involvement', even though they add the proviso that this will only happen in genuine schemes which give employees influence as well as income (p. 9).

The centre right of the party has taken the initiative in developing policy on how to manage the economy and how to involve employees and management in building new relationships. These policies are both a break with the statist public ownership traditions and an adaptation to the apparent success of the Conservatives' policies. Policy on employee share ownership also has its roots in the paternalism we have seen associated with the Liberal Party. Thus Roy Hattersley, for example, while denying the Conservatives' version of 'people's capitalism', does believe that:

> the possession of equity holdings which are organised to maximise the influence of employees within the company can produce a wholly different attitude, for the employee shareholder is doubly involved with the company. That such schemes reduce alienation and increase the feeling that the employee–company relationship is more than the expenditure of minimum effort necessary to ensure regular wage payment is beyond dispute. [1987: 202]

Hattersley's support for employee buy-outs, improved share ownership schemes, ESOPs, and worker co-operatives stems from the belief that 'the economy would benefit from the increased emotional involvement of employees in the company which now employs them and which, in the future, they would partly own' (1985a: 7). But for Hattersley share ownership must go hand-in-hand with a substantial extension of employee participation, and he recognizes the need for legislation to spread the best practice in this area. Only if share ownership schemes are combined with forms of employee participation will trade unionists come to support them. The ultimate goal is to increase commitment and to reduce employees' feeling of alienation, which proves a psychological barrier to change and innovation in British industry.

This analysis stands in marked contrast with that of the traditional left in the party as expressed by Tony Benn, who has argued that profit-sharing:

> does not resolve the basic conflict of interest that exists in industry, does not give the worker-shareholders any real share of power in the firm, and could put their savings and their pensions – as well as their jobs – at risk, if the firm collapses. [1979: 64]

However, Benn's view is now a minority position within the party, and leading party officials, such as the shadow Chancellor, John Smith, MP, are advocating the development of ESOPs as a more desirable and effective method of boosting employee motivation than the profit-related pay schemes favoured by the government.[8]

Financed by Unity Trust, with support from the Labour opposition and the government and the unions in the specific firms, ESOPs were first established in the UK in the first half of 1987 at Roadchef, People's Provincial Buses, and Armstrong Engineering in Coventry.

The strong support for ESOPs from both Labour and Conservative politicians should, perhaps, urge some caution on the unions involved. A review of the operation of ESOPs in the United States suggests that if an ESOP is to be successful, then:

> the appropriate union role must, almost necessarily, become less adversarial and less committed to traditional collective bargaining ... The union must become – a genuine partner in the business. It must become, at least in some measure, more like a Japanese company union and less like the craft or industrial union more familiar in the West. [Partnership Research, 1987]

A note of caution is introduced, as in some sectors, especially airlines and trucking, ESOPs have become associated with concession bargaining.

CONCLUSIONS

The position of the trade union and labour movement can be seen to be in a state of flux. The Labour Party's opposition to the Conservatives' 1972 and 1973 legislation on employee share ownership schemes was not based on firm principles. Labour could

55

therefore easily move to accepting profit-sharing as part of the Lib-Lab pact, and later, as the Conservatives' schemes became established, move from opposition to seeking ways to improve them and make them more equitable. The alternative vision propounded in *Capital and Equality* has never been a strong policy influence on Labour governments, and the new social ownership policy owes more to American than to Scandinavian experience. Running through all Labour Party policy is an acceptance, if not a firm belief, that profit-sharing and employee share ownership schemes can reduce 'them and us'. Thus the Labour Party is pulled towards the paternalism of the Liberals' approach but is drawn back from fully supporting it by the need to favour collective bargaining because of the links between the party and the trade unions. It is only in *Capital and Equality* that the co-partnership view is rejected.

> We believe that profit-sharing can all too easily encourage workers to accept the ideology of management that they are somehow part of a company 'team' with their role being simply to carry out the orders handed down from their management 'team-leaders'. What is more it can also encourage the belief that the interests of managers, and those of workers, are 'when you come down to it' really identical.

Labour Party thinking in this area is now dominated by the centre right of the party, particularly by Roy Hattersley and John Smith. While the party has developed its 'social ownership' vision, TUC thinking in this area has been extremely limited. From the 1974 statement on profit-sharing (as part of its Industrial Democracy policy) until the response to the government's Profit-related Pay document, the TUC has shown little interest in the question of profit-sharing and employee share ownership. The TUC was still tied to the Labour Party's traditional strategy of nationalization, but the lack of an unambiguous and attractive lead from the Labour Party has left the TUC somewhat adrift in its response to management initiatives in financial participation, or the development of viable alternatives for the labour movement.

The same observations can be made about constituent unions, although the unilateral introduction of various types of scheme in the late 1970s and early 1980s forced some unions to come to terms with a changed situation. But in most cases this was on an *ad hoc* basis, in particular firms or particular sectors. Although unions were aware of the TUC position, they responded as they saw fit, or in some cases, as their members pushed them. In particular, the overwhelming response of members in accepting free and reduced-priced shares as part of the privatization flotations in the face of union advice has forced a change of thinking.

This is most apparent with the moves to organize proxies in BA and in the support unions have given to the creation of ESOPs via Unity Trust. However, there as yet remain only indications of an attempt to think out the implications of profit-sharing and employee share ownership. For the most part the characterization of 'bored hostility' remains most apt. Unions are likely to stir into action over the non-negotiable nature of most schemes, especially where the benefits threaten their traditional collective bargaining aspirations. This is almost certain to be the case if many firms take up profit-related pay, as they are now being encouraged to do. The dangers to trade union organization stemming from non-negotiability are highlighted by the situation at Heinz. The company has introduced a profit-sharing scheme which was negotiated individually with employees via plant shop stewards, but outwith formal negotiations with full-time officers. Given our findings that schemes are found in unionized companies, any deterrence effect might be directed towards a goal of company unionism rather than non-unionism. The extent to which this might occur will be one of the issues addressed in our case studies.

NOTES

1. *Financial Times*, 10 December 1985.
2. ibid., 20 April 1986.
3. ibid., 4 October 1986.
4. ibid., 22–3 October 1986.
5. ibid., 27 January 1987.
6. *Glasgow Herald*, 23 January 1987.
7. *Observer*, 5 April 1987.
8. *Financial Times*, 9 April 1987.

Part 2

Company practice and ideology

4

Contours of profit-sharing and employee share ownership

Although the Inland Revenue publishes data on the number of schemes it has approved, and despite previous surveys of share ownership schemes,[1] neither source has provided the breadth of information and detail that is needed to create an accurate assessment of the current situation. The survey stage of our research set out to encompass the widest range of companies possible in terms of size and industrial sector, and data were collected on a variety of employees share ownership and profit-sharing schemes. They produced details of over 350 companies, of which nearly two-thirds,[2] employing just over a million people, operated at least one profit-sharing or employee share ownership scheme. In total, about 400 schemes form the basis of the analysis.

The methodology employed in the survey is discussed in appendix 2. In general we wanted data which would allow an assessment of the distribution of profit-sharing and employee share ownership by industrial sector and size of company. The characteristics of various types of profit-sharing and employee share ownership were also considered in the context of the economic, industrial relations, and physical environments in which they operate.

In this chapter we focus on the presentation of some of the general results of the survey, relating to the characteristics of the companies in the sample. Survey information relating to trade union recognition and organization and to aspects of management organization are addressed in the relevant chapters (see especially Chapter 3 and 5). We begin by reviewing some basic features of the respondents.

THE COMPANIES AND THEIR SCHEMES

Of the 356 companies responding, 231 (65 per cent) confirmed that they operated at least one type of scheme. In all, respondents supplied details of 396 schemes, as it is common practice to operate two or three schemes concurrently. This relatively high incidence of profit-sharing and employee share ownership[3] among our sample may be explained by some aspects of the survey methodology. Value-added and non-individual incentive bonus schemes were considered to be types of profit-sharing and accounted for slightly over 10 per cent of the total. Also, this study was carried out after the 1984 legislation which led to a boom in executive option schemes (23 per cent),[4] which will be reflected in our figures.

Although it seems probable that companies which operate profit-sharing schemes were more likely to reply to our questionnaire, it was found, by checking the Extel Data lists, that a similar proportion of both responding and non-responding companies operated profit-sharing and employee share ownership schemes of some kind. However, it is possible that the companies which considered their schemes to be operating successfully were more likely to reply. Also, smaller, unlisted companies are not included in the lists and therefore could not be checked in this manner.

In total, respondents returned details of schemes as in Table 2. Profit-related bonus (cash-based) schemes are the most commonly operated among our respondents, with SAYE and executive (discretionary) following. The Inland Revenue-approved ADST schemes appear less frequently, as do the company share options. These results do not match those produced by the Inland Revenue (table 1), which suggest that similar numbers of SAYE and ADST schemes have been approved.[5] Our sample produced eighty-seven SAYE schemes, compared with only twenty-six ADST schemes. The unexpectedly large figure for SAYE schemes may be partly explained by the skew in our sample towards large companies. Although both tend to be found in larger enterprises, SAYE schemes appear to be more concentrated than ADST schemes in very large companies[6] (cf. Table 7).

It is probable that the frequency with which a scheme is used will depend on its adaptability, its ease of application and on the advantages that it is perceived to offer the company and its employees. Until recently cash-based and incentive schemes have not been subject to any legislation and can be operated in a variety

Table 2 Incidence of type of profit-sharing or employee share ownership scheme

Scheme type	No.	% of total
Cash-based	123	31
Executive	91	23
SAYE	87	22
Incentive *	40	10
ADST	26	7
Company	21	5
Other	8	2
Total	396	100

* Incentive bonus not based on performance.

of forms and in a variety of environments. Secondly, a profit-sharing bonus may be used as a means of improving individual or departmental performance in both large and small companies, as a profit-sharing bonus can be geared to a small group, even in a large organization. Thirdly, a cash-bonus is a traditionally accepted form of payment of which most companies and employees have had experience and which can be introduced and withdrawn with relative ease.

Discretionary (executive) schemes may have become significant but, by definition, are unlikely to involve more than a small proportion of company employees. The tax incentives introduced in the 1984 Finance Act make the schemes attractive in remunerating senior and middle managers.

Table 3 outlines the total numbers of employees in firms operating profit-sharing or employee share ownership. Employees of firms operating more than one type of scheme will be counted separately for each scheme, and as indicated, may not necessarily be participating in the scheme. Schemes vary both in the proportion of employees who are *eligible* to participate and, where schemes are voluntary, in the numbers of employees who *choose* to participate.

Cash-based schemes figured most frequently in numerical terms and also involved one-third of employees in the sample. As Table 3 shows, ADST schemes involved only 18 per cent of the sample, yet, like cash-based schemes, they involve a large proportion of employees. As both executive and SAYE schemes tend to involve small proportions of employees within an enterprise their frequency in the sample is disproportionately large relative to the numbers of

Table 3 Employment in companies operating various types of profit-sharing and employee share ownership*

Scheme type	No. employed by companies operating PS or ESO	% employees in sample
SAYE	822,658	73
Executive	794,764	70
Cash-based	374,327	33
Incentive	241,137	21
ADST	198,125	18
Company	132,837	12
Share	55,076	5
Mix	5,215	0·5
Total	1,006,940	89
Total in sample	1,132,194	100

*These figures represent the number of employees who are working in companies operating schemes, not the number of employees who are eligible or who are participating. Therefore the apparently high proportion (89 per cent) of employees does not represent the actual numbers participating.

employees actually taking part. While executive schemes often involve no more than a few senior executives, the Inland Revenue rules for approval stipulate that SAYE schemes must include all full-time employees with five years' experience. However, the thirty[7] companies who supplied the relevant details had an average of only 23 per cent of employees participating in their SAYE schemes. The proportion of take-up seems to be lowest among manual employees, higher among non-manual employees and highest among management (Table 4). Factors influencing take-up may include size of disposable income; familiarity with share ownership both within and outwith the company's scheme; trade

Table 4 Take-up of SAYE option, by employee group

	Employee group	%	No.
1	Manual	8	16
	Non-manual	13	19
	Management	26	16
2	All groups	23	30

union membership and influence and the traditionally more positive orientation towards share ownership.

In all but a few cases, less than one in five employees participated in their company's SAYE scheme. Thus, in spite of the large numbers of employees eligible to join SAYE schemes, in practice only a small number actually do. Furthermore, as we see in Table 5, where share capital schemes exist the proportion of shares in employee ownership is also low, with 56 per cent of respondents indicating that less than 1 per cent of the total share issues belonged to employees. In our sample, of the companies operating Inland Revenue-approved schemes, in no case did the share capital owned by employees amount to more than 10 per cent of the total, suggesting that these schemes do not result in any substantial change in ownership relations. It appears that the Institutional Investors' Investment Protection Committee's guidelines which limit employee share ownership to less than 10 per cent are being adhered to, with only two respondents even approaching that level.[8] One of our objectives in this book is to discover why the employee take-up is relatively low and why greater inroads into capital ownership by employees have not been made.

Table 5 Proportion of share capital owned by employees in Inland Revenue-approved schemes

%	No.	%
Less than 1	60	56
1–2	22	20
2–4	6	6
4–6	6	6
8–10	2	2
Over 10	12	11
Total	108	100*

*As in some other tables, the figures do not add up exactly to 100, owing to rounding.

INDUSTRIAL ANALYSIS

Table 6 outlines the pattern of profit-sharing and employee share ownership, using the industrial sectors by which the sample was stratified. In our sample the incidence of profit-sharing and employee share ownership was not significantly dependent on industrial sector.[9] Although they were less well represented in the

Table 6 Industrial sector (SIC) and use of profit-sharing or employee share ownership

	Industrial sector (SIC)	Sample companies with PS or ESO	
		No.	%
1	Energy		
2	Metals	16	62
3	Engineering	38	73
4	Other manufacturing	45	82
5	Construction	18	60
6	Distribution	49	49
7	Transport	13	62
8	Banking	36	75
9	Other services	16	76
	Total	231	65

distributive and higher in 'other manufacturing' sectors, this almost certainly reflects the pattern of enterprise and unit size in those sectors, with larger unit and company sizes in manufacturing than in distribution, which also has high ratios of part-time and low-paid workers and high staff turnover.

SIZE, OWNERSHIP AND LOCATION

Our search for company characteristics which might be associated with particular types of scheme led us next to look at size, ownership, and location variables. We consider these in turn.

Size

It seemed likely that smaller firms would have more difficulty in mounting the resources and administration/financial expertise to deal with the problems of introducing a share-based scheme, particularly in view of the complexity of Inland Revenue regulations. The returns, analysed by size, are shown in Table 7. So far as share-based schemes are concerned, there is a suggestion of increasing incidence with size.

Multivariate analysis confirmed that companies with more than 1,000 employees were significantly more likely to be operating a

Table 7 Type of profit-sharing or employee share ownership scheme, by respondent size (by employment)

	Scheme size (by employment)															
	20-49		50-99		100-199		200-499		500-999		1,000-4,999		More than 5,000		Total	
	N	%	N	%	N	%	N	%	N	%	N	%	N	%	N	%
A. Share-based schemes																
ADST	1	3·8	3	11·5	2	7·7	3	11·5	2	7·7	7	26·9	8	30·8	26	100
Executive	3	3·3	4	4·4	6	6·6	10	11	8	8·8	27	29·7	33	36·3	91	100
SAYE	1	1·2	4	4·6	3	3·4	10	11·5	9	10·3	22	25·3	38	43·7	87	100
Company	1	4·8	2	9·5	1	4·8	5	23·9	2	9·5	4	19	6	28·6	21	100
Total	6	2·7	13	5·8	12	5·3	28	12·4	21	9·3	60	26·7	85	37·8	225	100
B. Cash-based schemes																
Cash	16	13	32	26	10	8·1	25	20·3	15	12·2	13	10·6	12	9·7	123	100
Incentive	6	15	7	17·5	1	2·5	2	5	5	12·5	6	15	13	32·5	40	100
Other	1	12·5	1	12·5	–	–	1	12·5	2	25	2	25	1	12·5	8	100
Total	23	13·4	40	23·4	11	6·4	28	16·4	22	12·9	21	12·3	26	15·2	171	100

share scheme than smaller companies. SAYE, ADST and executive schemes are concentrated in companies with over 1,000 employees, a result consistent with the hypothesis that larger companies are better equipped to develop and administer share-based schemes, and hence make use of the advantages offered by the Inland Revenue. Cash-based schemes, on the other hand, were more evenly distributed throughout the size ranges, and no significant relationship with size was discovered in multiple regression tests. Smaller companies may find cash-based and incentive schemes less complicated than share-based schemes. They require no outside intervention or approval, and although they offer no tax benefits, they may be seen as a means of employee motivation where company size and type of production allow a close profit share–reward/effort relationship.

Ownership

Public quoted companies seemed more likely to be participants in share-based schemes, independently of size, because the conditions that private companies have to meet to satisfy the Inland Revenue are quite stringent and may act as a deterrent. The Inland Revenue suggests that only around 15 per cent of its SAYE and ADST schemes operate in non-quoted companies.[10] Table 8 shows the pattern of ownership among the respondents, classified by profit-sharing and share ownership activity. This underlines the much higher proportion of public quoted companies involved in financial participation schemes.

Among companies owned by foreign multinationals, US-based companies proved more likely to have schemes (64 per cent) than their European counterparts (29 per cent). This may reflect the popularity of forms of company-based financial participation in the

Table 8 Profit-sharing, employee share ownership and patterns of ownership

Type of ownership	No. with PS/ESO	Total No. in sample	% within group with PS/ESO
Private UK company	147	260	56·5
Public UK company	84	96	87·5
Total	231	356	

United States, where knowledge and understanding of the various forms of financial involvement have developed to a greater extent. Unfortunately, the figures for the Japanese-owned firms were too small to allow any conclusions to be drawn.

Head office location

Larger companies tend to have their head office in the London and south of England area, but, even apart from the size factor, it seemed possible that closer location to the financial mainspring of the country might be an added incentive to financial participation schemes. Alternatively, differences in the industry structure may be reflected in locational distribution (e.g. with a high proportion of financial and banking services in London and the south). Table 9 confirms the higher density of profit-sharing and share ownership schemes in the south and London.

Table 9 Regional variations: location of head office

| | Companies with profit-sharing | | |
	No.	Density (%)	Total No.
London	78	78	100
South*	73	77	95
Midlands†	26	58	45
Provinces††	53	59	116
Total	230		356

*Includes south-east, south-west, and East Anglia.
†Includes east and west Midlands.
††Includes Yorkshire, northern England, Wales, Scotland, and Northern Ireland.

THE CONTEXT OF INDUSTRIAL RELATIONS AND EMPLOYEE PARTICIPATION

We focus next on the industrial relations and personnel environments in which profit-sharing and employee share ownership schemes operate. This is followed by a discussion of how profit-sharing and employee share ownership relate to other types of participative and mechanism, to the bargaining and industrial relations processes, and to the trade union and other employee representative bodies.

The industrial relations background

The survey set out to provide details of the degree of sophistication of the industrial relations and personnel backgrounds in which schemes are operating, and also of how profit-sharing and employee share ownership relate to pay determination structures at both local and national levels. Information was gathered on the following:

1 Patterns and levels of collective bargaining and their relationship to the operation of PS and/or ESO. Repondents supplied details about the organizational level at which pay is decided; whether it is negotiated and whether it is the subject of multiple or single-employer negotiations.
2 The status of the personnel/industrial relations function and its potential influence on the operation of PS/ESO. Respondents were asked whether their board included a director with particular responsibility for personnel/industrial relations. This may serve as a proxy for assessing the priorities and resources allocated to those functions.
3 The significance of capital and labour intensity for PS/ESO. The figures produced for PS/ESO by industrial sector showed no significant relationship; however, as there may be some relationship at company level, respondents were asked to give some indication of wage costs relative to total costs.
4 The relationship of PS/ESO to other types of employee involvement. Information on employee involvement schemes was analysed to see whether they are used in conjunction with, or as a substitute for, representative and workplace participation.

Consideration of the relationship between the work force profile of companies and their involvement with profit-sharing and employee share ownership yielded no significant association between the proportions of part-time/full-time, male/female and white-collar/manual employees and PS/ESO.[11]

For respondents as a whole, pay levels were most commonly determined at company level (roughly 40 per cent of cases). Manual workers (28 per cent) were much more likely than non-manuals (6 per cent) to have pay determined at national level by multi-employer organizations. Conversely, non-manuals were twice as likely to have pay determined by management decision (26 per cent, as compared with 12 per cent). When examined in terms

70

Table 10 Level of pay bargaining and profit-sharing or employee share ownership*

	Manual			Non-manual		
Level of pay bargaining	No. with PS/ESO	Total respond-ing	%	No. with PS/ESO	Total respond-ing	%
Multi-employer	52	100	52	15	23	65
Company†	84	130	65	90	149	60
Management decision†	27	43	63	61	92	66
Total	163	273		166	264	

*Excluding companies which operated executive schemes alone.
†These categories include plant-level bargaining.

of profit-sharing and employee share ownership the results were as in Table 10.

As we might expect, the proportion of PS/ESO schemes for manual workers is highest where there is company or workplace bargaining, but even in multi-employer bargaining situations just over 50 per cent had some financial participation scheme for manual employees. Among non-manual employees there was little to choose between the different forms of pay determination. Nor indeed was there a statistically significant difference between manual and non-manual employees in terms of pay determination systems.[12] More generally, multivariate analysis did not suggest any close relationship between bargaining structure and the frequency of PS/ESO: such differences as are indicated in the table may well reflect differences in company size and industrial structure.

When we turn to the proportion of pay received in the form of profit-sharing bonus,[13] the mode is between 2 and 4 per cent, but, as Table 11 indicates, just over one in five provided a bonus of more than 10 per cent. Overall, the evidence supports the view that in a majority of cases profit-sharing has a marginal influence on pay.

The personnel/industrial relations function

It seemed possible that the adoption of financial participation schemes by companies might be a reflection of a well developed

71

Table 11 Percentage of pay as profit-sharing bonus

% of pay as bonus	No.	%
Less than 2	18	13
2–4	43	31
4–6	22	16
6–8	11	8
8–10	14	10
Over 10	29	21
Total	137	100

personnel/industrial relations function in the company organization. However,we could find no significant relationship between profit-sharing and the existence of a personnel/industrial relations director on the board, although slightly more companies (47 per cent) operating a scheme did recognize that position, compared to 40 per cent of those which did not operate PS/ESO. This difference may be caused by factors such as company size.[14]

Capital/labour intensity

One hypothesis is that the larger the proportion of total operating costs taken up by employment costs the greater will be management efforts to control pay costs and returns in terms of productivity and efficiency, and this might favour the adoption of PS/ESO schemes. Alternatively, at lower levels of labour costs, the implementation of a profit-sharing or employee share ownership scheme might be easier because of the smaller number of employees. Of course other factors, such as unionization, which we discuss later in this section, will also affect this. As can be seen from Table 12, no clear relationship appears to exist between labour intensity and PS/ESO.

Profit-sharing, employee share ownership and employee participation

An important question is whether profit-sharing and employee share ownership are being used as a means of work and employee control, as a means of increasing employee involvement in the company, or as a mixture of both. Surprisingly, less than 10 per cent

Table 12 Employment costs (as a percentage of total operating costs, i.e. wages; salaries + National Insurance; pensions and other employee benefits) and operation of profit-sharing and/or employee share ownership

Employment costs (%)	Profit-sharing/employee share ownership		
	Yes (%)	No (%)	Total (N)
2–15	48	52	33
16–25	86	14	50
26–36	69	31	66
37–46	75	25	57
47–56	56	44	62
57–68	62	38	29
70–85	47	53	19
Total	66	34	316*

*Not all respondents supplied this information.

of PS/ESO users replied that employees had been consulted before or during the implementation of the profit-sharing or employee share ownership scheme: yet prior consultation could evidently be employed as a marketing exercise, particularly in the case of the voluntary SAYE schemes. This has implications for employee representative bodies where Inland Revenue-approved schemes are involved, as, once schemes have been approved, the few optional areas within them cannot be altered. Perhaps employers judged these types of employee participation to be limited to financial involvement, not requiring the active participation of employees in their implementation.

Compared with other types of employee involvement, it is apparent from Table 13 that profit-sharing and employee share ownership are both among the more popular types of employee participation being used by our sample. Table 13 reveals that profit-sharing and employee share ownership are of major significance if they are considered in terms of the number of schemes in operation, and, given the popularity of cash-based schemes in smaller companies which are less likely to operate other types of formal participation, the company's profit-sharing scheme may be the only form of employee participation open to many people. But while profit-sharing is the most popular type of participation in smaller companies, employee share ownership schemes are the more popular form in larger organizations (1,000+

Table 13 Size of company (by employment) and type of participation scheme

	ESO*	PS†	Pension trust	JCCs	Safety com- mittee	Chair- man's forum	Briefing group	Commn. scheme	Quality circle	Job enlarge- ment	Total No. in sample
Under 50	4	22	10	2	6	5	8	8	1		50
50–99	10	39	27	8	16	3	13	8	1	1	67
100–199	6	11	17	8	18	1	11	6		1	40
200–499	19	27	27	13	30	2	20	12	3	1	54
500–999	15	20	21	16	22	5	18	6	5	1	38
1,000–4,999	35	19	32	29	34	9	26	32	12	2	57
Over 5,000	53	25	39	42	43	12	34	28	14	4	50
Total	142	163	173	118	169	37	130	100	36	10	356

*Executive schemes were not included, as they typically involve few employees.
†Cash-based profit-sharing and incentive schemes.

Table 14 Employee participation in total sample and in firms operating profit-sharing or employee share ownership

Type of employee participation	(a) Total in sample		(b) Total with PS	
	No.	%	No.	%
Pension trustees	173	49	118	68
JCCs	118	33	92	78
Safety committee	169	48	116	69
Chairman's forum	37	10	30	81
Briefing group(s)	130	37	100	77
Communication group(s)	100	28	77	77
Quality circles	36	10	10	100
Job enlargement scheme	10	3	10	100
Other	32	9	22	69

The proportion of the total sample operating profit-sharing or employee share ownership is 64·9 per cent.

employees) and, not surprisingly, the latter display a greater overall tendency to operate a range of employee involvement schemes. The tendency for firms with PS/ESO to have a greater participation in a variety of forms of employee involvement is apparently confirmed by Table 14.

Column *a* in Table 14 refers to the number and proportion of all respondents employing various types of formal employee participation. While employee trustees on pension funds and health and safety committees featured strongly, briefing groups, JCCs, and communication groups were also in use in a substantial percentage of cases. Chairman's forums, quality circles and job enlargement schemes appeared to be less popular. In this case 'Other' often referred to social events, clubs, and works outings, etc. However, as the figures in column *b* demonstrate, respondents with some form of PS/ESO scheme were much more likely to be party to each of the other types of employee participation listed, particularly the less popular forms. This evidence is consistent with the findings of Poole (1987), who observes a strong association between PS/ESO and other types of employee participation. It is worth noting, however, that multivariate analysis just failed to produce a statistically significant relationship when other variables such as size, location, etc. were included (Baddon *et al.*, 1987).

Unionization

As we would expect, our survey results show that larger companies with PS/ESO showed a greater propensity to recognize unions, and the level of recognition is higher in manufacturing than elsewhere. The results in Table 15 suggest that unionized companies have a higher representation of PS/ESO schemes than non-unionized concerns, though unionization is in no sense a condition of PS/ESO participation.

Table 15 Trade union recognition by operation of profit-sharing or employee share ownership

| | With PS/ESO | | Without PS/ESO | | |
	No.	%	No.	%	Total
Unionized	142	69	64	31	206
Non-union	89	59	61	41	150
Total	231	100	125	100	356

CONCLUSION

From this partial review of the survey evidence, a limited number of conclusions can be drawn. The relatively widespread incidence of financial participation schemes of all sorts is consistent with the image projected by the current volume of debate and discussion in political and economic circles, in the press, and among practitioners. Such schemes are distributed across industry and the services and across a wide range of company sizes. Our evidence suggests that profit-sharing and employee share ownership schemes are among the most commonly used types of employee participation scheme.

However, even at this stage, there are some pieces of evidence which require a cautious approach to interpretation. There are suggestions, for example, that cash-based incentive schemes may be more suitable for smaller companies in which the limited management and administrative resources available make it easier to cope with cash rather than share-based schemes. In larger companies the organizational problems of Inland Revenue-approved schemes are easier to take on board, and share ownership will commonly figure as an element in a 'package' of involvement covering a variety of aspects of participation.

Share-based schemes, then, tend to be concentrated in larger companies, and SAYE and executive schemes usually involve small proportions of employees. Share schemes appear to have made little impact either on wage levels, constituting a small proportion of total wages, or on patterns of share ownership in the companies in which they operate. In all but a few examples employee-owned shares made up a tiny proportion of the total, and in the vast majority of cases even the 10 per cent limit imposed by the Institutional Investors' Investment Protection Committees was in no danger of being reached. On the other hand, cash-based schemes tend to involve more people, both within the companies in which they operate and in the range of companies which operate them. However, like share schemes, profit-sharing bonuses seldom make up more than a very small proportion of total wages, and their use appears to be limited to that of effort/reward exercises. Cash-based schemes tended to be perceived as a means of rewarding employees for improved performance, and of developing business awareness. Neither type of scheme offers opportunities to individual employees or their representative organizations to participate in the running of their company, nor are the schemes themselves often open to consultation or negotiation.

Although the propensity of larger firms to use profit-sharing and employee share ownership means that there is a greater probability of finding profit-sharing and/or employee share ownership in unionized firms, the nature and distribution of the type of scheme involved has meant that schemes seldom enter negotiating or consultative procedures (see Chapter 5). Inland Revenue rules leave little room for negotiation after they have been approved and are almost never subject to negotiation before approval. Also, the two most popular Inland Revenue-approved schemes in our study, executive and SAYE, require the minimum involvement of employee representatives, given the exclusive nature of the former and the voluntary nature of the latter.

These differences between cash-based and share ownership schemes underline the fact that it is misleading to lump all forms of financial participation together, a conclusion which will be further substantiated in later chapters. Even at this point, however, it is worth recording that further statistical examination of the survey evidence, reported in Baddon *et al.* (1987) suggests that whereas cash-based schemes have a fairly random distribution across the population of organizations, share ownership schemes exhibit well formed relationships with variables such as size, head office location and public quoted company status. These variables may be regarded as 'enabling' in the sense that they reflect the greater ability of some organizations to cope with the administrative problems of the more complex employee share ownership schemes. In addition to the enabling characteristics, we may also think in terms of motivating factors; that is, influences which would encourage companies to participate in share ownership schemes, such as pay determination structures, capital intensity, the presence of the participation arrangements, and so on. Our analysis suggests that some of these motivating factors play a part in determining the adoption of share ownership schemes, but a lesser part than those we have termed 'enabling'. It also indicates that there are quite distinct differences between the cash-based and employee share ownership schemes in this respect.

These suggestive findings will be explored in later chapters, using evidence from the case studies to supplement the survey data, which, in the last resort, are a somewhat blunt instrument with which to explore the underlying relationships involved in this discussion.

NOTES

1. See for instance, D. W. Bell and G. G. Hanson (1984) or Copeman (1986).

2. A small number of companies did reply but did not co-operate, and the accuracy with which some respondents replied to the questionnaire may be doubted. During follow-up telephone calls some respondents denied all knowledge of the profit-sharing schemes which company returns had intimated they operated. (This applied only to cash-based and incentive schemes, and in no case involved the Inland Revenue-approved schemes.)

3. Blanchflower and Oswald (1987, using WIRS data for 1984) found that more than 40 per cent of establishments in the private sector had at least one of the following: an employee share scheme, a cash profit-sharing scheme or a value-added bonus scheme.

4. These percentages are relative to the number of schemes, not the number of companies operating them. Consequently the combined effect of these schemes will not be their cumulative value, as several schemes may operate in a single company.

5. Although the Inland Revenue maintain that all ADST schemes which they have approved are still in operation, Smith also reported more SAYE than ADST schemes (see Smith, 1986).

6. While almost 70 per cent of SAYE schemes were found in companies employing more than 1,000 employees, the figure was 58 per cent for ADST schemes. While 44 per cent of SAYE schemes were in

companies of over 5,000 employees, only 31 per cent of ADST schemes were found in companies of that size. Also the mean number of employees in companies operating an ADST scheme was found to be 7,620, while, for SAYE schemes, it was 9,456.

7. Only thirty companies provided statistics on take-up of their SAYE schemes, probably because few companies keep up-to- date figures on this, and when they do they are held not by Personnel but by Payroll, the department which makes the necessary savings deductions.

8. One company reported 100 per cent take-up and another reported 80 per cent. Without these figures the overall average proportion of employees participating in their company SAYE scheme would have been less than 20 per cent rather than 22.5 per cent.

9. The relationship between industrial sector and use of PS/ESO was found not to be significant using a chi-squared test at the 0.5 level of significance. Multiple regression analysis reinforced this result. The multivariate analysis reported in various parts of this chapter is more fully described in Baddon et al. (1987). A brief account may be in order here. Our sample of PS/ESO companies was divided into two groups, those with some form of share ownership scheme, and those without such a scheme but with a cash or incentive scheme. We sought to determine by means of multiple regression methods, using logit techniques, the probable relationship between the presence of either type of scheme with a set of independent variables, namely size, ownership type, regional location of head office, type of pay determination system, labour intensity, the presence of other forms of participation, whether unions were recognized, and type of industry.

10. Not unexpectedly, multiple regression analysis revealed type of ownership (whether the company was quoted or unquoted) to be strongly correlated with operation of *employee share ownership schemes*. Profit-sharing, on the other hand, did not appear to be dependent on ownership.

11. This was ascertained for all levels of significance using a Pearson's correlation coefficient one-tailed test.

12. A chi-squared test of independence was used.

13. The supply of figures for the proportion of pay paid as a profit-sharing bonus was limited, possibly because this may fluctuate and is therefore difficult to report accurately, because (a) often companies do not keep accurate, up-to-date records, (b) companies were reluctant to divulge what might be regarded as personal and confidential information, and (c) only profit-sharing bonus was relevant to this question, not employee share ownership.

14. A chi-squared test there showed no significant relationship between the operation of PS/ESO and the existence of a director with responsibility for personnel or industrial relations.

5

Management objectives

Financial participation is almost invariably a management initiative. Such initiatives are not necessarily prompted by conditions of management's own choosing, of course, and at least some proportion of schemes will be reactions to circumstances beyond their control. Financial participation may even form part of an attempt to restore management's grip in such circumstances. Just occasionally, there may be more direct pressure for the establishment of some form of profit-sharing or employee share ownership from employees or unions. All the evidence suggests that employee initiation is rare, however. Even where it does occur, management acts as the gatekeeper for the introduction of any scheme and thus exerts a determinant influence on its contours. For these reasons a careful examination of the intentions and reasoning behind management actions on the financial participation front is essential to any attempt to understand the dynamics and consequences of such schemes. In this chapter we draw on our survey and second-stage interviews with company representatives to map out the major features of management approaches and the contingencies which help to shape them.

Historically, profit-sharing and employee share ownership appeared in Britain and elsewhere as a paternalistic response to the challenge of labour as it developed in the nineteenth century. That paternalism had two interwoven strands: a benevolent (at least in outward intent) response to perceived moral danger if workpeople were not reasonably appeased; and a more direct and blatant dislike of trade unionism. Today, though, the rawer forms of parental authoritarianism might be expected to have given way to less ideological, more 'rational' and substantial reasons for sharing profits. It is possible to construct a list of possible goals for such schemes, although in many cases these overlap or have somewhat blurred edges. In fact this blurring remains a notable and significant feature of management policy in this area, it will be argued.

THE OBJECTIVES OF FINANCIAL PARTICIPATION

A working classification indicates five broad types of objective which management may seek to achieve through the various types of scheme under discussion:

Financial incentives are the most direct and potentially measurable type of objective in the management repertoire. A number of variants are detectable:

1 Rewarding past efforts in producing good company results.
2 Inducing future efforts to enhance performance.
3 Attracting personnel in a competitive labour market or section of the labour market.
4 Creating wage flexibility, allowing an automatic reduction of labour costs if profit margins are squeezed (one stated intention of the 1987 Finance Act provisions for tax relief under profit-related pay arrangements).
5 Creating an employee stake which industrial action might threaten (possibly with explicit penalty clauses).

Motivational objectives cover more diffuse aims to increase employee cooperation and effort in less directly calculative or instrumental terms. Again there may be a number of aspects to such an approach.

1 Increased effort by the employee arising from greater identification with and commitment to the employer.
2 Employee co-operation in operating or changing work practices, accepting new technology, and so forth.
3 Economical attitudes to use of company resources.
4 Reductions in absenteeism, turnover, and possibly industrial action.

Attitudinal changes tend to be still more broad and vague, encompassing management aspirations which are not necessarily readily observable in employee behaviour, although they are expected to shift the ambience of motivation at some level. They include:

1 A unity of purpose and harmony.
2 A sense of loyalty, identification and commitment to the plant/company/wider corporation.
3 Increased business awareness, legitimation of profits.

Defensive/deterrent effects, to adopt the terms coined by Creigh *et al.* (1981), may be seen as a distinctive form of motivational and attitudinal aim directed against trade unions or other employee organization. Again there are a number of possible emphases:

1 Excluding a union or restricting its recruitment.
2 Seeking to take the initiative from unions in meeting employee demands/desires.
3 Seeking to delimit the areas of union influence and the scope of employee attachment to the union.

Ownership per se is often the stated objective – of a share ownership scheme in particular, of course. It may be expected that this goal will be less prominent in management circles than among business ideologists or in the Conservative Party, for example, but it may still emerge in its own right for a number of reasons:

1 A desire to give an 'instinct of ownership', to make the employee feel as much a capitalist as a worker, and so reduce class divisions and attitudes.
2 A wish to give a direct stake in the company a person works for.
3 A moral obligation on equitability grounds to extend ownership rights.
4 As part of a wider strategy to create employee involvement.

These objectives tend to overlap with various of the earlier categories, but, given the centrality of ownership to much of the current discussion of PS/ESO, it seems important to recognize its distinctive status.

MANAGEMENT STRATEGY

While the categories outlined above offer a useful starting point, they do not of themselves make sense of management actions. It is possible, however, to consider how such goals for profit-sharing might fit with a wider typology of management strategies or styles. The notion of management strategy has received welcome attention in recent years, although efforts to produce an adequate and helpful typology have run into problems of inclusiveness and applicability to the real world. Thus many companies either do not readily fall into any category, or operate in ways which seem confused or even contradictory in terms of the rationale imposed by the research categorization yet are not necessarily irrational in themselves. Moreover, some writers have argued that the search for strategy itself misconceives a far more inchoate activity (Rose and Jones, 1985), though others have suggested that a consistency of style may be regarded as constituting an implicit strategy (Child, 1985).

Notwithstanding these unsettled issues, and the further provisos articulated below, we have found it useful to draw on existing discussions of management strategy in seeking to comprehend patterns in the observed incidence and operation of PS/ESO. In particular the typology advanced by Fox (1974) and developed by Purcell and Sissons (1983)[1] affords a useful initial categorization which we have elaborated and modified below, particularly with reference to the concept of paternalism:

Traditional authoritarian management operates on a unitarist basis, with no concession to participation and with hostility to trade unionism.

Traditional paternalist management is also unitarist in outlook, but is prepared to consider welfare and consultative approaches, if with a fairly clear limit on the degree of influence employees may exert through participation. Although many such companies may be anti-union, in a large number a *pragmatic* or tolerant view is taken of unions. This variation is one we have found on several occasions in this and other research, though it remains absent from existing typologies.

Standard modern companies concede union recognition, but reluctantly. This ambivalent pluralism is backed by an *ad hoc*, fire-fighting industrial relations style, often leading to confrontation. Consultation may well exist, as with other formal procedures, but its influence is likely to be rote and trivial.

Sophisticated modern approaches entail a more positive and developed pluralist view of unions, backed by a coherent personnel/industrial relations policy. Consultation and other participative forms may well play an active part in this policy, in

83

many cases in an effort to demarcate and limit union influence by creating a separate, consensus-based channel of discussion. It is possible that such a channel will allow informal information access and airing of views on areas outwith the scope of collective bargaining, however, a possibility shown by research on consultation[2] but not considered by Purcell and Sissons. Fox suggests that this approach overall remains liable to revert to the management anger and confrontation characteristic of the standard modern firm in the event of a major dispute.

Sophisticated paternalist styles involve the granting of participative rights and the pursuit of other unitarist and integrative strategies (quality circles, job reform, welfarism) in an effort to promote enterprise consciousness and restrict or prevent union influence.

Attempts to echo what are thought of as Japanese management practices also seem to belong in this category (though this may involve only a core, permanent work force receiving integrative attention). Again, however, it proves important to add a pluralistic or *pragmatic* variant, since a number of companies may be observed to combine paternalistic approaches with extensive and sometimes pre-emptive acceptance of trade unionism – as, for example, with ICI, or Nissan and other Japanese companies seeking single-union deals.

Bureaucratic detente is a term taken from Thurley (1984) to denote a situation where change has long been avoided and this remains possible and acceptable to the key actors. Union recognition leaves management clear areas of discretion, with consultation existing as a ritual which deadens rather than promotes innovation in labour–management relations. Thurley predicts that it will be found most typically in those parts of the public sector governed by Whitleyism, though in recent years that seems less appropriate, while at the same time it seems to fit some public corporations nominally at least not covered by the Whitley mantle, and perhaps a number of private-sector establishments as well[3]. By and large, though, it is not likely to be discovered by our survey or by management interview methods.

This typology is still not without its problems. Notably, it lacks a sense of dynamic response for the most part,[4] which, given the particular potential for change introduced by the recession, is a significant failing. It also tends to presume a singularity for an organization which may be especially problematical for large multi-plant companies, and particularly for conglomerates and enterprises built by the acquisition of independent units with their own cultures. Uncertainty, lack of policy definition, and contradictory actions will also make it difficult to fit any real-world company to what are basically ideal types. Another difficulty concerns the implicit evolutionism in concepts like 'traditional' and 'modern', a problem particularly evident now that paternalism, often regarded as rooted in past circumstances and values, is enjoying a ready revival in 'japanized' and other forms seemingly at least as popular in high-technology and expanding service sectors as anywhere.

Finally, there is a potential problem of circularity in using the strategy typology to analyse financial participation or other forms of employee involvement, since these are themselves significant implicit inputs to the typology and to the allocation of any empirical example within it. To avoid this, it is important, for example, not to attach the label 'sophisticated' without clear evidence that financial participation is associated with a wider-ranging, coherent policy on employee relations, within which participative arrangements should not be merely a formal or token arrangement. The extent to which this proves to be the case is itself an important aspect of the analysis of financial participation in practice.

Our evaluation below is based on both survey results and the more textured observations in the second-stage interviews. The case studies seek to explore further some of the themes aired here, and apart from occasional linking comments they are not included in the discussion in this chapter.

STRATEGY AND FINANCIAL PARTICIPATION

It seems reasonable to posit two contrasting ideal types of style or strategy associated with PS/ESO. On the one hand there may be a primarily short-run and calculative intention to promote employee effort. The most obviously appropriate method here will usually be a value-added bonus or some form of cash-based profit-sharing closely related to performance, and so emphasizing financial incentives and related motivational objectives. Although such an approach is conceivable under any of the strategy types identified above, it seems most likely in a standard or sophisticated modern setting. Two examples of this approach are provided by a north-west England study of participation (Dowling *et al.*, 1981), both entailing the use of value-added bonuses. Standard (and perhaps some 'sophisticated') modern settings might also be expected to yield the strongest use of deterrence, as in the Telecom and other cases noted later, though this may also fit with anti-union paternalism.

On the other hand, an ideological role for financial participation may be advanced, though long-term employee behavioural consequences are usually anticipated also. Here ownership *per se* and less specific but more sweeping attitudinal effects are the target, with in some cases a genuine sense of obligation to the employee (as in the welfarism of some Quaker firms). This seems most likely with paternalistic or related integrative strategies, as with the long commitment to share distributions by ICI, or the proclamations of more recent converts to employee share ownership such as retail chains like Habitat, Boots, or Marks & Spencer, though it also has a potential role within a portfolio of longer-term 'sophisticated modern' approaches. Once again, a distinction between approaches at least tolerant of trade unions and those hostile to them should be drawn. Any defensive motive at work will probably differ sharply here from the deterrent, aggressive style envisaged in the previous paragraph, tending to emphasize keeping unions at arm's length through employee involvement and persuasion rather than a frontal offensive.

Some companies may not fit within the continuum between these extremes because of the sheer vagueness of their policy ('It seemed like a good idea,' 'Everyone seemed to be trying it'). In general, though, both our survey and the interviews suggested that a tendency to 'go for the lot' was a more common sign of policy fuzziness, with every type of objective being thrown in. Only occasionally was there much indication that this was a considered evaluation of multiple and linked aims. None the less, some tendencies towards either the short-term/calculative or the longer-term/ambient emphasis could be discerned and will be discussed later.

In order to clarify the nature of management's commitment to financial participation, it will first be useful to map out a profile of objectives from our company survey. Management respondents were asked to indicate which of a given set of objectives were appropriate for the scheme they were operating. Financial aims were represented by the options of providing cash-efficient remuneration, and of attracting and retaining key staff, together with that of rewarding improved performance (which may be regarded as partly direct incentive, partly motivational). The encouragement of employee co-operation and involvement embodies attitudinal aims with a potential for a more direct behavioural (motivational) result, e.g. co-operation in promoting technical or organizational change. The development of business awareness, and particularly the encouragement of identification with the company, are more diffuse attitudinal aims, while share ownership *per se* has been allotted a separate status, for reasons given earlier.

The findings of the survey are given in Table 16. In total 679 choices were made by the 231 company respondents, an average of just under three selected objectives per case. This shows the spread of aims, a tendency confirmed and extended in the elaboration afforded by company interviews. More specifically it will be seen that financial objectives (items 1, 2 and 3 in the table) account for just under one-third of all responses, the most popular being the rather less direct reward for past performance, which was found in 44 per cent of companies. The most popular responses concerned co-operation and involvement and company identification. When business awareness is added, the attitudinal objectives (items 4 to 6), all of which emphasize integrative or consensual purpose, account for 56 per cent of total expressed aims. Share ownership accounted for just 12 per cent of selected objectives, though it does entail mention in 36 per cent of cases, a significant minority.

Whilst the primacy of integrative but diffuse attitudinal objectives over more direct incentive or motivation seems clear from these findings, it may be expected that management goals will vary according to which group of staff is being targeted. It seems plausible that staff retention will apply particularly at senior levels, for instance, and perhaps that other efforts to induce enhanced effort will also be seen as most efficacious for those individuals in a position to affect company performance personally.

In the event, an analysis of selected objectives for different groups of staff confirms these expectations, but only to a mild degree. As Table 17 shows, the attraction of staff is seen largely as an objective for non-manual and managerial groups. This came through a little more strongly for the last group in some of our interviews. The differences are small for the other two financial objectives, however, so that overall the incentive categories account for 20 per cent of selected objectives for manual workers, 27 per cent for non-manual, and 32 per cent for managerial staff.

Conversely, attitudinal or integrative goals were more

Table 16 Management-stated objectives of profit-sharing and employee share ownership

Objective	No. of choices indicated	% of total choices	% of companies
1 To provide a cash-efficient way of improving the overall remuneration package	43	6	19
2 To attract and retain key staff	65	10	28
3 To reward employees for past performance	102	15	44
4 To create a sense of business awareness among employees	97	14	42
5 To encourage the co-operation and involvement of all employees in improving the business performance of the company	159	23	69
6 To give employees a sense of identification with the company	124	18	54
7 To enable and encourage employees to become shareholders	84	12	36
8 Additional reasons	5	1	2
	N=679	100	N=231

Table 17 Management objectives for different groups of staff

Objective*	Manual No.	%	Non-manual No.	%	Managerial No.	%
1 Employee remuneration	19	5	26	5	41	7
2 Staff retention	9	2	21	10	65	10
3 Employee reward	52	13	68	13	92	15
4 Develop business awareness	62	15	79	15	84	13
5 Encourage co-operation	105	26	137	26	142	23
6 Company identification	87	22	110	21	110	18
7 Encourage employee shareholding	65	16	77	15	82	13
8 Additional reasons	4	1	5	1	5	1

*For the full version of options see Table 16.

prominent for non-managerial employees, though again not greatly so for any of the three objectives concerned. Overall, they accounted for 63 per cent of aims concerning manual workers, 62

88

per cent for non- manual employees, and 54 per cent for managerial staff.

Thus far, management objectives have been analysed *en bloc* for all types of profit-sharing and employee share ownership. As the earlier analysis of the survey has shown, however, the incidence of different types of scheme is quite markedly affected by company size, and to a lesser extent by other contingencies. This differential distribution suggests that it may be important to distinguish between schemes in an analysis of objectives, and a breakdown of the results to this end is provided in Table 18. It will be seen that certain marked differences do emerge between the objectives seen as appropriate to different types of scheme. As would be expected, cash-based schemes (including incentives) are more linked to financial and performance-related objectives. Thus the three financial objectives plus business awareness account for 55 per cent of the total for cash-based profit-sharing but only 34 per cent for ADST and SAYE schemes. This is of some added interest, given the rough equivalence of such schemes to profit-related pay, which seeks to extend tax incentives for profit-sharing beyond share-based schemes.

None the less, apart from the obvious appropriateness of share-based schemes to the goal of employee ownership, the differences from type to type are not as great as might be expected. This can be seen by considering in combination the two attitudinal variables of co-operation/involvement and identification. As would be

Table 18 Management objectives by type of scheme (%)

Objective*	Incen-tive	Cash	ADST	SAYE	Exec-utive	Com-pany
1 Employee remuneration	6	8	5	4	5	14
2 Staff retention	8	10	6	8	12	7
3 Employee reward	15	21	10	9	11	10
4 Develop business awareness	16	16	13	12	12	13
5 Encourage co-operation	25	23	24	22	21	16
6 Company identification	19	14	25	22	19	23
7 Encourage employee shareholding	11	7	16	20	17	22
8 Additional reasons	0	1	0	2	2	7
Number	128	368	93	302	319	69

*For the full version of options see Table 16.

expected, these account for a larger proportion of all objectives for ADST (45 per cent) and SAYE (44 per cent) schemes than for others, and for the smallest proportion for cash schemes (37 per cent). The differences are not great, however, and the figure for incentive schemes (at 44 per cent) is higher than for executive (41 per cent) or company share option (39 per cent) schemes. This apparent lack of discernment between types of financial participation suggests once more a lack of specification of objectives in at least a considerable proportion of companies.[5]

We now turn to a closer examination of particular objectives through the medium of our company interviews, before turning attention once more to the nature and cohesion of objectives *in toto qua* strategy. In these accounts, while some rough idea will occasionally be given of what proportions of companies interviewed adopted a particular stance, the account largely confines itself to providing the more textured impression to which this research stage was directed.

FINANCIAL PARTICIPATION AS DIRECT INCENTIVE

As we have seen, there are a number of ways in which various forms of financial participation may be related to incentives. Indeed, critics of the idea as far back as Marx and as recent as the TUC response to government proposals for profit-related pay have argued that an essential management goal is to subject at least part of workers' wages to the risk of variability according to company performance, and to intensify their effort in the process.

Notwithstanding this aim, which occasionally emerged in our interviews as a hidden agenda for schemes which were publicly (and in one case in the company's original questionnaire response) presented as integrative in intent, in many companies it played at most a subsidiary role, and one of which no great things were expected. One company saw it as some reward for effort but, it was stressed, 'We didn't go into it expecting to increase productivity,' while two others, both with pragmatic paternalistic styles, argued that the link from any attitude changes to effort was too remote for a realistic expectation of financial participation forming an incentive. Thus for these companies the main material element of any scheme was seen as the integrative one of applauding and sharing the fruits of past company performance.

For senior staff, however, a few company spokespersons

expressed the view that performance, and particularly recruitment and retention, could be enhanced by a stake in the company. The method here, unsurprisingly, was usually an executive or other share plan, sometimes described as a 'golden handcuff'. While this reinforces an expectation that was only weakly apparent in the survey, it remained an occasional factor only, and one on which opinions differed. On the one hand, managers were best placed both to feel they could influence performance by their own efforts, and to perceive the results of those efforts. On the other, while offering shares as an incentive in a competitive labour market for managerial skills might be a necessity, it was also thereby no more than a means to match the opposition (as the proliferation of executive schemes recorded earlier confirms) and afforded little expectation of preventing career moves in which PS/ESO benefits could either be dwarfed or replicated in the distracting offer.

Similarly, a number of companies admitted in their elaboration of objectives that profit-sharing and employee share ownership were becoming simply part of a 'good employee benefits package' (in the words of a manager whose company's scheme has received praise in business publications), with some additional spin-offs for attitudes. While cash schemes were preferred by some for this purpose, the balance seemed to be tipped in favour of ADST or attractive offer prices for SAYE by the prevailing tax concessions in other instances, including for the publicized case noted above. 'We always had the criterion that we wanted it to be a tax-efficient scheme,' was the comment in one large, traditionally paternalistic company that saw itself as 'modernizing' its employee relations. The same company explained its choice of SAYE over ADST or cash schemes, both of which would have been preferred in other circumstances, as due to the low cost of the former, and the fact that its capital/labour and profit/employee ratios were too low.

In another case, again a company whose scheme has several times been reported as an exemplar, a public emphasis on employee relations was displaced by the admission of a major goal of buying out an expensive and ineffective bonus scheme – with an additional advantage of penalizing strikers (see discussion of this tactic later). At the same time several companies acknowledged a tendency for pay-outs to become little more than a bonus themselves, so ceasing to have any worthwhile incentive effect. The only solution to this for management is repeatedly to clarify the relationship between the profit-sharing payment and performance, so that 'if you have got purely instrumental people ... then we are now giving them a reason to start taking an interest' (manager in 'standard/ sophisticated modern' company).

The problems of gearing up any form of financial participation, even a cash-based one, to act as an incentive have been well rehearsed. Most employees are simply too remote from those activities which generate profits, or their individual efforts seem too much a drop in the ocean, for any link between personal performance and a profit-related reward to induce strenuous efforts. In any case, factors beyond even management control (market shifts, currency movements, and so forth) may easily outweigh even a collective effort. For a number of companies the disaggregation of results, and so payments, to sufficiently small units carries the added risk of exposing information on operations to employees and/or competitors that they regard as sensitive. Only one company in which we carried out interviews, in the travel sector of 'Other services', had felt able to disaggregate department results and set performance targets against which a profit pay-out was determined. Considerable problems in setting reasonable and comparable targets between departments were acknowledged, and in one large department in particular the impact of uncontrollable currency fluctuations had undermined the scheme, but overall it was claimed to have had a strong and popular incentive effect.

One further advantage of financial participation for management is that it takes one element of pay outwith the context of normal negotiations, and so beyond the trade union purview (although a number of companies reported tacit bargaining, including profit-sharing, and the odd one claimed its more formal inclusion in benefits negotiation). This was seen as useful for the promotion of acceptance of change in technical and working methods, a point made by two companies we interviewed, both in highly organized and fairly 'confrontational' parts of the media sector.

MOTIVATION AND FINANCIAL PARTICIPATION

Although the example cited at the end of the previous section indicates ways in which financial participation may smooth the pathway to change, in general the expectations of a direct behavioural effect through motivation of employees did not figure prominently in the extended rationalization of schemes offered by managers in our interviews. In several companies the link was explicitly dismissed; the quotations below are taken from a small, service-sector company classifiable as 'sophisticated paternalist', and from a 'sophisticated modern' multinational in non-metal manufacturing:

...I honestly don't believe that people wasting money in November relate to the fact that they're wasting that money for their profit-sharing next April and therefore they won't be somewhere on [on holiday] in July ...

For the shop floor earnings are the key ...[they are] just doing a job of work ... [profit] in terms of a motivator – let's just say that in the end it is virtually non-existent.

The management spokesperson in a company with a long history of paternalist welfarism (though shifting to a harder style in the process of restructuring) was critical of schemes in his organization for being unable to motivate through their remoteness and ill-conceived target structure. But even for cash schemes this was a common problem, such that in the words of a small distribution company manager it becomes 'more of a hand-out' than a motivator.

About two-thirds of managers interviewed expressed this downbeat judgement. A few companies did take a less jaded view, however. Motivation was perceived as relevant, although usually it was cast as an indirect consequence of other, attitudinal changes. For one pragmatic paternalistic engineering company this came from 'sharing in the success ... we want to be a high-performance company and we want everybody to share in the success'. Another somewhat similar company with a more 'modern' style insisted that there was no benevolence or welfarism involved: 'It's fairly remote, but to some extent it is a performance-related activity.' A non-union finance company, a travel company in similar mould, and a retail chain, all categorized under the general heading of 'sophisticated paternalist', were the most bullish about the motivational advantages, the first arguing that 'a key objective [is to] improve the growth of average profitability, the feeling that employees will give of their best'. In all three cases it may have been that the style of management, the lack of 'unionateness' on the part of employees, and the awareness that service quality was a very direct contributor to success, together created favourable circumstances for this approach.

INFLUENCING EMPLOYEE ATTITUDES

We identified earlier a number of aspects of attitudes which management may seek to affect through the introduction of financial participation. The most active (i.e. near-motivational) of these were the encouragement of co-operation and the sharpening of business awareness, while the more passive entailed employee involvement and a degree of loyalty to and identification with the enterprise.

From a management point of view a focus on attitudinal advantages may be taken for the most part to imply a longer-term commitment to financial participation, probably as part of a wider involvement strategy, and in this guise it would be expected to be most common among paternalistic and the more sophisticated 'modern' firms. This expectation was confirmed by our interviews, as, however, was the extent to which reliance on the supposed benefits in this area amounted to a weakly specified policy, more an 'act of faith' in many companies. In this it hovers uneasily on the borderline between being targeted on definite objectives and merely servicing a management ideology of underlying unity and harmony. If there is a logical progression in articulation of objectives in this area, it runs from this diffuse invocation of unity and involvement to the slightly more focused inculcation of loyalty and identification. The latter connects to a perceived need to develop a corporate image in large and diverse organizations in particular, as well as to the general development of business awareness among employees. We now look a little more closely at each of these aspects.

Although involvement is a predictable objective in companies with a paternalistic style, it may also appear an optimistic gesture on the employee relations front in more confrontational firms. In one of the media companies, for example, it was intimated that in considering the establishment of their cash and SAYE schemes 'it was felt it would improve the situation if people felt a greater affinity with the company'. The SAYE scheme was seen as particularly important in this respect, and several companies indicated that the fact that people had to commit their own money of their own volition separated the wheat from the chaff in terms of employee commitment. In the media company it was suggested, 'the more people who you can get feeling that they are part of the company and not simply employees as such, that they must have something beyond their salary for the work that they do, then the better that must be'. At the same time, this respondent did not claim any improvement in profits, and expressed disappointment that the tenor of union–management relations had not visibly improved, either. On the other hand, involvement was recognizably something of an easy explanation in management terms, a justification that was almost automatic, particularly where an element of public relations presentation was involved. Thus one large petrochemical company (which with most of that industry fits the sophisticated pragmatic paternalist category) told us that their employees were sold their SAYE scheme in terms of involvement, but in practice management viewed it as part of the benefits package (which still leaves the question of whether SAYE was really a very adventurous step on the benefits front by comparison with ready alternatives).

The accretion of employee loyalty affords a slightly more substantial expression of involvement, but one which is expressed in very much the same terms (and breath), often hard to distinguish in the typical loosely defined account given by managers of their aims. Identification with and loyalty to the company were particularly apparent as stated aims in, though not the exclusive preserve of, companies with paternalist styles. Elaborations ranged from talk of 'warmth' or 'friendship' (in a retail chain) to the rather harder 'identification with the long-term interest of the company' and less elegantly 'all part of one heap' (from a medium-sized manufacturing company with a 'modern' approach).

In one area, identification became a rather more coherent and significant objective. In well over half those companies interviewed where a large number of employees were split across at least several sites, the importance of achieving a corporate image to the employee was stressed. This became particularly important where the company had grown by acquisition or merger, creating pockets of confused or parochial identification. A reward or ownership scheme spanning these different enclaves was seen as a way of broadening employee awareness of the corporation in a way that localized incentives, for example, would even militate against. Thus for a retail chain it was 'very much a cohesion exercise', while one multi-divisional chemical company described its scheme 'as one which brings the whole group together'. Another chemical company explicitly rejected any significant link to motivation by insisting, 'It was much more to do with achieving a realization of the interconnectedness of [the company] ... It's aimed at the corporate consciousness level.' Conversely, several companies with share option schemes observed that the take-up varied with the extent to which employees in different areas (rather than just different grades) identified with the company as a whole.

Approximately one-third of the companies interviewed spoke in specified terms of the effect of schemes on the business awareness of employees. In some cases this was still at a rather general level – that employees would read reports on company performance or even just watch share prices more closely. A more powerful reinforcement of management efforts to communicate its view of reality and have it accepted was articulated by others. One large manufacturer spoke of the 'increased understanding of the need to accept change' as a hoped-for result, while a petrochemical concern opined that all employees 'will share in the management's view that profit is important' so that everyone would 'bend our minds to making profits rather than arguing about other nonsense'. It is thus hard to disentangle awareness *per se* from an endorsement of management in these accounts. Others were tougher still in their view, however. For one North American manufacturer the idea to be put across was that 'if the performance is poor the money's not there'. A pragmatically paternalist chemical company supported participative and welfarist styles, but also celebrated the fact that one year when a profit share pay-out had not taken place it had caused grumbles in the consultation machinery which showed 'triumphantly' that people had been reminded of their attachment to profit-sharing and sharply reminded of its link with performance. On the other hand, a sophisticated modern manufacturer took the view that such an increase in business awareness was contradicted in its beneficial effects by demotivation.

Others, too, expressed more caution on this front. A retail chain was concerned that profit orientation did not become a narrow cost orientation with negative effects on the quality of customer service. One manufacturer felt that any meaningful impact on awareness would be restricted to non-manual employees, and in other companies this was used to justify separate executive schemes. Another paternalist manufacturer felt that awareness and effort were little influenced, and rolled back the attitudinal impact to the assessment: 'but they're appreciative'.

DEFENSIVE AIMS

Explicit anti-unionism or other defensive objectives were voiced in only about one-fifth of the companies we interviewed. This approach seems to be particularly common in paternalistic companies where involvement and identification strategies could be seen as a means for management to reinforce its authority, and where unions are hard pressed to gain a foothold. Examples among firms whose innovations in financial participation have attracted widespread attention might include Marks & Spencer, Habitat, or the John Lewis Partnership (all, notably, retail companies). Aggressive deterrent or other defensive aims may none the less be latent rather than non-existent in many circumstances, susceptible to reinvocation at times when conflict draws forth any quiescent unitarism. The examples we did encounter suggest that financial participation retains a potential for adaptation to an anti-collectivist view, even if welfarism or attitude massage were its original intended aim.

Where unions have gained a substantial footing, the most concrete expression of management efforts to control labour organization are found in anti-strike penalty provisions written into the profit-sharing arrangement. Several examples of this are cited in recent reports,[6] including the possibility of charging management's assessment of the imputed 'cost' of a strike against strikers' profit share (e.g. Hotpoint, Southern Newspapers). A variant of the British Telecom decision to penalize its entire work force for a strike by some employees (see Chapter 3) by cancelling the entire profit share-out for the year was operated by one of the companies in our study. In published accounts this scheme had been presented as principally concerned with employee involvement and business awareness, but that, it was made clear, was basically a public relations presentation:

> Clearly we used words like 'beneficial for companies to help their employees to be closer to profitability' ... Very nice, and to some small extent true, but I think we accept ... that people working on the shop floor are so far removed from profitability that it doesn't really motivate them, not in the least.

Instead the manager concerned went on to celebrate the efficacy of the sanction of stopped profit-sharing payments, as used on several occasions already, in deterring strikers. The one drawback, however, was that if used too often it would lead to the feeling that profit-sharing was entirely as management's discretion, and it would lose altogether its other desired impacts on performance sensitivity, involvement, and other attitudes.

The British Telecom tactic lacked precision by requiring to dispossess the entire work force, including non-strikers, thus threatening to increase rather than reduce conflictive solidarity. Another way of seeking to contain union influence and scope has been exemplified by Norwich Union (IRRR, 1987). Following a dispute with the Association of Scientific , Technical & Managerial Staffs (ASTMS), management decided to insist on a three-year salary deal, including profit-sharing as a measure of flexibility which none the less left the union little room for negotiation. Alternatively, one of the manufacturing companies we visited had established a profit-related bonus system at a higher rate for non-unionized groups of staff, justifying it in terms of their lower resistance to such schemes and by their generally greater ability to influence performance (as they were mostly in the higher grades).

Such deliberate use of financial participation was not a particularly common feature in our interviews, however. If a less 'unionate' or otherwise less militant or resistant work force was mentioned, it was more typically in the context of a somewhat pious hope related to diffuse attitudinal shifts. In one case, in a manufacturing company with a long history of paternalism and a union with a well established reputation for moderation, the union itself was seen as a channel of control over its members: 'Now the workers' representative [dealing with a strike threat] will say, "You are placing your profit-sharing payment at risk because the company can take disciplinary action".'

OWNERSHIP: MAKING WORKERS CAPITALISTS

Where companies choose to operate a share option scheme or to give shares away, rather than pay cash, then it might be expected that an intention is to tap the effects of ownership in itself. Several companies with SAYE schemes did talk in terms of getting employees to own shares as 'a good thing' in its own right, the same phrases cropping up each time. Two manufacturing companies in the 'modern' mould indicated their allegiance to ideologies associated with the Conservative Party and discussed in Chapter 2, one describing its commitment as 'semi- political, right there with the government and the CBI', while the other suggested that the 'whole exercise' was 'part of a philosophy to encourage moves towards a share-owning society'.

A number of paternalistic companies did talk in kindred terms, but generally the impression was that ownership *per se* was something of a token, a makeweight point thrown in for good measure alongside other reasons for having schemes, or occasionally a convenient justification where rational reasons seemed a little thin on the ground. One company saw its ADST scheme as fostering ownership, yet its SAYE scheme was represented as serving only instrumental, tax-saving purposes. One or two companies explicitly rejected ownership as a significant factor, but more than half the companies we interviewed did not invoke ownership at all in its own right.

Finally, a few companies did see employee share ownership as relevant in an age of take-overs. Two felt that the wider spread of shareholding among people with a deeper commitment to the company (and perhaps a fear for their jobs under a new regime) would be beneficial in fighting off predators, but at least one other feared that it would increase the number of shares accessible to bidders. The actual behaviour of employees in such contexts will probably depend on their feelings about their employers as well as their concern about the future of their own employment, and it will be interesting to observe the outcome in different circumstances.

THE COHERENCE OF MANAGEMENT OBJECTIVES

There was a wide range of degrees of articulation and coherence of management strategies on PS/ESO. This was expected to some extent following the patterns (or lack of them) evidenced by Table 18. Such coherence as may be found is in part masked by the widespread tendency, noted earlier, for almost all objectives to be articulated in some form in a *post hoc* managerial rationalization of the purpose and achievements of a scheme. It is also problematical given the adaptability of financial participation to various roles within different strategies between companies or within any organization across time and circumstance.

Analysis of the survey data did indicate some differences between categories of companies in their indication of objectives for financial participation. Most evidently, smaller companies tended to emphasize rewards somewhat more, while larger ones placed greater stress on co-operation, identification, and ownership. This was consonant with the concentration of share schemes in the larger companies, although a notable exception here was that foreign-owned companies did not see ownership as an aim

99

of their schemes – starkly bringing out their subsidiary status, perhaps. Sectoral analysis indicated no decipherable pattern, auguring poorly for the explanatory power here of one major element in management strategy distinctions. Trade union recognition and higher densities were associated with greater emphasis on ownership, less on rewards, with little effect on the indication of attitudinal objectives. The first two relationships are statistically explicable by the company size effect, but intuitively the rewards de-emphasis may be attributed in part to the union presence itself. One finding was especially disturbing for those who believe that evolving management sophistication and attention to labour matters should sharpen objectives and increase the emphasis on the importance of attitudinal factors. This was the lack of any discernible relation between companies having appointed a board member to deal with industrial relations issues and their choice of objectives. If anything, this ran counter to the direction predicted by the greater typical size of this sub-group, with such companies on average selecting attitudinal options slightly less often.

Reported origins of schemes give the first clues in this area. It was not uncommon for even senior interviewees to be hard pushed to know (or even guess) where the proposal had arisen from. Even when a source was indicated, it was sometimes left strikingly vague: in one manufacturing company it had 'grown like topsy'; for a small construction company 'there is no particular source in a small company like this'; while in a large chemical producer it was 'an idea that had caught its time'. In contrast, a traditional paternalist company in the process of shifting to a more conflictual style reported the origins as 'lost in the mists of time', kept going by inertia alone. Another variant had the idea descending from 'The Board' (with its originator commonly being seen as someone, perhaps a non-executive director, who had picked the idea up elsewhere). In one company it was reported that after an initiative for an ADST scheme from the finance director had been discussed, a proposal to 'throw in' an SAYE scheme as well was put forward and accepted on the board at the tail end of their discussion of the matter.

In just under half the companies we interviewed, none the less, a fairly clear source of the scheme was identifiable. There was no obvious pattern, however, with Personnel (alone, or more commonly in alliance with another management functionary) and Finance or the company secretary figuring fairly evenly. Nor was reported origin notably associated with a particular style of management, or with a particular type of stated objective for the scheme (e.g. it was not perceptibly the case that personnel initiation meant that a scheme was less likely to be calculative on this limited evidence).

If we turn next to the stated objectives of schemes, it will be informative first to consider these against a broader attempt to classify the companies within the typology of management strategies outlined earlier. Given the problems with the categories employed, we regarded them as heuristic and intuitive guidelines rather than closely specified labels. On this basis, in practice we found it reasonably easy to classify companies as either 'paternalist' or 'modern', with the proviso that a number of 'modern' companies professed or exhibited paternalist strands to their approach, usually seen as gradually fading or being eased out, while a number of paternalist companies likewise showed signs of, or declared themselves to be, moving towards a more 'modern' outlook. Within the paternalist category, classification as 'pragmatic' rested chiefly on whether unions were recognized or not. The 'traditional/sophisticated' distinction largely followed industrial lines, with long-lived and community-based (originally, at least) companies being placed in the traditional category, but petrochemicals in the sophisticated group, along with service and retail-sector companies (though one of the latter was difficult to locate between traditional and sophisticated).

On the 'modern' side, classification proved far more problematical – not surprising, given the observed potential instability in any sophistication or pragmatism. Only a few companies seemed clearly 'sophisticated' in their approach, one having an extremely elaborate set of participative structures, and two others being in the service sector but in the highly unionized media subdivision thereof. At the same time, since financial participation was rarely the only move from simple confrontational labour relations, most modern companies could not readily be labelled 'standard' (which makes that term particularly hard to sustain). Thus, with the three exceptions noted above, we regarded the modern companies as indeterminately or semi-sophisticated, a somewhat tentative classification which encompassed about one-third of all the companies in which we interviewed.

We argued earlier that one would expect a paternalistic approach to generate a longer-term view of financial participation, stressing the attitudinal or ambient effects, and perhaps also a partly ideological commitment to the aim of employee share ownership.

A modern approach might be expected to yield a more calculative and possible short-run view of any such scheme. More sophisticated modern approaches might be more long sighted in their aims once more, though the extensive union role where it permeates any employee participation arrangements could detach this from financial participation as an involvement strategy more firmly than in paternalist companies. Although ownership *per se* has a less obvious place in such a style or strategy, the contingent and insecure nature of the management commitment to pluralism, and the potential attraction for employees of ideas of worker capitalism could make employee share ownership a viable element of many a modern approach also.

In addition to Fairbrush, dealt was as a case study later, three companies we interviewed fell into the *traditional paternalist* pattern. All three (and Fairbrush also) recognized and dealt extensively with trade unions, and all three had high levels of union membership thus contradicting one of the defining features of paternalism in the Fox/Purcell and Sissons typologies. In all three there had been a notable shift towards less welfarist approaches, with greater emphasis on competitiveness and a growing willingness to restructure in recent years, this change being related in all three cases to merger or threatened take-over in the recent past. In all three there were both SAYE and executive schemes, but all three also operated cash-based profit-sharing. In one case the cash scheme was offered to employees in tandem with a tax-exemptable ADST option, but only 4 per cent took the latter.

In all these companies the origins of financial participation did seem related to a degree of employee welfarism in the firms' cultures, and there was a history of employee share ownership initiatives long predating the statutory innovations of the 1970s in two of the companies. Indeed, in one of these the scheme in operation was seen as having emerged more in response to this vague commitment than to any logically tailored aims, and so as in need of considerable rethinking in the changing climate. Employee share ownership was advanced as an end in itself in two of the companies; the third had operated only a cash scheme until 1981. In all three, however, identification was well to the fore of pronounced objectives, and so the expectation of an ambient, attitudinal emphasis was fairly well fulfilled. This said, there was also a distinct and advancing calculation of results, not so much with expectations of direct incentive or motivation, but with at least more effective linkage to employee business awareness and consequent co-operation with management. On the participation front, all three companies had consultative and other arrangements. In two of them, financial participation was represented as part of the participative approach, though in the third this was rejected for a claim to a more generalized but less strategic human-relations style.

Three companies also fell into the category of *sophisticated pragmatic paternalists*, two being large petrochemical producers and the third in metal manufacturing. Of the case studies, Norbrew may also be placed in this group, although with important traditional vestiges. All three interviewed companies had SAYE and executive schemes, and one also operated an ADST scheme. In this last company financial participation had a clearly articulated role in a widely based integrative strategy which had entailed numerous other involvement schemes over a long period. Both of the other companies also boasted extensive formal and informal participative arrangements, though financial participation seemed far less definitively located as a coherent element of this approach. Ownership figured in stated objectives, as suggested by the presence of SAYE schemes, but, significantly, in the company with the ADST scheme it was noted that prior to the legislation a plan was under way to change a share distribution into a cash-based scheme, implying that tax advantages were now more important and ownership itself less so than previously. In another company it was stated that involvement was more the public justification than the real reason for the scheme, which was primarily providing an ancillary benefit with a few advantageous, integrative overtones. The third company also spoke of the desirability of reducing union influence by winning employees across with financial participation among other things. None the less, with the exception of the chemical company, where employee share ownership played a definite if somewhat marginal role in management's sophisticated paternalist strategy, there was no strong sense of a significant place or coherently purposive direction for the schemes.

The six interviewed companies outside our case studies who fell in the *non-union sophisticated paternalist* group were markedly more heterogeneous in their approach. Two companies in business services and one in the travel industry operated cash schemes. All six had (or, in the case of a retail firm where a take-over had made it impossible, had once had) at least one share-based scheme, including four with executive schemes, and three with company share options. Two, a finance company and a retail company, had

SAYE schemes, while the retail chain and a business service company also had ADST schemes.

The particular clustering retail and of financial and business service companies in this group is confirmed by other well published cases falling into a similar mould, in particular Marks & Spencer and Habitat in the retail sector. Bossguide, from our case studies, also falls in this grouping. Beyond this sectoral concentration, and a commitment to saving and ownership in all six companies (the counterpoint of varying degrees of hostility to employee collectivism), the emphasis of these various schemes shows little consistency. The three companies which had chosen to operate share options appeared particularly enamoured of the ownership and related attitudinal atmosphere of partnership that they felt went with it – in many ways most in tune with the paternalist stereotype. The other three saw their schemes more in terms of financial perks for employees, which they sought to set within a participative ethos as a somewhat secondary issue. Only one felt there was a directly effective incentive involved, however, and this was achieved, it was claimed, by a disaggregation of pay-outs by department as described earlier.

Apart from one small construction firm with a traditional authoritarian style and a cash-based scheme, the rest of the companies we interviewed (and Thistle and Goodbake from the case studies) fell into the broad '*modern*' Church, with varying (and apparently variable) degrees of sophistication. As other evidence had led us to expect, any supposed pluralism rarely stretched to any significant union involvement in the design or implementation of a financial participation scheme. Three operated only cash-based schemes, but (leaving aside executive schemes) SAYE schemes were particularly popular, while only two companies had an ADST scheme. The use of SAYE was commonly a minimal step, in the sense that it involved no actual pay-out, merely an 'opportunity' for employees. The potential for different solutions is best illustrated by two companies in the media, facing very similar work-force organization and attitude, and basically the same market situation, one of which opted for an SAYE and a cash scheme, the other for ADST and executive schemes.

Although many of the companies in this group had fairly developed formal participation arrangements, the linkage between financial participation and the schemes was often poorly if at all articulated. The three companies we felt were relatively unproblematically 'sophisticated' were rather more explicit in tying financial participation into other involvement strategies (typically outwith the sphere of union influence), but only in one with no fewer than five types of scheme was an explicit, elaborate, and coherent account of the claimed role of financial participation provided. Ownership also presented a low profile in the reasons given for financial participation in the firms in this category; it had often been checked off on the questionnaire, but with one or two exceptions it faded into the background in the interview elaboration. The emphasis on incentive and motivation, or at least on sensitivity to business situation and so co-operation in competitive efforts, was more prominent in this set of firms than elsewhere, though for most the objectives retreated to rather vaguer attitudinal aspirations if pressed.

Overall, then, there does seem to be some accord between management style or strategy in general and the objectives claimed for PS/ESO. The paternalistic companies were more likely to be seeking ownership and integrative ambience, while the modern firms were somewhat more inclined to calculative and shorter-term perspectives. This generalization conceals considerable variation within groups, however, and also over-rationalizes a situation where a choate and articulate strategy with a consentient role for financial participation was the exception rather than the rule. In general, any strategy remained indistinct and uncertain. This seems to confirm the relationships indicated by our survey, as summarized at the start of this section. We did note a size effect, which is tied to the feasibility of employee share ownership options, and also, like other participative forms, to the tendency towards more formal and elaborate arrangements in larger settings. Beyond this, the impact of varying circumstance and characteristics on selection and outward coherence of management objectives seems remarkable for its limits rather than its extent.

CLAIMS AND CONSEQUENCES

When it came to asking management about the bottom line, how successful financial participation had been and in what ways, the balance of the answers tended, unsurprisingly, towards positive achievements. Since public relations impulses, rationalizations, and sometimes personal career stakes, all tend to push such reporters towards a favourable presentation of the outcome, these claims must all be leavened with a consideration of the case studies discussed later. None the less, some features of their comments remain worthy of note.

When sought after, the markers of claimed success became blurred: 'People can now see what they're worth', or 'There is no doubt about it at all, extremely successful', were typical assertions, these both from non-union paternalist retail companies. But the strongest enthusiasts were likely to be stressing broad attitudinal gains, and the difficulty was that these were unmeasurable, and almost an act of faith. The interviewee manager in the chemical company which was probably the most sophisticated exponent of 'strategy' that we encountered showed a ready awareness of the auditing problems when he described benefits as 'impossible to quantify ... All we can say is we have a thorough scheme of consultation which gives us favourable feedback, and that people appreciate it, and they see how it is related to corporate performance.'

Some optimists among management nevertheless admitted problems. One manager disappointed with the SAYE take-up still declared himself 'sure it's going to achieve the desired objective'. Another acknowledged, 'there's a long way to go, but we're moving in the right direction', while a third allowed that there had been 'little impact so far', and averred that a scheme needed to run for a few years to build up sufficiently substantial benefit to participants.

Sceptics were particularly likely to doubt the motivational or direct incentive effect, as we saw earlier. For some more pessimistic commentators this was accompanied, ironically, by an employee enthusiasm which was generated by big windfall gains from rising share prices and unlikely to mark a transformation of loyalties. One or two were still more negative. Two companies openly admitted the absence of the hoped-for impact on the atmosphere of industrial relations, though, as we have seen, other managements did expect to exert some defensive or deterrent influence against collective employee organization.

In our interviews we finished by asking managers to indicate their agreement or disagreement with claims that PS/ESO had helped in specified ways. Only a minority thought it had helped to increase productivity, and even fewer that it had reduced employee turnover or helped recruitment. Other factors were felt to be determinant in these areas. On the other hand, a clear majority felt that their schemes had increased employee loyalty and corporate identification, and in the end not one failed to agree, on balance, that interest in and understanding of company performance had been enhanced. In each of these two attitudinal areas the paternalist companies of all types were notably at the forefront of enthusiasm.

One final area concerned the impact of schemes on employees' say in the running of the company. Only a small group of companies thought there was a move in this direction through financial participation, and of these one restricted the effect to obtaining limited information in the company accounts, while another insisted that there was a formal opportunity for workers to speak up as shareholders, though it had never happened. This non-participative nature of schemes was confirmed by comments on the extent to which the schemes were themselves the subject of any employee influence. In almost every case we were told that there was no discussion either with the unions or with employees themselves. Sometimes this was forcefully deliberate: 'This was very much a management initiative; we felt very strongly that it should be.' In several cases we were told there was no consultation but that there were attempts to communicate after the decision had been made. These were not genuinely participative, though: 'To be honest, it was more of a question of management designing the scheme and then going out and selling the ideas to the employees,' as one manufacturer of agricultural equipment told us. Only two companies had undertaken consultation, both paternalists and one the chemical manufacturer with a particularly sophisticated participation strategy. Even here SAYE was admitted to be a 'management creation', and indeed many managers observed that all Inland Revenue-approved schemes, in particular SAYE, were so constrained as to allow little management room for manoeuvre, let alone employee input.

The potential role for PS/ESO schemes in management approaches can be usefully considered in terms of whether they afford participation, whether they involve employees more actively in other ways, or whether they are primarily means to control labour. Since 'involvement' and 'control' may be seen as two sides of the same interpretative coin, the data do not adjudicate between them but do suggest the extent to which either is realized.

The lack of meaningful participation noted above echoes the finding in our survey that only 9 per cent of our respondents claimed to have consulted employees before or during the implementation of any type of scheme. This is surprising in some ways, in that it suggests a missed opportunity for a marketing effort by management, particularly for voluntary share purchase schemes.

This may be taken as evidence either of the lack of effective strategy in this area, or of the marginality of financial participation within any such strategy.

If PS/ESO is marginal to any involvement strategy in substance, this is despite a frequency of occurrence which rivals that of the most popular forms of participation, as Table 13 in Chapter 4 shows. In some small companies, where other formal arrangements for participation are relatively rare, a financial scheme (probably cash-based) may well be the only way in which many employees can 'participate' at all. Employee share ownership, meanwhile, is more popular in the larger companies, and as such is particularly likely to coincide with other formal participative arrangements. As Table 14 in Chapter 4 indicates, there is a strong relationship between PS/ESO schemes and other forms of participation, increasing for some of the less common reported types of participation.[7] This correlation has also been noted by Poole (1987).

One possible conclusion is that profit-sharing is being offered as part of a 'participation package' by firms, providing a financial or even ownership dimension alongside the contractual job relationship and other forms of involvement. This would imply a strategic coherence which, however, our interviews failed to confirm in this strong version. Rather, earlier discussion suggests a stylistic consistency, particularly in firms adopting a paternalistic line, which to date is rarely thought through and applied as a conscious and effective strategy for control. Our statistical analysis also tends to support this correction of the 'participative culture' implied in Poole's account, since multiple regression reveals that the financial participation/other participative form relationship can be better explained by factors such as company size, location, and ownership.[8] This suggests a weaker contingency relationship consistent with the less vigorous variant of the strategy model developed to date.

In practice the capacity of management to construct effective control mechanisms, or in other terms to involve employees comprehensively and successfully, does not seem convincingly high in most companies, on the evidence presented here. There are few signs that most companies with PS/ESO have any effective means of assessing the role or contribution of schemes to profitability or other aspects of management authority and control. If there is a significant effect, it may be in the decollectivization of at least a part of employee income regulation, and thereby further on the attitudes of employees. To ascertain whether these tentative conclusions hold true, and if so under what circumstances, it will be necessary to turn to our case studies.

NOTES

1. See also Deaton's (1985) elaboration. Deaton was unable to reproduce clusters of factors corresponding to such strategies in his reanalysis of the Workplace Industrial Relations Survey data (see Daniel and Millward, 1983), a result which seems to confirm our own observations on the 'fuzzy' nature of real-world management strategies. Other classifications may be found in Thurley and Wood (1983), Gospel and Littler (1983), and in Thurley (1984).

2. See, for example, Marchington and Armstrong (1981, 1983, 1986), Cressey et al. (1981).

3. A private-sector example is provided in the case study outlined by Bate and Murphy (1981).

4. This is less true of Fox's original discussion – which allows, for example, for management lapses from sophisticated modern approaches in the face of manifest conflict – than it is for Purcell and Sissons. Most existing analyses remain paradoxically static yet evolutionist, however.

5. One qualification here is that the question on objectives did not ask for separate specification of the aims of different schemes where companies had more than one scheme. Since, as we have seen in Chapter 4, this is a common occurrence, some blurring of differences between schemes is possible. This could explain, for example, how cash and incentive schemes seem linked with the aim of share ownership in Table 18. To check the extent of this effect, we analysed the returns for companies with cash/incentive schemes only and share schemes only. These served largely to confirm the relationships observed above, though with some sharpening of differences. Co-operation and identification together accounted for 36 per cent of selected objectives for cash schemes, but 45 per cent of those for share schemes, for example. On the other hand, items 1 and 3, emphasizing financial incentive, accounted for 3 per cent of selected objectives for cash schemes against just 14 per cent for share schemes. These differences still imply that most managements lacked discernment (for instance, 19 per cent of companies with cash-based schemes only still put down employee ownership as one objective), thus leaving our conclusions concerning the weakness of strategic selection intact.

6. See, for example, Labour Research Department (1986), TUC (1986), *Industrial Relations Review and Report* (1987).

7. The correlation is strong but crude. It survived multiple regression analysis, but short of satisfactory statistical significance. (See n. 8.)

8. The multiple regression analysis showed that the common relationship with size, in particular, dissolved much of this apparent correlation.

Part 3

The case studies

6

Setting the scene

This chapter explains the reasons behind our decision to include a case-study element in our research, in addition to the more general survey evidence and the follow-up interview programme in a sub-sample of surveyed companies. The chapter describes the methods used and the problems encountered in the case study stage as well as identifying the main issues we wanted to examine by means of the case studies.

RATIONALE OF THE CASE STUDIES

First, then, we consider the rationale for the case studies in general. The postal survey returns were intended to permit us to analyse the structural features of profit-sharing and share ownership schemes. It was expected that the coverage of the survey would be sufficient to define a broad picture of the incidence of different kinds of scheme, their objectives in general terms, the organizational characteristics of the firms that participated in different schemes and the extent to which they differed from non-participant enterprises. In general these objectives were satisfactorily achieved, and the results have been reported in previous chapters.

In addition, we wanted to gain a better understanding of how participant enterprises approached the inception of profit- sharing and employee share ownership, how they made their selections and how these related to the established aims. This could not be achieved through the postal survey method, involving as it did a need for some analysis in greater depth of the processes of management in developing their strategy. For this reason we introduced an intermediate stage of investigation which involved extended interviews in a sub-sample of the survey population. These interviews were for the most part conducted with a single member of the management of the enterprise, and proved to be helpful in underlining some of the differences in the philosophy and approach to the issues of profit-sharing and employee share ownership. However, these interviews could take us only so far. They could reflect only one aspect of the management view – that of the manager primarily responsible in the organization for the administration of the scheme or schemes adopted. As we shall see, there are reasons for being interested in the approach of different elements in management, and above all it was important to determine what the reaction of employees and trade unions was to the schemes in operation. Did employees respond in the way management expected when they introduced their schemes? What were their attitudes to the ideas of profit-sharing and share ownership? Did trade union representatives at the enterprise level reflect a distinctive point of view, different either from the employees' or from the position of the trade union movement in general? Such questions, clearly, required the development of our enquiries into the workplace itself, and in order for that to be meaningful the responses had to be set in a framework which represented a sound appreciation of the rationale and *modus operandi* of the schemes at enterprise level. Equally evidently, that implied a case-study approach, to be developed as a complement to the two broader approaches which had their own distinctive, but limited, contributions to make to our understanding.

The case studies, then, were viewed as a fundamental stage in our investigation, designed to nest into a wider background in which the general parameters would be better defined, but in which details of response and process could not be properly appreciated.

METHODS AND PROBLEMS

In developing the case-study approach we had a number of problems to resolve. We had first, to determine more precisely the issues we wanted to explore. Both the survey and the initial interview with management helped to define these issues, and to suggest a general structure for our approach to individual cases. Second, we had to choose our cases for closer examination. These were expected to derive from the management interview programme, which served both to highlight interesting cases and to provide sufficient depth of information to permit specific issues to be identified in the context of individual companies. This information, together with the structural characteristics derived from the survey, and with a developing sense of cases where the necessary co-operation could be obtained, allowed us to narrow our focus to perhaps a dozen or so. The third issue was to narrow these down to six or seven which were within the scope of our resources and which would provide a variety of schemes operating in different contexts. Two companies, though initially willing to co-operate, withdrew because of internal pressures or changes in management, while a third became the subject of a take-over at a critical moment and the case had to be abandoned. In the end, we conducted six case studies in five companies which largely fulfilled our requirements. The characteristics of the six can be summarized as in Table 19. This selection gave ample range in terms of size and geographical location, and was inclusive of both private companies and public limited companies. It contained a variety of scheme types, but was more oriented to manufacturing than we would have preferred: two companies which dropped out at a late stage were in service industries. All but one were unionized: a deliberate choice, since we wanted to explore the nature of union reactions and any interactions with collective bargaining and other union-based procedures. In addition to the variables shown, we hoped to find a variety of management styles which would allow us to explore some of the issues developed in Chapter 5.

Approaches were then made to the companies to request their formal co-operation, including access to management, employees, and, where relevant, trade union representatives. Management interviews were normally conducted with three or four different managers covering general management, personnel, finance, and the administration of the scheme(s).

For the purposes of the interviews we prepared an outline of the topics to be covered, including company history and background, the PS/ESO schemes employed, how they were developed and how they related to other types of participation, and the attitudes and responses of management, trade unions, and employees to them. We recognized that the emphasis and content would vary from case to case, and that it was up to the interviewer to develop and improvise questions in response to the material that emerged. The interviews, then, were semi-structured, lasting from one to two hours. Many of the interviews were tape-recorded and transcribed for subsequent analysis.

Table 19 Characteristics of case-study companies

Company	Ownership	Sector	Unionized	Type of PS/ESO scheme(s)	Approx. employment size	HQ location	Case study location
Bossguide	Ltd	Management services	No	Discretionary profit-bonus; share option	70	Midlands	Midlands
Fairbrush	Ltd	Manufacturing (tools)	Yes	Cash-based: employee trust	340	Midlands	Midlands
Goodbake	PLC				30,000 (group)	South-east	
(a) Breadline		Manufacturing and retail	Yes	SAVE: (discretionary profit-sharing)			Scotland
(b) Scotcake		Manufacturing* (food/drink)					Scotland
Norbrew	PLC	Manufacturing (food/drink)	Yes	ADST: SAVE	6,000 (group)	North England	North England
Thistle	PLC	Manufacturing	Yes	SAVE	20,000	North-west	Scotland

*In this case there is also a productivity bonus scheme.

KEY ISSUES IN THE CASE STUDIES

Four main areas were identified as being of particular importance in the case-study stage: (1) management objectives, (2) trade union reactions within the enterprise, (3) the interaction of financial participation schemes with 'conventional' industrial relations processes and practices, and (4) employee attitudes and behaviour. Each of these is briefly introduced in turn.

Management objectives

The basic problem can be stated quite succinctly. As we have argued in Chapter 5, management will typically have some set of corporate objectives, and some sense of philosophy or style which will influence the range of policies and strategies it adopts in pursuit of these aims. Some styles will lend themselves to a strong emphasis on employee participation, particularly those which have a unitarist foundation. Thus policies and schemes for employee involvement may be expected to have quite explicit functions in relation to management objectives. Schemes for financial participation should be no exception to this. That is, they will have different design features which will seek to influence worker behaviour or attitudes in different ways, and it is possible to think of different schemes for financial participation which provide a menu from which selections can be made according to the particular management objectives and the style of management adopted.

There is, therefore, a hypothetical chain such as has been developed in the last chapter, linking management style, corporate objectives, and the selection of methods used to secure these objectives through their influence on employee attitudes and behaviour. This was, for us, the fundamental reason for wishing to explore what management believed it would achieve by the pursuit of one or more schemes of financial participation. The matter does not, however, rest there.

First, we know that the introduction of tax concessions consistently produced a flurry of new activity in profit-sharing or employee share ownership schemes. Was management in those cases simply participating in a fashionable trend induced by financial prompts from government, without explicit objectives or benefits in view, or was its reaction the result of a clearly thought

117

out decision which taxation benefits had moved into the 'worthwhile' category?

Second, did the adoption of a particular financial participation scheme represent the company's only approach to the securing of specific objectives, or was it seen as an incremental device which could significantly add to the effectiveness of a variety of other measures or schemes already in force? In other words, were financial participation schemes plugging specific gaps in the range of managerial objectives or were they closely related to a broader grouping of schemes aimed at a particular attitudinal or behavioural change on the part of the employees?

Third, we already had available (cf. Chapter 5) a variety of classifications of management styles or strategies and a sense of the main range of motives which management might have in mind when it adopted a scheme for financial participation. But these general motives each have a number of operational counterparts, such as the effects of financial incentives on attracting personnel or inhibiting industrial action; or the effects of motivational schemes on employee effort and productivity, or on reductions in absenteeism, turnover, and industrial action. To the extent that general objectives could be related to operational strategy, we might expect that companies opting for financial partnership schemes would be interested in monitoring their effect, setting up appropriate methods of measurement and undertaking periodic analysis of the outcomes.

Clearly, then, the examination of management objectives was a basic building block in the development of a better understanding of financial participation, and required the depth of treatment that a case study could yield. The questions we have posed above, furthermore, give a natural shape to the design of questions to test the sort of approach that different managements would adopt.

Trade union reactions in the workplace

In examining trade union reactions and responses to profit- sharing and employee share ownership we needed to distinguish policy and practice at three different levels: (1) official TUC policy, (2) official policy on the part of individual unions, and (3) the practice of both lay and full-time officials at company and plant level. The first two of these were pursued by direct application to the TUC and individual unions, as described in Chapter 3. The third would be obtained only by investigation in the company case studies themselves.

The starting point here is the need to acknowledge that, whatever formal union policy may be, management can introduce schemes of financial participation without reference to trade unions, whether recognized or not. Our general evidence indicated this to be the norm: unilateral management initiative. Is this, then, to be seen as an attempt to bypass trade union organization and appeal direct to the employees as individuals rather than as a collective group? Such a strategy might reflect outright opposition to the union organization, or it might be a more defensive response, seeking to reduce reliance on union-dominated channels of communication or to limit the scope for possible extensions of union control.

How, then, did local union representatives react to this kind of move by management? How important to the representatives was the TUC or individual union policy (if any), and how did it influence their response? The representative is potentially in a difficult position, since he may be caught between a measure of employee enthusiasm for financial gains and an official policy that is suspicious at best and perhaps quite opposed. If local representatives identify with the company, they are in a sense aligning themselves with a 'company union' concept – a tendency which has in any case increased in recent years, with emphasis being placed on company and workplace bargaining. Such alignment clearly has implications for the company, for the employees as a whole, and for the union, and beyond that for TUC and political party policy.

These then, were the issues we wished to pursue in the course of interviews with full-time officers and local union lay representatives.

Interaction with other industrial relations practices and procedures

We have already noted above that a scheme for financial participation may be part of a set of measures jointly designed to achieve certain management objectives, and there must then be some possibility of interaction among different participative measures. More generally, financial participation schemes may interact with existing elements and processes in the industrial relations framework of the enterprise or workplace.

The extent of interaction seems likely to depend in part on the overall objectives of financial participation. For example, where profit-sharing is introduced to provide an incentive to employee effort or performance, it may have implications – positive or negative – for other forms of incentive already in operation. Again, a share ownership scheme aimed at creating a greater sense of employee 'belonging' and organizational commitment may interact with other ingredients in an internal labour market strategy seeking to achieve the same objectives. However, of at least equal importance to the kind of objectives pursued will be the industrial relations mechanisms and institutions of the enterprise or the individual workplace.

We can identify three broad areas epitomizing these mechanisms: collective bargaining, consultation, and communications. The central issue is whether and to what extent financial participation schemes are dealt with in any significant way through any of these devices. We have already observed that, even where unions are recognized, profit-sharing and employee share ownership schemes appear largely to be introduced by management *fiat*, not through collective bargaining channels. But does this mean that the *consequences* of financial participation schemes are necessarily neutral with reference to collective bargaining? To what extent are the terms of a profit-sharing scheme, once introduced, subject to adjustment or improvement through collective bargaining?

On the consultative front, interaction effects are likely to depend on the types of consultative mechanism employed. Where consultative channels are part of the regular management–union machinery, profit-sharing and share ownership schemes could readily be integrated into the machinery – but is this done in practice, or is profit-sharing kept aside as part of a specifically management initiative to influence the individual employee? On the other hand, consultation procedures may already be established by management as a form of 'voice' alternative to trade union channels of representation and opinion.[1] Financial participation schemes may then be seen as a further means of strengthening the extra-trade union channel linkages.

Third, what part is given to financial participation in the communications strategy of the enterprise? Is the regular communications machinery used to promulgate the scheme and report on its progress, or is it in some way enlarged to incorporate the PS/ESO initiative? Is there evidence that the information conveyed to employees through the communications channels is directed to productivity, motivational, and loyalty ideals which are consistent with the financial participation scheme objectives?

In essence, consideration of these questions should help us to understand how far companies view their financial participation measures as relatively independent, 'tack-on' devices which they believe will contribute to some corporate objective; and how far profit-sharing is seen as an integrated part of a fully fledged industrial relations apparatus.

Employee attitudes and behaviour

In some measure, a sense of how different schemes shaped up with respect to the three foregoing areas of inquiry could be obtained from the survey and management interview stages, though the case study would allow greater penetration into each. The last area, the impact on employees, was one which could be tackled only through the case-study approach, and was our strongest reason for adopting it.

Here again the basic issue is quite simple. If management has particular objectives in introducing financial participation, how far do employees behave and respond as management would expect? While some aspects of behaviour may be measurable (e.g. effects on turnover and productivity) on the basis of management data, others are not, especially employee attitudes to the principle and practice of financial participation. This, we believed, had to be covered in our study to complete the picture.

A double-pronged approach was adopted, a combination of a limited number of in-depth interviews with individual employees, and a questionnaire distributed to the whole or part of a plant labour force. From these we wished to obtain:

1 Information on personal characteristics (age, sex, job or skill level, union membership status, involvement in union or representative activities in the workplace, etc.).
2 Reasons for participation or non-participation in the scheme(s) available and, for both groups, their reactions to characteristics of the scheme(s).
3 Attitude to management and the company in general, in the light of the financial participation scheme.
4 General attitudes to profit-sharing, share ownership, trade union

121

power and management–employee relations in the United Kingdom.

This approach, we believed, would enable us to determine whether there was any discernible pattern of participation according to personal or attitudinal factors, and whether participants and non-participants were sharply differentiated in their attitudes either to the scheme or to the principle of financial participation. It would also provide a guide to the extent to which individuals responded to the stimuli perceived *by management* to be the means of fulfilling corporate objectives.

This approach, however, has its own limitations, of which we have to be aware. First it could not tell us about the way in which attitudes or behaviour had *changed* as a result of the scheme. Nor, secondly, for the same reason, could it really distinguish the cases where employees had long-standing predilections which led them to favour opportunities for financial participation from those where attitudes or prejudices had been influenced by the opportunity or the experience of financial participation. Third, we were not able in any assured way to locate the responses we obtained in a framework which would permit sample weighting procedures to be applied. There was no generally available sampling frame for the selection of our samples for interview and questionnaire, and it was probably to be expected that we would get different response rates from different parts of the employee population. However, despite such limitations, we were in no doubt that the issues raised by employee response to financial participation schemes had to be addressed along these general lines. The particular methods used in each case are briefly summarized in the context of each presentation.

Note

1 The 1984 WIRS study reports some tendency for non-union representation on consultative committees to increase in the recent past.

122

7

Bossguide: managing the consultancy

Bossguide is a successful and rapidly growing management consultancy firm, offering a wide range of services, including the engineering and production control aspects of technological change and manufacturing systems rationalization, other management systems such as maintenance, stock control, or accounting systems, office automation, and various elements of human resource management. Bossguide's philosophy of consultancy emphasized a 'practical implementation' approach, in which consultants also took responsibility for seeing through the application of their recommendations. The company was originally founded in the USA in the 1950s, but its expansion into the UK proved so successful that the UK operation became the driving force of the group. Eventually in 1980 the UK company became independent and locally owned, in effect through a management buy-out, and the new company then bought a 50 per cent stake in the former US parent.

At the time of the research Bossguide had several offices in the UK, with its headquarters in a small town a few miles outside a major conurbation. There were subsidiary operations in France and Australia, facilitating a cross-frontier consultancy service to internationally spread customers. It was still a private limited company, despite which an extensive share ownership system was operated, as described below.

THE 'HUMAN RESOURCES'

The staff size of the company had grown quite rapidly during the 1980s from a very small base, to reach over seventy at the time of

123

the study. Sixty of these were male, and all but two female employees were full-time. Five-sixths of the total were consultants with various specialisms, the rest being secretarial and administrative staff. With only one or two exceptions, this distinction followed the gender division, office-based staff below senior management level being almost entirely female. In our analysis of attitudes, discussed later, we divided our sample into 'clerical', 'administrative management', 'consultant', and 'top management' groups. The second of these groups included posts such as office manager, administration training manager, and a number of service operations (e.g. marketing support) carried out from the headquarters building.

In terms of relations with the market environment, and so assessment of the company by customers, the key role was played by the consultant group. Bossguide, the financial director emphasized, was 'operations-driven', and so those in the 'operations environment' out in client companies 'must be the heart and soul of the company'. It was the abilities and performance of this group which was essential to Bossguide's success. Either individually or within a project team they had to be able to enter another organization, familiarize themselves with and gather information on those aspects relevant to their assignment, and produce recommendations in plausible format and superior to propositions current inside the customer in a relatively short period of time. Given the Bossguide approach, they had, then, to demonstrate their workability. The pressure of work could be extremely high and individualized, also exposing it to evaluation. The motivation, control, and assessment of this category of staff were therefore crucial to the operation of Bossguide, and are discussed in the next section. Usually those in post had established themselves in management jobs elsewhere but had moved to Bossguide for the challenge and the financial rewards of this line of work.

Those consultants who survived the first year or two and performed well could expect to progress into the upper stratum of the category, the project managers. Beyond them, and classified as top management for our analysis, lay a smaller group of senior project managers, who also carried out personnel management functions in effect, and the directors of the company.

MANAGEMENT STRATEGY AND EMPLOYEE RELATIONS

The approach of top management at Bossguide was shaped by the contingencies described above. Sustained success and growth in a lucrative market, one which was apparently enhanced rather than threatened by the need for restructuring in large parts of industry, gave it a good deal of room to manoeuvre. A general atmosphere of thriving prosperity prevailed and, given rapid expansion, prospects were good for security and, for the proficient and ambitious, advancement.

At the same time constant staff intake, and the increasing numbers themselves, generated pressures that were forcing a reappraisal of approach. The number of employees by the time of our study (in fact any total above forty) was regarded as creating dilemmas by the managing director. It stretched the point where close personal contacts could be maintained, and these management saw as the mainstay of good relations: communication and the ability of the top management to monitor activity. The combination of these was seen in turn as essential to sustain the desired motivation and commitment of the key consultant group. They were also desirable on grounds of philosophical consistency and, perhaps, demonstration to clients, in that like most consultants Bossguide advocated integrative, involvement-oriented employee relations policies in the field.

Pay was determined by top management, in accordance with their judgement of performance during the previous year, through a system of appraisal and merit rises. Assessment for consultants and project managers drew on estimations of performance from senior project managers, and clearly the perceived competence and fairness of their evaluations and those of still more senior management were important to the motivation and morale of this critical group. This appraisal was also closely linked to both share and profit bonus schemes as described later, so that its effect on total remuneration was very considerable. Senior management expressed concern that sheer size and rate of growth could jeopardize the effectiveness of the system, and so also of the profit and share option systems themselves, since it was so heavily based on their personal knowledge and judgement of individual employees.

One pressure common to our other case studies was absent in this instance. There were no trade unions or staff associations in Bossguide, nor was there any visible prospect of such emerging in

125

the foreseeable future. The individualization of consultancy ('professional') staff, through both work and appraisal, made this a foregone conclusion, while the relatively isolated village location, the management ethos, and other factors common to predominantly female clerical and administrative staff in small companies, ensured that this applied also to 'non-professional' staff. This distinction was used in conversation by the managing director, incidentally, though it appeared to make him uncomfortable by implying divisions management preferred to blur by personal approachability and seeking 'to make everyone part of the company'.

This integrative approach entailed a commitment to employee involvement through communication and informal accessibility. Indeed, all the management views expressed to us from observations of client companies emphasized faulty communications as the greatest problem encountered, making the stress on this element of employee relations internally all the greater. Company size as yet still made much in the way of formal provision for involvement superfluous, though there were briefing groups and employee trustees for the pension fund, together with the opportunity for shareholders to take part in the quarterly company meetings and occasional weekend trips. The managing director described the Bossguide philosophy in this area as follows:

> I suppose I would describe it as trying to be as open as we possibly can with information – not really sensitive information, but we're very open. We hold regular briefings and will tell what's going on, whether it's good or bad, and we encourage involvement and participation, we encourage people to contribute. We have a management structure and we don't believe in management by committee. Certain people have responsibilities, and they have to have the authority to get on with the job. So we try not to compromise that.

The extent to which this arrangement again relied on personal style and approachability was made apparent several times in our efforts to get a closer specification of such channels. The problem of getting many staff to contribute to public briefings and discussion was acknowledged, but it was claimed to be bridged by the willingness of people to make their views known in informal and less dauntingly public encounters with senior management. Formal consultative arrangements were not seen as any substitute for this, but the continuing development of the company was already putting some strain on the system without, as yet, suggesting a ready alternative.

Although there were some aspects of senior management's approach which were fairly loosely defined by their nature, and which relied to a significant extent on the personal inclination and manner of the managing director in particular, it was sufficiently coherent and articulated to merit being termed a strategy rather than just a style. It is fairly readily classified as sophisticated paternalist in terms of the taxonomy adopted in Chapter 5. There is evidently no noteworthy challenge to management control, and so it is possible for management to proceed on unitary, integrative principles, and to define the extent and limits of involvement and 'openness' unilaterally.

THE EMPLOYEE VIEWPOINT

Our attitude survey among Bossguide employees was distributed to all seventy members of staff, and produced fifty returns (71 per cent), spread in fairly representative proportions across the company population. Percentage figures are quoted at times in the following discussion for convenience of presentation, but the small numbers should be borne in mind.

In many aspects it will be found below that Bossguide employees had a relatively favourable and unchallenging view of the authority structure and management approach in their firm. Any expectations of blanket deference and legitimation which might follow from the above description of the unusually auspicious circumstances from a management viewpoint would be disappointed, however. On the subject of trade union power in British industry, 53 per cent thought the unions had too much, but 43 per cent believed their share was about right for instance. Since there were no unions in Bossguide, the company-specific version of the question had no relevance. To give other examples, 62 per cent disagreed that management knew best and should be left by employees to make the decisions, 78 per cent disagreed that workers should never strike, for reasons of loyalty to the company, and 84 per cent agreed that a good management always consulted its work force. There was a fairly even split on the view that most management had its workers' welfare at heart, with 46 per cent agreeing and 36 per cent dissenting. Finally, 82 per cent felt that there was a combination of shared interests and conflict between management and employees in Britain as a whole, with 13 per cent seeing the two as basically on opposite sides and only 4 per cent perceiving an identity of aims and objectives.

At the same time, when questions explicitly or potentially entailed more direct evaluation of the state of affairs at Bossguide itself, the dissent from unitarism was markedly more muted. The statement 'Most management tend to treat people like me as numbers' was overwhelmingly rejected, as, rather more significantly perhaps, was the view that 'People like me have no opportunity to use their real abilities at work'. Overall, 62 per cent rated Bossguide a 'very good' employer, 28 per cent 'moderately good' and 10 per cent 'average'. The ratings given on specific aspects of the employment relationship in the company are shown in Table 20.

Table 20 Employee ratings of Bossguide (%)

Rating	Pay	Manage-ment openness	Management skill	Chances to get on	Job security	Employee partici-pation in decisions
Well above average	4	38	27	39	14	16
A little above average	38	35	37	41	33	49
About average	43	21	31	16	35	16
A little below average	15	4	6	4	16	12
Well below average	–	2	–	–	2	6
Number	47	48	49	49	49	49

While there was some spread of opinion, the overall results still cast Bossguide in a good light in the employees' eyes, and this among a work force which was probably unusually well informed about alternative regimes. The company was rated above average by a majority on everything except pay and job security. As might be expected, the chances of advancement were rated particularly high, but of particular relevance for our discussion is that three-quarters rated openness above average, and two-thirds rated participation likewise (though here almost one in five put the company *below* average). On workplace relations the respondents' opinion of Bossguide was again markedly more favourable (i.e. less conflictual) than for Britain as a whole, with three-quarters seeing these in terms of common aims and objectives, and the remaining quarter perceiving both shared interests and areas of conflict. Interestingly, the main source of dissent from the outright unitarist view of Bossguide in this question was the consultants, two-fifths of whom selected the more pluralistic option.

THE FINANCIAL PARTICIPATION SYSTEM

Apart from the system of salary determination itself, two forms of profit-sharing were operated at Bossguide at the time of our study, together combining a cash-based and a share-based approach. Both worked largely on the same basis of senior management judgement of merit as did the system of salary appraisal. That judgement therefore had to carry a lot of weight, and its perceived fairness and accuracy were important to the viability of the system of human resource management. The managing director claimed that apart from the odd grumble there were 'no major difficulties'.

The *profit bonus* was an arrangement inherited from the original American company. Operating profit was divided into that amount the directors judged necessary for development, with the residual considered for distribution between dividends and profit bonus. Bonus took the lion's share in most years – probably five to ten times the amount for dividends, it was claimed, but again this was at management discretion. The bonus was then divided among employees according to assessment of performance during the past year. Typically, we were told, bonus would range between 15 per cent and 30 per cent of pay, although it could be far lower in a bad year (which Bossguide had not yet faced). In practice, we were told, sums were initially allocated for categories of employees by the board. This allocation was roughly in line with the proportion of salary accounted for by each group, although the process by which it emerged was described somewhat surprisingly as an approximate and subconscious estimation rather than a formula. Within each group the managers responsible for those lower down the hierarchy would then propose a level of bonus from the group 'pie', which the board would usually approve. These managers would themselves be assessed directly by the directors.

The levels of bonus reported by our respondents in the attitude survey confirmed both the size and the wide range of bonuses allocated. For analysis, we classified them as 'low' (up to £1,500 for the year), 'medium' (£1,500–£4,500), and 'high' (over £4,500). Overall, 35 per cent fell into the low category, 44 per cent into the medium, and 21 per cent into the high group. This amounts to a very considerable performance-related element of pay, affected by overall company achievement and attributed individual contribution thereto.

The *share ownership* scheme was operated outside the Inland Revenue guidelines, so attracting no tax relief, and again on a discretionary basis. It was introduced when the company became British-owned, taking its present form in 1980. Each year a decision to create new shares was taken, and an opportunity to purchase those shares was given to employees at management invitation. To be invited or omitted was a further affirmation of top management's judgements. Not all would be able to raise the money to accept in any year, although most apparently do take up at least some proportion of the shares offered.

In general it was regarded as unusual if shares were not offered after a year's service, and at the time of our first visit participation in the scheme was estimated at two-thirds. None the less it was accepted that 'the scheme is in a sense arbitrary'. One question concerned the possibility that a failure to take up shares would be taken as a sign of suspect involvement in the company by the employee in question. The managing director was at pains to deny that anyone would receive a black mark in this way, but two other senior managers reflected on the matter and conceded that there was an element of this. The financial director observed that take-up by individuals was certainly noted on the board, and that limited or non-purchase was liable to be read as a sign of transience. He acknowledged that this might well lead some employees to feel obliged to apply for a full quota of shares. Rather more forcefully, the other senior manager commented that 'the more shares they've got, the more committed they are to the success of Bossguide'. Elaborating on the different aspects of management's employee relations strategy, he averred that communication was targeted at involvement, and that the share scheme did not seek to offer participation but was a mark precisely of commitment.

On a later visit we were told that a decision had been taken to lessen divisiveness by offering shares still more widely, so that figure had probably risen to five-sixths (this was confirmed by calculation from a list of shareholders). This was also in preparation for a shift towards free share issues in place of part of the bonus, partly to reduce the drag on company valuation by having to deduct the bonus as a cost. This would have the implication that the share scheme, through the payment of dividends as well as the free issue, would come to play a far more central role in management's approach. It also seemed that in consequence the scheme would have to become somewhat less discretionary, with significant implications for the management strategy thereon. The new proposal was being sold through discussion groups of employees, but these were organized in a cascade down the hierarchy which meant that it was not known to those below senior level at the time of our study, so we were unfortunately unable to raise it and assess reactions in our interviews.

All the shares were owned by employees, it being laid down in the company's articles of association that only active members could hold shares. If a shareholder left, his or her holding had to be placed on the internal Bossguide 'market'. In practice, if the number were small, we were told, a favoured person or someone who had performed well but had been unable to buy shares as yet would be picked out and offered some or all of them. At other times bids for numbers (at the fixed valuation of the time by which leavers were compensated) would be taken. The shares were allocated a book value based on an estimation of the worth of the company divided by the cumulative number of shares issued. That book value had more than doubled between December 1984 and June 1986, suggesting that ownership was potentially extremely lucrative. The average shareholding value worked out a £10,400 by the middle of 1986, with a wide variance; the directors with maximum holdings possessed over £70,000 worth each. None the less management told us that no holding stood at above 11 per cent, and claimed that the long-serving directors had avoided the temptation to build up a controlling proportion, diluting their holdings in the interests of the scheme. This view of top management was not shared by some of those we interviewed. Shares could be sold if individuals chose, but this was reported to be rare. The fact that most employees owned shares in Bossguide was regarded by management as a selling point to potential customers, and the extent of share ownership was celebrated on a display in the reception area of the headquarters and in the company literature.

The original questionnaire response from Bossguide checked every reason for introducing the schemes that we listed. Though this suggested a possible lack of specification, we were obviously interested to see how well defined and evaluated the objectives of employee financial participation would be in what it seemed reasonable to assume was an exceptionally sophisticated management milieu. In the initial interview the schemes were adjudged successful on every score provided, including a say in running the company, and with only increased productivity sinking from strong to unadorned agreement. In a later interview, it should be added, the finance director opined that participation in decisions was not really connected with financial participation: 'because shareholding is spread so widely, it is also a fact that most people are shareholders as well, but their capacity to influence decision-making stems more from their responsibilities in the organization than from having shares'. In the view of another senior manager, 'Share ownership is more about commitment than involvement.'

None the less there was clearly an immense confidence in the schemes on management's part, reflecting in turn the exceptionally large incentives and control thereof which permeated both schemes. An evaluation had been made of the Inland Revenue schemes offering tax relief, but despite this advantage they had been rejected as too complicated. In reality the fact that 'they were so hedged around with rules and various things that they really just didn't work for us' (managing director) may well have been a euphemism for the potential loss of management discretionary powers that they might have entailed. In addition, we have seen that the approved schemes rarely seem suitable for unquoted and small companies.

Size also came up as a factor in the workability of financial participation. One senior manager took the view that 'profit-sharing wouldn't work in a large company'. Two reasons were given: the problem of achieving the communication and approachability required to tap the potential motivational value of the arrangement; and then, 'for a start you'd have a trade union ... and then before they went into any agreement they would want to know all the rules'. This would entangle and destroy the point of such schemes, it was argued.

Although there seems a strong coherence to these policies from the evidence so far, management replies on why it had chosen the particular schemes in operation led us to qualify this conclusion.

'I'm not sure there is a specific reason,' the managing director opined when asked more closely about the rationale of the share scheme:

> At the time we didn't adopt a scheme, we simply adopted a policy allowing members of the company to acquire shares. It was a policy we set, as we want shareholders to be in the business. We were more concentrating on that than the specific sort of mechanism for allowing it. If there had been these sort of sophisticated schemes maybe we would have gone for one. But several years into it, it's a different thing altogether.

In response to a query as to whether the share scheme had emerged somewhat *ad hoc* from a general approach rather than being carefully and specifically designed, the managing director agreed. 'Yes. It evolved rather than a sudden decision one day, "let's do this." It seemed natural.'

The line adopted on the profit-sharing bonus was more definite but far more restricted than the questionnaire response: 'Motivation, that's all. Just to make people that much more motivated to profitability and the business such that everybody in it can influence profitability to a higher extent than in most companies.' There was, moreover, some contradiction between theory and practice. Asked how far the bonus affected the way pay was decided, the managing director mused for a moment, then commented:

> Good question. In theory it's independent; in theory we determine basic salaries and the bonus is a separate issue. In practice I think when we look at the competitiveness of the packages we're offering in the market place then we would tend to include bonus in the assessment. The total package is worth this much because you all know that you can expect bonuses in between. So in theory it's separate, in practice I'm sure they're not.

Either way, it was clear that management at Bossguide wielded a powerful weapon in the form of profit-sharing and employee share ownership. 'I can't imagine running the business without it,' was one comment from the managing director, and elsewhere he commented on a feeling in some circles that a more predictable recognition through the bonus would have been desirable, but rejected it for the time being as costing 'flexibility'.

EMPLOYEES AND THE IDEA OF FINANCIAL PARTICIPATION

Those searching for radical undertones to the views of Bossguide employees on the notion of financial participation would have to read a rather deep and obscure meaning into the runes cast before us. In response to the general question on profit-sharing and employee share ownership posed in this case study as in the others we conducted, the aggregate expressed attitudes did not divert far from a unitarist, managerial viewpoint, as Table 21 indicates. Large majorities at Bossguide may be seen to disagree that employees should get profits by right, and that if employees did have shares they should elect managers. These were two possible 'labourist' conversions of the managerial predilection for profit-sharing/employee share ownership. That almost two-fifths felt that employees should own the companies they work for shows an interesting division of views, but not a subversive one for Bossguide, where in an important sense the company was entirely employee-owned. Finally, just over half of employees accepted the argument for loss-sharing as the reasonable counterpart of getting a slice of the profits, this implying a substantial internalization of the employee capitalist notion when considered along with the apparent legitimation of top management control in the rejection of election and at various other points in the findings discussed in this chapter.

All this is not to say that there is no element of dissent at Bossguide. An analysis of the employee responses reveals that almost all the support for non-managerial views came from the overwhelmingly female employees at the bottom of the

Table 21 Employee views on profit-sharing and employee share ownership in general (%)

	Agree	Disagree	No opinion
Profits should belong to employees, not shareholders	10	86	4
Employees with shares should elect managers	18	78	4
Employees should own the companies they work for	38	45	16
Employees should share losses as well as profits	53	41	6

N = 49 throughout.

organizational hierarchy. Thus almost half this group agreed that profits should go to employees, not shareholders, while two-thirds supported employee shareholder election of management. Though numbers here were small, the contrast with other groups was consistent and striking. At the same time, half the clerical respondents supported loss-sharing (a higher proportion than all but top management's 85 per cent), and there was little difference between groups on the more ambivalent question (for Bossguide) of the desirability of employees owning their company.

VIEWS OF THE BOSSGUIDE SHARE OPTION SCHEME

In our sample four-fifths of respondents reported having been offered and taken up share options in Bossguide, this being close to the figure given to us for the entire work force at the time of the survey. Only five indicated having bought shares before 1980, and most were fairly recent additions to the list of shareholders. Of those without shares, apart from one person who cited not wishing to tie savings to the job, all said the reason for non-participation was not having been offered shares as yet. This limits the value of an examination of the differences between shareholders and non-shareholders by comparison with option schemes in our other case studies, since it becomes a surrogate for length of service combined with broader management assessment of the person concerned, rather than a distinct and autonomous choice by the respondents themselves. In our survey there was some sign of lower opportunities of involvement for clerical staff, though, since just under half this group were shareholders, compared with all responding middle managers in the office, and all top management along with three-quarters of consultants.

Those who had become participants were asked to indicate the importance of various advantages of share purchase. The results are summarized in Fig.1. It will be seen that gaining a stake in the company and involvement in its future were the most important reasons which respondents claimed they had considered in purchasing shares. Financial rewards also played a prominent part, but the lack of risk was much less to the fore, and not much importance at all was attached by most to having an easy route to share purchase itself. Particularly for those with a potential career stake in the company, and something to prove to their superiors, the offer of a chance to buy was an important achievement, and refusal

135

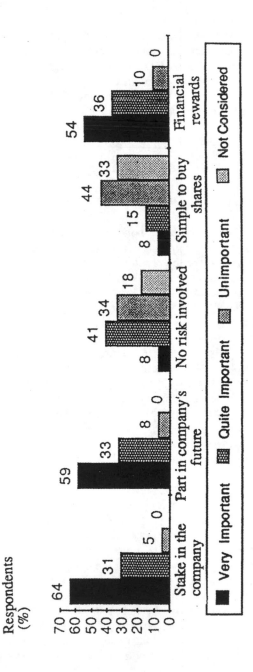

Figure 1 Motives for participation: Bossguide

would be feared to seem a signal of poor commitment to the company. That acceptance of offered shares was seen as a measure of commitment was confirmed by all but one of the employees we interviewed.

This puts a different slant on the high support for the first two reasons selected for share purchase. Given the confirmation by the senior managers quoted earlier, it seems likely that this pressure is of some importance, for recent additions to the consultant force in particular. Almost three-quarters of the clerical and consultant groups, and more than four-fifths of the office-based middle management reported two years' service or less, so that most staff might come under this scrutiny.

A breakdown of the results by length of service gives some credence to this argument. Taking the three most significant reported factors, the proportion classifying rewards as very important was similar whether service was low (up to two years), medium (two to five years) or high (over five years). For both 'stake' and 'company future', those reporting the factors very important ran at around two-thirds for the low service group, dropped to a third or less for medium service, then rose to over four-fifths for long service (mostly top management).

When we examine the reasons for taking up options by occupational group, the above suspicions are not entirely borne out, however, With only half rating a stake in the company very important, consultants were easily the *least* likely participants to place maximum emphasis on that factor. The same proportion rated involvement in the future of the company very important, well below top management or middle management in the office (everyone in the latter group), but in this case all the small group of clerical respondents rated it only 'quite important'. The clerical and consultant groups were in any case less likely to rate any factor 'very important' than the other two groups.

Another possible explanation of this apparent division in the consultant ranks is that our interviews offered some indications that a fair proportion of those who entered as consultants saw their attachment to Bossguide as a lucrative but highly pressured and probably fairly short-lived one, with a danger of burn-out or neglect of family over a long period. These individuals would not be expected to feel obliged to get more involved in the company than their job already required.

That a significant group existed for whom share ownership (in Bossguide and elsewhere) was merely a matter of financial return

137

was confirmed in the employee interviews, though the interviewees were divided as to whether they belonged to that group. Those who did not tended to add, almost paradoxically for the objectives of a scheme, that their commitment was in any case to the job and company regardless of the inducement of Bossguide shares. Further, several comments were made as to the potentially divisive effect of selective offers of shares over time. Finally, a common view of the consultants interviewed confirmed that of top management on the impact of size: financial participation would mean little or nothing in a large company, and in any case played only a supporting role to the critical influence of good communications. Examples from well known large companies, from past employment, or from consultancy experience were usually cited.

OPINIONS ON THE PROFIT BONUS

The profit-sharing element of the system of financial participation was unreservedly supported by a small majority of Bossguide employees, but almost half said they had some reservations, and one had no strong feelings. When we broke these results down by occupational group we find that the locus of reservations is chiefly the consultant and top management groups, with half of each qualifying their support, compared with only one-third of clerical staff and under one-fifth of office management. The proportion with reservations was highest among the middle-service group (60 per cent), just over one-third of those with short service having any criticisms.

These figures may, however, give a false impression of the aggregate view of the scheme *in practice* and the pattern of critical attitudes. Although a majority accepted the salary differentials in the firm as fair, and only one in seven thought them too high, when it came to the fairness of the bonus allocation only a quarter gave it unqualified endorsement. This implies that the support for the bonus system noted above was in some measure for the principle or idea rather than for the implementation. The overall level of doubt was mild but distributed across the organization in a rather different way to questioning of the principles of the system. (Table 22)

Top management now appeared as the chief defenders of (their own) operation of the allocation. Several clerical staff were notably disgruntled in some degree, while no consultants at all rated the

Table 22 Expressed fairness of profit share bonus allocation, by employee category (%)

Rating	Clerical	Office management	Con-sultants	Top management
Fair	25	40	–	57
Could be improved	25	60	67	21
Unfair in some instances	50	–	22	14
Unfair altogether	–	–	6	–
Indifferent	–	–	6	7

implementation completely fair. An analysis by length of service showed that those with two years or less were most divided in their views, perhaps reflecting their differential treatment and also possibly their doubts about the impartiality of a system which handed down judgements and associated rewards from on high with little or nor discussion.

The implied criticism was hardly harsh, and it is hard to imagine a system in the real world which everyone thought fair; but again the location of restrained questioning was informative. Moreover, in almost every interview the perceived arbitrariness and unfairness of the bonus system came across as the most persistent criticism recorded. More than once mention was made of the feeling that being in good favour with top management near the time of the assessment could count for a lot, and that much might rest on whether an influential figure had been crossed in the recent past. Reference was made to management jokes about taking care to remember that the review was near. The need for a more open and formally evaluated system was widely canvassed.

Although only 14 per cent of employees reported seeing their bonus as an essential part of their pay, 70 per cent described it as a welcome addition, an assessment echoed in the interviews. Given the scale of payments reported earlier, this judgement is hardly surprising, and brings the scheme some way in line with the more ambitious of the current ideas for profit-related pay. However, since the bonuses paid were in practice tied up with salary assessments, as described earlier, their level was also therefore related to occupational place. Thus whereas half of top management received 'high' bonuses, consultants were evenly split between low and medium levels, while almost all clerical and office management staff fell into the low category. Thus while a small

139

group of office management, consultants, and top management admitted regarding the bonus as essential (and one in each group regarded it as making little difference), all the clerical staff saw it as a welcome addition only. Perhaps not very surprisingly, too, whereas 86 per cent of those on high bonuses thought them completely fair, this went for only 14 per cent of those on medium bonus and 7 per cent of those on low.

THE EFFECTS OF FINANCIAL PARTICIPATION

It is difficult to disentangle the effects of these financial participation schemes, whether on attitudes or on behaviour, from many other factors which could feasibly act as either cause or effect in the system. This is particularly true where, as here, numbers are too small to attempt any meaningful complex variable analysis for the attitude survey results. We will none the less attempt a few tentative observations here before concluding.

First, we asked respondents to consider the overall effects of profit-sharing and employee share ownership in their experience. The results are summarised in Table 23. It will be helpful to consider the responses in sets of topics. Incentive and related calculative issues are covered in items 3 and 6 to 9; other motivational (and so potentially behavioural) matters are dealt with in items in 4 and 5; awareness is covered by item 1; and the question of employee influence is dealt with in 2 and 10.

On the incentive front, a very high proportion agreed that profit-sharing did allow the sharing of the fruits of hard work. Most agreed that the unpredictability of the bonus prevented planned spending (this applied across the range of length of service in the company), and almost two-fifths that part of employees' earnings were put at risk. This last result may be read as loss-sharing (of which a management view tends to approve) or as a labourist critique of double insecurity, but in this instance the concentration of this response in top management suggests the former was most operative. There was a clear gradient, too, from low service with the company (25 per cent agreed) through medium (40 per cent likewise) to high (70 per cent support). Almost half the replies agreed that profit-sharing was just another kind of bonus, a view at odds with many of the management objectives reported earlier (and confirmed by the lower support for this view at the top in the survey). Length of service had little effect on these proportions.

Table 23 Bossguide employees' views of the effect of financial participation schemes, by occupational group (%)

| | Proportion of each group agreeing | | | | |
	Clerical	Office manage- ment	Con- sultants	Top manage- ment	All
1 Creates awareness of management problems	17	33	39	46	38
2 Enables greater participation	33	50	44	69	50
3 Can share results if work hard	83	100	78	100	88
4 Less likely to move to another job	17	67	30	39	35
5 More likely to notice if colleagues don't pull their weight	17	67	48	71	53
6 Are better ways of improving benefits	33	50	41	23	36
7 Just another kind of bonus	50	67	48	31	46
8 Part of employees' earnings put at risk	17	17	39	54	38
9 Cannot predict bonus and so cannot plan spending	50	100	70	69	71
10 Employees should have more say in fixing profit share	33	33	35	36	35

Finally, over a third agreed that there were better ways of improving benefits, with a smaller proportion disagreeing and a final third (far more than for the other statements) checking 'no opinion'. Here length of service produced an apparent relationship, with seven-tenths of those of medium service agreeing, compared to one in three with low and one-fifth of those with high service.

Only a third were less likely, on their own assessment, to move to another job as a result of the company schemes, with the figure for clerical employees very low and that for office management

141

high. Again the interviews confirmed the limited impact of financial participation on this decision. A majority, but excepting the clerical staff, felt they were more likely to notice colleagues slacking. In neither case did length of service exert an important influence.

A greater awareness of management problems was most popular as a detected consequence of profit-sharing with top management, consistent with our interviews with key policy-making figures. Overall, however, the proportion agreeing that it resulted was less than two-fifths, and exhibited a clear downward gradient as we moved down the hierarchy to the clerical staff. The figure for those with low and medium service was similar at around one-third, but leapt to almost three-quarters for those with long service.

Finally, on the matter of participation, half the employees felt that the schemes enabled them to participate more in the working of the company (again with some occupational gradient, and a much stronger one by length of service). One-third agreed (and over half disagreed) that employees should have more say in fixing the profit share, however, a result almost unvarying by occupational grouping or length of service.

It would appear that, to judge by these findings, it is the financial rewards and their potential motivational effects which carried most weight with Bossguide employees. Other effects were more attenuated, particularly for the clerical employees, although attitudes did not incline to demand the greater influence over decisions that the pessimists among managerial commentators fear will follow from employee share ownership.

To examine other possible effects, or at least concomitants, of the profit bonus and company share ownership, we examined the relationship between these factors and other expressed attitudes. Those participating in the share option schemes were more likely to see Bossguide in terms of unitary or shared interests (73 per cent to 60 per cent), to feel that employees should own the company they work for, and to support loss sharing, while being less likely to support the idea of profits belonging to employees rather than shareholders (5 per cent, compared to 30 per cent of non-participants). Both participants and non-participants were four to one in favour of electing managers. The two groups expressed similar support for the profit bonus system, though none of the non-participants thought its allocation was completely fair, while almost one-third of the participants opined thus.

Intriguingly, participants were *less* likely to concur that financial participation schemes increased business awareness (33 per cent to 56 per cent of non-participants), and were somewhat more likely to see profit-sharing as just another bonus. They were markedly more likely to agree that such schemes constituted a risk to earnings (44 per cent to 11 per cent), and that they would be less likely to move as a result of the schemes (44 per cent to none), but on the questions around participation and watching colleagues differences were minor.

Overall, then, the effects of participation in the share option scheme were haltingly in the direction of greater support for some managerial views. If we turn next to the profit bonus scheme, we can divide the work force as described earlier into low, medium, and high bands of bonus payments received. The relationship between these levels and support for the profit bonus scheme was far from uncomplicated, for while half of those with a low bonus and almost all those with a high one lent unreserved support to the scheme, only a quarter of those with a medium level of bonus did so. This seems to have been a result of lower support among the consultant group and top managers with only medium levels of bonus, but nevertheless it seems to show the potential for disgruntlement being generated by disappointed expectations or relative deprivation once a scheme is in operation. This conclusion is reinforced by the fact that only the group with high bonuses bestowed an unqualified judgement of fairness on the system of allocating bonuses (86 per cent, by comparison with 7 per cent on low and 14 percent with medium bonus levels).

Those with a high bonus level were twice as likely as those on lower levels to agree that their awareness of management problems was enhanced by the schemes. They were also more likely to scrutinize the efforts of colleagues, though their reported likelihood of moving jobs did not seem significantly affected. They were much more likely to disagree that profit-sharing was just another kind of bonus, however, and none agreed (in contrast to almost half on medium and low bonuses) that there were better ways of providing benefits. They were much less likely to feel that employees should have more say in fixing the profit share (partly as senior managers, and partly, perhaps, because the existing system served them well) but much more likely to agree that the schemes enabled greater participation.

Finally, we can examine the relationship between perceptions of the fairness of the profit bonus allocation and the perceived effects of schemes. Here a clear gradient appeared on a number of factors,

Table 24 Views of the effect of schemes by the perceived fairness of the bonus allocation (%)

	Fair	Could be improved	Some reservations
1 Creates awareness of management problems (disagree)	30	42	75
2 Enables greater participation (disagree)	30	32	63
3 Can share results if work hard (disagree)	0	5	0
4 Less likely to move to another job (disagree)	40	47	63
5 More likely to notice if colleagues don't pull their weight (disagree)	22	42	38
6 Are better ways of improving benefits (agree)	30	39	25
7 Just another kind of bonus (agree)	30	58	25
8 Part of employees' earnings put at risk (agree)	40	42	38
9 Cannot predict bonus and so cannot plan spending (agree)	80	84	50
10 Employees should have more say in fixing profit share (disagree)	73	53	25

as shown in Table 24. The table lists proportions taking the expected management line, this sometimes entailing agreement with the statement and sometimes disagreement, as indicated. It will be seen that on awareness of management problems, the effect on participation, the likelihood of moving jobs, and the right to a say in fixing profits, greater criticism of the allocation was associated with a non-management line on the effects of schemes. On the other hand this relationship did not hold, for example, on whether there were better benefits and whether profit sharing was just another kind of bonus.

To some extent, then, the profit bonus scheme did seem to affect other attitudes, though this could be read in partly negative terms, since the clearest relationship was between a critical view, in some degree at least, on the system of allocation and the rejection of outcomes management would have wished for from the schemes.

CONCLUSIONS

In many respects Bossguide must count as the most successful environment for management control that we examined. Employee attitudes generally indicated a strong legitimation of management, with at most mild criticism particularly likely from part of the consultant group and from the clerical staff on a few matters. It also had the most extensive financial participation system (in terms of the sums involved for beneficiaries) and, as one would expect, given its business, a relatively aware, articulate, and refined management strategy on employee relations in general and financial participation in particular.

None the less it proved hard to pin down specific and demonstrable benefits to management objectives from the schemes, and even the management itself was sometimes pushed to define precisely what it hoped to achieve. There were signs that the attitudinal and motivational effects of financial participation were sometimes attenuated or ambivalent, and it seems more plausible to suppose that such enthusiasm as existed was born of the size of the benefits, the widespread approval of top management's efforts to be approachable, and extensive arrangements for communication, rather than participation generating attitudinal approval in itself.

Finally, several senior managers recognized the problems posed by a rate of growth and the attendant quantum transition in scale which undermined an approach facilitated by personal contact in a small company. Some of the limitations on support for the schemes which we found were probably partly a result of the transition Bossguide was beginning to attempt at the time of our study. Whether the more formal and rule-governed arrangements which seem likely to develop will fulfil management aspirations it would be fascinating to discover. Certainly, a more fertile ground for financial participation schemes to be effectively implemented and to work successfully in management terms would be hard to imagine.

8

Fairbrush: the Quaker tradition

Fairbrush was a medium-sized, family-owned, private limited company. Its headquarters and main manufacturing centre were located on a greenfield site some miles from the nearest urban centre in the English Midlands. The company predominantly produced high-quality D-I-Y tools. Formally the company may be described as a multinational, with a number of geographically scattered overseas projects in merchandising and manufacture. However, these appeared very much as peripheral outposts of the single UK base for management, both economically and psychologically.

Fairbrush had its origins in the enterprising development of a small individual trading operation by the founder in the late 1920s. In the early 1930s a manufacturing operation was begun, assembling the tools directly, and a few years later the founder decided to move from the large conurbation where he had begun to a small village some twenty miles away. Shortly after this the profit-sharing scheme described later was commenced, prompted in large part by the founder's commitment to Quaker principles.

The present factory was constructed in stages during the 1940s and 1950s on a large piece of land not far from the village. This period was for the most part one of rapid expansion and optimism. Although Fairbrush was not the first substantial employer in the area, it remained a major presence in the local economy. In the post-war years demand was boosted by the start of the D-I-Y boom, and considerably outstripped production, given the shortages and restrictions, while in addition the company manufactured and sold extensively around the world machinery which had been designed and made operational at Fairbrush. The capital-goods demand became saturated and the excess demand for the company's product

146

fell abruptly at the same time in the early 1950s, but a successful drive to seek new retail and industrial customers allowed the slack to be taken up fairly quickly.

The company had claims to be an innovator in production methods, operating a primitive form of assembly-line system with the small work force of the late 1930s and extending these at the new factory in the 1950s. In his innovations the founder admitted to seeking to follow the production methods of Henry Ford on a small scale. Despite these efforts, however, the crises of the 1950s, which had been ridden out without significant sustained setbacks in staffing, were followed over the next decade and more by a series of challenges in overseas markets. In response to these, which usually took the form of local restrictions on imports, a number of manufacturing or licensing operations were begun, in countries as diverse as South Africa, Kenya, Ireland, and Sri Lanka. None was very large, most being *ad hoc* responses aimed at local markets only. No international strategy was apparent, nor any intention to relocate to make use of cheap labour such as might be projected by international division of labour theories. A similar approach to marketing left the company heavily dependent on the rather restricted UK market.

After a time the detailed problems of this period were replaced by more severe and intensifying competitive pressures in the 1970s and 1980s which compelled the introduction of new methods and a steady reduction in numbers employed. Despite further mechanization and the introduction of some new techniques, however, it was generally agreed that the factory layout required systematizing and updating by the time of our study. Meanwhile, the general state of manufacturing decline in the region and beyond was compounded by what was seen as mass dumping of substitute products from the Far East, and the use of cheap imported components in British assembly plants. The result was low-quality products, but sold at a considerable price advantage.

The growing concentration of the retail market into large chains of warehouses served to focus and intensify these pressures. It also created a major dilemma of corporate identity, due to the demand by these oligopsonistic outlets for 'own-brand' products. To adapt to this, which Fairbrush had done to date only for one customer in the American market, would force a change in style and presentation of a distinctive product, and also threaten the brand-name claim to elite quality on which the company had long relied.

THE WORK FORCE AND THEIR JOBS

Some 350 employees remained on the company's UK books at the time of our study, four-fifths of them on the one main site where our study took place. Senior managers claimed to know many by name, aided by a pattern of long service among a large proportion of the work force, and in recent years by declining numbers. The figure had been maintained around the 600 mark from the 1950s until the pressures of the last decade had taken their toll. All but two (both female) employees were reported to be full-time, and of the full-timers almost three-quarters were manual employees. Of the manual employees 64 per cent were male, while the figure for white-collar staff was 72 per cent. There were also approximately 200 employees in the various overseas operations.

As the commitment to Fordism implies, much of the labour process in the Fairbrush factory involved fairly routine, semi-skilled manual work, with maintenance workers and electricians and specialist skills in joinery and wood-turning providing the main exceptions. That changes in production methods of recent years had tended to deskill and reduce job satisfaction was confirmed by our survey (where three-fifths agreed that 'People like me have no opportunity to use their abilities at work') and interview evidence, and was also acknowledged by management.

Staff reductions through new manufacturing methods were paralleled in the offices by a limited introduction of computerization – though here the reduction in the number (as distinct from volume) of orders entailed particularly by the shift of custom to the large chains had also exerted an important influence. On the shop floor, new equipment now required shift work, and for some tasks had increased the spacing along the line, making social contact with fellow employees far more restricted. One senior manager expressed the view that job redesign to increase interest should be a priority, though it was one to which the company had devoted little attention in the past. An interest in quality circles was also raised, but changes of this sort were also linked with ideas of flexibility seen as required for future survival. Initial attempts at QC meetings had not been judged successful by either side.

MANAGEMENT PHILOSOPHY AND EMPLOYEE RELATIONS STYLE

At the time of our study the company was widely perceived, among both management and employees whom we interviewed, to be in a transition towards a more calculative, production-oriented management style. This was embodied in the shift of control from the old guard to the younger, more recent arrivals (though most still had a good many years' service in Fairbrush by most standards). The change was viewed somewhat ambivalently by employees. In the face of the difficulties confronting the company it was seen as unavoidable, and even as dangerously sluggish and half-hearted, but at the same time as a regrettable abandonment of the relatively personal and even (in some ways) indulgent style of the past.

The founder had grown up in a Quaker family, and 'in the shadow' of the Bournville chocolate factory, and seems to have been much impressed by the moral outlook and attendant welfarism of the Cadbury management philosophy. He had assumed like obligations to his own employees, within a paternalistic framework that produced ambivalent attitudes to trade unionism and to other forms of communication. He and his senior managers voiced a judicious, constrained, but none the less substantial respect for the rights of employees and the moral responsibilities of management towards them. The company had long played an active part in the Industrial Co-partnership Association (having joined in 1948), and several managers stressed to us their commitment to employee participation. It was with an air of disappointed puzzlement that they each recounted the periods of enthusiasm and then decline which had plagued their efforts on this front.

A formalization of participative arrangements had begun with the rapid increase in scale after the Second World War. The company had initiated joint consultation in 1946, in common with a great number of companies at the time, but after an active period, and despite management claims to have taken great care in implementing employee suggestions to prevent the system being seen merely as a talking-shop, interest had waned, and after about five years the arrangement had become defunct.

Next an effort was made to set up 'free discussion groups' on a basis proposed by a Scottish management consultant James Gillespie. Employees were given time to discuss problems and 'let off steam' with no management present. Grievances were expressed which the founder admitted were unsuspected, but to which he claimed management assiduously attempted to respond. Despite this, the same pattern of decline ensued, and after eight years the groups were abandoned. The latest effort to revive participation, once again a management initiative, took the form of

149

briefing meetings led by the managing director (now the founder's son), but these too were flagging after a couple of years, and no sessions had been organized for some time when we arrived, partly for lack of demand and partly through management inertia. In addition, regular monthly meetings of supervisory staff, and annual meetings of sales staff, gave these groups a chance to discuss company matters.

Although there had been periods when it was necessary to reduce the work force, particularly in recent years, Fairbrush management claimed to have stuck to a policy of no compulsory redundancies, motivated by its welfarist commitment to the employees. According to the founder, the company had always sought to give employees' interests a high priority, and to allow some channel to express views through the participation exercises mentioned earlier (though never feeling that they should intrude on management's right to manage, he made clear).

Because of these policies the founder professed himself unable to comprehend why trade unions had been able to establish a foothold in the company. He declared himself in favour of unions in industry at large, to protect worker rights against less scrupulous employers. But, he added, 'I must admit I was disappointed to hear that our workers felt they had to combine into a union to get fair treatment from the firm; I liked to think they always had it anyway.' None the less in the early 1970s the management was approached by a group of employees seeking recognition for the Transport & General Workers' Union (TGWU) to represent shop-floor workers. Despite management disquiet, it seems, no major obstacles were put in the way of this. Subsequently non-manual employees also gained recognition, for the Association of Scientific Technical & Managerial Staffs. Management reported membership in the 25–49 per cent range for manual employees, but in the 70–89 per cent range for the offices, claiming that after reaching a peak of about 60 per cent on the shop floor it was now in decline there. That decline was not confirmed by the manual union itself, but a persistent weakness *vis-à-vis* management was admitted in the absence of a much higher density.

That weakness was expressed most emphatically in the pay bargaining arrangements. Negotiations were conducted separately by the two groups of employees, both unions reporting that occasional joint discussions had never yielded close collaboration. Although this seemingly created a mild bitterness, on the manual side in particular, the implacability of management's stance on bargaining seemed to undermine rather than fuel any move towards unity on the labour side. The management view was that they decided each year what sort of wage increase the company could afford, usually starting from at least a cost-of-living increase, and that that was put to the unions as a *fait accompli* in 'negotiations': 'We put forward the highest figure the company can afford and we are not prepared to move.' The unions saw it no differently in substance, if in a less positive light. The manual union confirmed that 'they decide and tell us ... There's no negotiation.' Complaints every year had brought a promise from management to hold some discussions before its final decision next time, but little hope of any material change was held out. For the white-collar union, too, there were 'no negotiations here about anything ... We do a bit of begging sometimes.'

The problem, as perceived by the manual union, was that without total or near-total membership it would never get the management to listen beyond token concessions on marginal fringe benefits. On the white-collar side, despite high membership levels, it was felt that militancy was non-existent: 'Stand 'em up against the wall and shoot 'em but they wouldn't go on strike.' It was apparent that management's genuine commitment to paternalism, combined with a certain familiarity (the senior managers were almost always referred to by their first name in interviews and to their face in our presence), played their part in maintaining this ambivalence of union membership yet inaction. Of at least equal importance in this passivity, though, was the widespread belief that the company was in a parlous state.

This was reinforced by a widespread respect for the moral validity and achievements of the founder, though the uncertainty concerning the younger and more recent managers also came through and may bode some change in the future. Additionally, the attitudes of employees, discussed in more detail later, were suffused with contradictory perceptions of management legitimacy and of conflict. One office worker sought to explain why she was a union member despite her support for management in many respects, and despite the union's inability to achieve much:

> I joined because you tend to have more to say to the management about anything that's happening if you're in the union. They recognize them and they do tend to be informed of things ... I think that there's a lot of people who don't want to stand up in front of the management ... they tend to want to do it through

someone else ... not because they want to be militant or anything like that, it's just because we do tend to have more say about anything that's happening.

A little influence, it seems, is still better than none at all.

THE FINANCIAL PARTICIPATION ARRANGEMENTS

In 1938, shortly after learning of the arrangements at the Quaker company Kalamazoo (see Farrow, 1964) and the textile firm J. T. & T. Taylor (Pollard and Turner, 1976), the founder established the *profit share bonus* scheme. Initially it covered just fifty employees, but despite changes in scale it survives virtually unchanged to the present. It was explained in terms consistent with the employee relations philosophy described above:

> When I started out on my business career, my main ambition was to be a successful manufacturer. I certainly hoped to obtain a good standard of living for myself. But I was not mainly motivated by the idea of acquiring large personal wealth. I wanted to share my commercial success with those who worked with me.

The original questionnaire response to our survey from Fairbrush had rejected pragmatic objectives for profit-sharing, instead articulating solely 'a moral obligation to share the profits between employees'. This morality suffused discussions in subsequent interviews, and did appear to be a genuine belief of key managers (particularly among the 'old guard'), not just the common unitaristic posture found in many companies. The founder none the less elaborated his own views a little more illuminatingly when he expressed his wish to share the profits '*to a reasonable extent*' (emphasized in his own intonation) and added:

> I hope that (*a*) it was morally justifiable and (*b*) probably good business anyway ... because they would feel some interest in the firm. Whether it in fact provides any incentive I rather doubt, frankly, because [given the size of the company] whether an individual can really affect the profits of the firm is rather doubtful.

This 'small piece of social justice', as the founder also described it, was thus targeted at attitudinal objectives also, but the limits here were recognized. The founder felt that 'they appreciate it', but added that he was sure the company had co-operative staff in any case.

It was reported that since profit-sharing antedated the unions by far, and since it varied with profits only, whereas salary was set primarily with reference to the cost of living, there was no history or prospect of negotiations on the subject. The unilateral nature of the payment went unchallenged by the unions, and fitted closely with the management philosophy of benevolent but non-participative paternalism.

The scheme was reported by the founder to have been designed in an effort to give a 'reasonable' share of the profits with some element of stability in the pay-out. There has been at least some payment every year except 1951, when a loss was made. The bonus is paid once a year, at Christmas, a choice which reflects its status in management eyes and helps shape the employee perception described later. The provision is not simply left to the management's discretion, however, but is prescribed in a formula laid down in the company rule book, and explained with examples for employees, reflecting a wish to be seen as consistent and fair by the founder. A base figure of 10 per cent of profits (net of all but tax and the profit-sharing pay-out itself) was stipulated, but with the provision that if profits fell the previous year's total *sum* would be maintained up to a maximum of 15 per cent of the current year's profits. The founder reported that the average payment over the years had amounted to about 13 per cent of profits.

The share of the resulting sum that each person received was weighted by two factors, which combined to provide each person with a certain number of 'bonus points'. Firstly it was calculated in proportion to the individual's salary. Secondly, there was an indexing by length of service, as shown in Table 25. The result is a fairly steep differential between employees in the amount they receive in profit-sharing: someone with over twenty years' service and a management salary could well be getting ten times or more the share of a recent shop-floor recruit, for example. The founder was aware that some people favoured minimal bonus differentials, but he himself disagreed, and that appeared to settle the matter.

However, the impact of this differential was lessened by the timing and overall size of the sums involved. As the founder himself admitted, the timing meant that employees 'have come to

Table 25 Fairbrush profit-sharing bonus calculation

Length of service at 31 December	To find bonus points multiply weekly wage in pence by
Under six months	Nil
Six months and under one year	6
One year and under two years	7
Two years and under three years	8
Three years and under four years	9
Four years and under five years	10
Five years and under six years	11
Six years and under seven years	12
Seven years and under eight years	13
Eight years and under nine years	14
Nine years and under ten years	15
Ten years and under twenty years	16
Twenty years and under thirty years	18
Thirty years and over	20

Example
Your weekly wage: £100
Length of service on 31 December: five years three months
According to the table above, multiply 10,000 times 11, which makes
110,000 points.

Value of bonus points in pence: the total sum available for distribution will
be divided by the total of bonus points for all employees of the company
to give the value of each bonus point in pence.

Extract from Fairbrush 'Handbook for the Guidance of Employees'.

look upon [it] just as "the Christmas bonus", without relating it
much to profits'. For the year of our study, moreover, the total
pay-out was expected to be around £60,000, which thanks to sale of
forestry lands adjacent to the factory was a major improvement on
the last few years. For many employees the bonus had amounted to
perhaps little more than an extra week's wages in recent times, as
profitability declined. The founder regretted this limitation, which
meant that 'Distributions by more profitable and larger companies
such as the British-American Tobacco Company and Kalamazoo
have given employees two or three times more than ours'. None the
less, he observed, many companies had no scheme at all, 'and I
think our workers have appreciated their regular pay-outs'.

In addition to the profit bonus scheme Fairbrush also boasted an
employee share trust. The founder observed that in some Quaker
companies such as Kalamazoo, or the John Lewis Partnership, the

original owners had decided to move towards actual ownership of the company by their employees, with over half the shares in employee hands in the former and all of them in the latter. He had made a provision in this direction, but less radical and without direct implications for employee control.

All the shares in Fairbrush were owned privately, for the most part by the founder's family. In pursuit of his principles, however, he had decided in the late 1950s that should the company ever be sold he wished employees to retain at least some stake in the firm. To this end he had set up the trust to hold one-fifth of the company's shares in perpetuity. Asked for the reasons behind the scheme and the choice of the proportion of shares, the founder replied, '... it was just arbitrary, really. I didn't feel myself willing to give control to the employees, but I did feel I wanted the profit-sharing scheme to carry on after my death'. At present there were no dividends paid on the shares held in trust, so that the profit-sharing bonus remained the only form of financial participation experienced by employees. Were the company to be sold or the profit-sharing scheme to be discontinued, however, the trust would be activated, and the 20 per cent of distributed profits accruing to the shares would then be allocated to employees (less one-fifth for a contingency fund to fill the gap should profits fall), effectively in lieu of the profit-sharing bonus.

According to the employee handbook, 'Trustees have been appointed from the employees.' It took even the personnel director a little time to discover the precise meaning of this phrase; it turned out that trustees had been appointed from the founder's family together with the company secretary when it was first set up, and they were still in sole occupancy of this role.

EMPLOYEE VIEWS OF FAIRBRUSH AND BEYOND

Our survey of Fairbrush employees somewhat disappointingly yielded only forty responses (around one in six of the questionnaires actually distributed). Union representatives attributed this above all to the state of apathetic gloom among the work force concerning the company's prospects. The sample was reasonably representative of the work force profile in gender and occupational distribution, and in the proportion (just under 60 per cent) of union members. The possibility none the less remains that those sending back the questionnaires were not entirely typical in their views. The small numbers also entail that for the most part broad indications of results rather than precise percentages will be quoted, and that analysis of findings is unable to demonstrate high levels of significance, although this is partly ameliorated by the additional source of views through the employee interviews.

Respondents were divided on the question of trade union power in Britain, two-fifths reckoning the level about right, one-fifth too low, but almost a third that it was too great. Their perception of the situation at Fairbrush reflected the reality described by shop stewards and management rather than a deference to managerial authority, however, with no one feeling that the unions had too much power in the company, and over two-thirds feeling they had too little. On the question of interests, the proportions were very similar for views of Britain generally and of Fairbrush in particular, with about half seeing things in terms of a combination of conflict and shared interests, a third or so as opposite sides only, and just over one in ten seeing interests as basically shared.

These findings suggest a work-force outlook that may not have been militant but was at best tentative in its acceptance of management authority. Other findings tend to bear out this impression, as did our interviews. Looking first at general views on labour–management issues, we find that three-quarters of respondents disagreed that 'management know best and employees should let them make decisions', three-fifths agreed that 'management tend to treat people like me as numbers', and only just over a quarter agreed that 'most management have the welfare of their employees at heart'. Nearly everyone agreed that 'a good management always consults its work force', while only a quarter disagreed that 'workers should never strike, for reasons of loyalty'.

These views have an obvious potential carry-over to and from views of Fairbrush itself. Again the survey results bear this out. For instance, as Table 26 shows, the company was rated poor as an employer by only a few respondents, but the majority saw it just as average. These figures are not high by the standards of responses to this question in our own and other studies. More telling still, while the company's rating on pay about matched the overall judgement, and that on security improved on it, a clear majority rated Fairbrush below average on management openness, chances to get on, management skill, and most severely on employee participation. More significant still for the profit-sharing scheme, three-fifths thought the top-to-bottom pay differentials too high.

This ambivalence was also apparent in the interviews conducted

Table 26 Views of Fairbrush relative to other employers (%)

	Aspect of employer				
	Well above average	Above average	Average	Below average	Well below average
Pay	3	14	50	19	14
Management openness	3	10	31	21	36
Management skill	3	3	40	34	21
Chances to get on	3	10	36	26	26
Job security	23	38	28	5	8
Employee participation in decisions	0	5	26	21	49
	Very good	Moderately good	Average	Rather poor	Very poor
As employer overall	20	20	53	5	3

with both shop floor and office employees. Interviewees tended to acknowledge that the company had good intentions, but also that its approach restricted the impact of any accessibility. One long-serving employee, when asked about management approachability, hesitated for some moments, then commented, 'Yes and no ... It depends on what the situation is or what you're talking about.' Another interviewee, commenting on the briefing groups, supported the idea, but 'it's all one way ... if you say something, you're talking to yourself'. The impression we gained was that the observable familiarity and tolerance of management in everyday exchanges was not felt to extend into openness on matters of substance, partly as a consequence of the same paternalistic view that encouraged first names being used in conversation.

Many of the interview exchanges seemed to reflect the general disquiet on the future of the company, and doubts about the ability or existing policies to escape difficulties. 'It's a shame, its a beautiful place – everyone who comes here says it's a beautiful place,' was the gloomy observation of one union convenor about the factory site. The sense of foreboding also concerned the changes that were expected to follow from the completion of the passing of power to the newer generation with impending retirements among senior management.

In the light of the above findings, it is not surprising that, as

Table 27 shows, half the employees replying to our questionnaire thought profits should belong to the employees, not shareholders, and that employees with shares should elect managers, but disagreed that employees should share losses as well as profits. However, almost three-fifths disagreed that employees should own the company they work for. None the less these findings imply a potential spoke in the wheel of the existing profit-sharing and trust arrangements, and again fail to indicate a consensus behind the philosophy of management.

Table 27 Employee views on general issues related to financial participation (%)

Statement	Agree	No opinion	Disagree
Profits should belong to employees, not shareholders	47	11	42
Employees with shares should elect managers	50	11	40
Employees should own the companies they work for	26	16	58
Employees should share losses as well as profits	36	15	49

EMPLOYEES AND THE FAIRBRUSH PROFIT BONUS

'To me it's a gift, however small – something they give me ... it's something they needn't give you ... I don't know why they do it really, it's always been that way.' This view was typical of those expressed to us in interviews. As more than one manager (indeed, the founder himself, as we saw above) suggested, the profit-share pay-out was seen essentially as no more nor less than 'a Christmas bonus – comes very nice sometimes' (office worker). Few people could recall what they had received the previous Christmas, nor did they pay much attention to any link between their own actions and what they would get the next time round. As the year drew on, it was reported, joking references might be made. As often as not comments were critical of management rather than exhortations of effort, though – for instance, a piece of machinery seen as poorly selected provoking the remark 'There goes our Christmas bonus.' More typically, though, as a clerical worker opined, 'It doesn't change behaviour ... it's just a bit extra.' Or, in the words of the shop-floor worker quoted at the start of this section, 'I never think about it, to be quite truthful.'

Nevertheless, this worker was critical of 'the moaners'. 'It's never enough for some. To me it's a gift, so you can't complain.' Ironically, of course, this legitimation of management works precisely against any likely motivational effect, since the bonus is seen as beneficence rather than being earned. Thus one white-collar employee, asked if the bonus affected attitudes significantly, replied, 'No, not really ... you're always grateful for it.'

The survey results lend support to these impressions also. Almost half the respondents expressed themselves 'very much in favour' of the Fairbrush scheme, while a third had 'some reservations' and the rest either had no strong feelings or (in a couple of cases) were opposed to the scheme. When asked about the fairness of the existing allocation of the bonus, though, only one-fifth thought it 'fair and equitable as it is', just under a third thought it 'could be improved', a similar proportion that it was 'unfair in some instances', and almost a sixth that it was 'unfair altogether', an overall result evenly divided between fairness and unfairness. The interviews revealed further that often people had given the issues only passing thought. When the specific matter of different payments for different length of service was raised, almost every person interviewed thought it unfair, including some with long service as a vested interest in the system. Indeed, in our survey, length of service and amount of bonus received the previous year were only marginally associated with increased support for the system of profit-sharing allocation. The following remarks exemplify this:

I feel everyone in the company should get the same – they've all made the same contribution to that year's bonus, whatever their service. [Eight years' service]

Somebody who's been here only twelve months really has worked all through that year, and to my mind they should be entitled to the same as me. [Twenty-five years' service]

This also created occasional cynicism: 'The people who decide the system are all long-service people, aren't they?' With only a little less force, these views were also carried over to the inequality caused by making payments proportional to salary. The company subsequently reported to us that supervisors had discussed and firmly rejected more equitable arrangements, though they remained hopeful of introducing some modifications.

Yet these views to some extent were drawn to the surface by our questions, and the effect of our investigating the issue at all. The profit-sharing arrangement was just not important enough to count as a major factor in most employees' attitudes. Typically 'I don't know a lot about it myself,' or 'People don't really talk about it' were qualifications thrown in with these comments. Thus only one person reported depending on the profit-sharing bonus as 'an essential part of my pay', two-fifths described it as 'a welcome addition', and almost three-fifths as making 'little difference'.

The marginal impact of the profit-sharing bonus also comes through in the assessments of experience reported in Table 28. For clearest presentation we shall comment mainly on the contrast between agreement and disagreement with the various statements (i.e. net of 'no opinions'). On this basis, if we look first at the kind of objectives we might expect managers to emphasize (1, 3, 4, and 5), the response is not encouraging. Very few respondents believed they were made more aware of management problems, with almost five times as many disagreeing as agreeing. The link from effort to profit share gets somewhat more support, but there were still almost twice as many rejections with a similar result for likelihood of noticing fellow employees not pulling their weight. Meanwhile three and a half times more disagreed than agreed that they were less likely to move jobs.

From the standpoint of more employee-oriented benefits which might still have a spin-off for management (2, 6, 7, 9) the replies were, if anything, even less propitious. Thus eight times as many disagreed that participation had been advanced as agreed, while comparable proportions agreed that there were better forms of benefits, and that profit-sharing was just another kind of bonus. A like majority concurred that unpredictability made planning spending impossible, which was an unfortunate finding, given the intention in the original design to build in stability in payments (see above). Moreover, a majority agreed that employees risked losing part of their earnings (8), which implied a view of the profit-sharing payment contrary to management's that it lay outside the purview of normal pay settlements. Finally, and again echoing an implied criticism of the management approach at Fairbrush, two-thirds overall agreed that employees should have more say in fixing the profit share, four times as many as disagreed with this challenge to the *status quo*.

Table 28 Employee experience of profit-sharing (%)

Statement	Agree	No opinion	Disagree
1 It has made me more aware of the problems management faces	12	32	56
2 It has enabled me to participate more in the way the company works	9	21	70
3 If I work hard, I know I can share in the results	32	9	59
4 It has made me less likely to move to another job	18	21	61
5 I am more likely to notice if my colleagues are not pulling their weight	24	27	49
6 There are better ways of improving benefits	73	21	6
7 It is just another kind of bonus	70	12	18
8 Employees risk losing part of their earnings	24	21	55
9 As you cannot predict the bonus, you cannot plan spending	78	11	11
10 Employees should have more say in fixing the profit share	67	17	17

For reasons already given, we did not pursue the analysis of the Fairbrush questionnaire returns beyond a few cross-tabulations. A few of these yield findings worthy of comment, however. By and large non-manual workers were no less favourable towards the profit-sharing scheme than manual workers, for instance. Nor were union members less favourably disposed to the scheme or any more critical of the fairness of the allocation system than non-members. They were, however, more likely to reject notions that various managerial objectives might be met, and particularly that they would watch colleagues more closely, while agreeing that there were better ways of providing benefits. Gender also had no significant effect on judgements of the scheme overall or the system of allocation, though women were in some cases less likely than men to discount the effects of profit-sharing on participation, ability to share the benefits of effort, and keeping them in their job. On the other hand, they were also a little more likely to agree that there should be more participation in fixing the profit share-out.

Attitudes to union power, or to the state of labour–management relations in Britain as a whole, did not seem to have much effect on views of the profit-sharing schemes; rather than these general views, it was perceptions of Fairbrush itself which showed some relationship with opinions of the scheme. As one might expect, evaluations became somewhat more negative for those feeling the union had too little power in the company, as one moved away from a common interests view of employee relations, or as the company was rated less positively as an employer.

There were no strong tendencies for 'labourist' judgements, e.g. on employees owning companies, electing managers, or having a greater right to profits than shareholders, to lead to more than averagely negative evaluations of the effects of profit-sharing in management terms. However, the idea that employees should have a greater say in the allocation of profit shares did attract markedly more support (in fact at least four-fifths backing in each case) from those who supported these three proposals. Interestingly, this demand for participation in running profit-sharing gained equally strong support from those who agreed that employees should share losses as well as profits, this being a good deal greater than from those who rejected loss-sharing. The implication is that loss-sharing is not necessarily a view associated with deference to management perspectives; here it appears to be linked instead with a demand for the fairness of the principle to be matched by scrutiny of management fairness.

THE TRUST ASSESSED

Despite management's insistence that employees would be well aware of the existence, status, and potential of the trust from the handbook, our predominant impression from the interviews was of a vacuum of knowledge, matched by an absence of concern about the subject. Actual hostility in any degree was confined to mild resentment in some quarters that the system had 'never really been explained', and that for all its place in the handbook there were no signs of its substance. One union representative reported having gone to management to 'see if I could do anything with it', but had found them merely vague on the matter.

In our questionnaire we asked how much people felt they knew about the trust arrangement. Only one person claimed a clear knowledge of how it worked, the rest reporting that they 'only know it exists' (two-fifths, including one fairly senior manager) or professing 'no knowledge at all' (almost three-fifths). This lack of knowledge, though significant in its own right, made it problematical to pursue any further questions, but we did ask how people viewed the idea of replacing the annual cash bonus with dividends from the trust. One in six approved, a couple rejected the idea, but predictably the main responses were two- fifths with 'no opinion', and almost a third who checked 'It depends'. Some of the things it might depend on were outlined in our interviews: in particular, the state of the company was seen as crucial by several people, since it was felt if things continued badly the shares would be worthless. With a little further explanation of the possible system, a few interviewees did welcome the idea of shareholdings rather than just the bonus, though none in a very forceful way.

In the end, it is impossible to make any real judgement of employee opinions on the employee share trust. It simply has too little meaning to them for any worthwhile judgement to be sought – and this lack of significance is the only clear conclusion to be drawn.

CONCLUSIONS

In some ways the Fairbrush schemes attracted less support than we had expected. Our interviews with management left us with the impression that the claim to a primarily moral commitment to sharing with employees had a genuine basis in the philosophy of the founder and many of the senior management. What emerged, however, was that, although the work force was not 'militant', it was not greatly moved by paternalist welfarism, particularly given two things. First, approachability was not felt to run very deep, and was prevented by paternalist views of decision-making from allowing either negotiation or other convincing participative styles to operate. Secondly, the company was not seen to be doing very well, and its fragile prospects cast an additional shadow across management legitimacy, reinforced by the mixed auguries of the management succession which was under way. If this has a wider significance, it is probably that profit-sharing relies for its effectiveness on levels of payments to employees sufficient to grab their attention, at least, and that it is therefore likely to be blighted by poor profitability and company prospects. The research reviewed in Chapter 1 confirms this primacy of financial determination of positive employee judgements on profit-sharing. As a motivational solution to crisis, though, this gives profit-sharing little leverage.

At Fairbrush the profit-sharing bonus was widely seen as a marginal addition to wages, with no feasible links to employee efforts, and with little to offer in an era of declining company performance. This in turn linked with a low assessment of management's capabilities and of its perceived unwillingness to give genuine attention to suggestions from below. The trust arrangement was so latent that it held no meaning worth speaking of for most employees, although at least it was not regarded in a hostile fashion. None the less, the most definite attitude we encountered was to the unfairness of the existing allocation, and the need for greater participation in the operation of the system. Overall, though, the experience of financial participation at Fairbrush had left all but a minority of employees untouched in their attitudes or motivation.

Finally, we took the opportunity offered by the interviews to raise with management and employees the possibility of profit-related pay. On the employee side the notion was met with solid disapproval, for a number of familiar reasons. First, wages which had at least matched rises in the cost of living would be severely threatened by the company's performance. Second, this would impose on the work force a burden they had not deserved: 'You would have to rely on management to make profits; if they didn't, you'd suffer, having to pay for their mistakes.'

Interestingly, management tended to agree. The founder himself felt that such a system would cause a lot of resentment. 'People are entitled to a reasonable amount of stability in their income, and it shouldn't be subject to the effects of trade depressions and so on ....' This reasoning is partly embedded in the logic of paternalist authoritarianism, of course, – i.e. it is up to management to provide, whatever the circumstances. But it also contained an element of pluralism: that such an arrangement would disturb (and perhaps sharpen) the bargaining relationship rather than by-pass it. It is certainly noteworthy that profit-related pay ideas seem to find a less receptive hearing in a private company with a cash-based profit-sharing scheme in existence than simple analyses might predict.

9

Goodbake: SAYE in a multidivisional company

Goodbake is a large UK public limited company operating primarily in the food, drink, and tobacco industry, although it also has interests in other sectors. Within the food industry it operates in manufacturing and distribution, both wholesale and retail, producing cakes, biscuits, nuts, chocolates, and frozen food. Through the holdings PLC the company operates a divisionalized structure with eight UK divisions: biscuits, snack foods, frozen foods, distribution services, restaurants, small businesses, group research, and management services. In addition the company has interest in North America and Europe. In the UK it employs around 30,000 people, the majority of them women, in a large number of separate establishments located the length and breadth of the country. There have, however, been a number of major closures in the 1980s. The case study took place in two locations: one a major factory located in Scotland (henceforth Scotcake), part of the main manufacturing division; the other, part of the small businesses division engaged in the manufacture and distribution of bakery products throughout Scotland (henceforth Breadline).

Scotcake produced a range of branded and 'own label' biscuits and employed nearly 1,450 people, the majority of whom were hourly paid women. This number had declined in recent years and was expected to decline further. Employees were paid on a banding system, and managed by a senior management team of seven. The factory was highly unionized (more so than the company as a whole); the General Municipal Boilermakers' and Allied Trades' Union (GMBATU) represented the production workers, ASTMS organized clerical and junior managerial workers, while the Amalgamated Engineering Union (AEU) and EETPU covered the craft workers. Each union had its own shop stewards and senior steward, but only GMBATU had a full-time convenor. Collective bargaining was conducted at divisional level, but separately for production, craft, and salaried staff. Representatives of factory management and unions were involved in the negotiations. Certain matters such as abnormal working arrangements were negotiated at plant level. Interviewees expressed a view that the company was being firmer with the unions in negotiations, and new working practices for craftsmen had just been agreed after an ultimatum from the company.

Scotcake operated a Factory Advisory Committee (FAC) in which senior managers met employee representatives monthly. These representatives were elected directly by employees and were not necessarily section shop stewards, but all the union convenors were ex-officio members of the FAC. The company operated a number of other participative institutions such as departmental FACs, a pensions consultative committee, *ad hoc* briefing groups, and task forces to study problems jointly. The health and safety committee was part of the FAC. Minutes were distributed widely and a weekly factory brief was issued. The PLC distributed employee reports.

Industrial action was reported to be quite rare. There had been a two-week strike over pay some four years before the case study and a similar length of strike involving electricians the year before that. Absenteeism was running at some three percentage points above the divisional average, but there were no difficulties in recruitment or retention.

The senior management team included a head of personnel who was also deputy factory director and responsible to the factory director. The factory director reported to the production director of the divisional board, but the orientation of most employees was to the factory, and indeed many still referred to the workplace by the family name of the original owners.

Breadline controlled three bakeries which produced bread and cakes for sale through its own chain of over a hundred retail shops, but also produced for supermarket chains. The company's trading position was not good; nearly half the employees in one of the bakeries had been made redundant earlier in the year of the study, and other parts of the company had been restructured. The vast majority of the 1,200 employees were employed in the shops, and most of these were part-time women workers. By contrast the bakers were nearly all full-time and male. The head office was located in the same building as one of the bakeries and employed about forty people. This company was much less unionized than Scotcake but there were marked variations among groups. The small team of drivers and the employees at the main bakery were highly unionized in the TGWU and the Union of Shop Distributive & Allied Workers (USDAW) respectively. On the other hand the shops and the other bakeries have virtually no union members. The TGWU and USDAW both had a senior shop steward, but neither was full-time. Collective bargaining for the bakeries was conducted through an industry-wide joint negotiating committee in which the company personnel director, but no plant union representative, participated. The drivers negotiated directly with the company, while the Retail Wages Council rates were followed for shop assistants. Shop manageresses and headquarters staff had their pay determined solely by management.

Management perceived the company as a large family firm which was closer to its workforce than in a large factory. Formal participative arrangements were less well developed, compared to our factory study. A joint consultative committee in the main bakery had recently been revived, but the main means of communication to employees was oral via management. Industrial disputes were reported as being rare.

FINANCIAL PARTICIPATION SCHEMES

The PLC holding company operated two of the types of profit-sharing and employee share ownership under discussion: a discretionary scheme open to a relatively large number of senior employees, and an all-employee SAYE share option scheme. The latter was the main focus of the case study, although Scotcake also operated a productivity bonus whereby performance was measured quarterly and a bonus paid on the improvement over the equivalent figures from the previous year. At the time of the case study a payment of over £70 had just been made. All employees, except senior management, participated in this scheme. Management regarded the scheme as a significant motivator of employees in that it operated across the factory and employees were aware that a good factory performance helped the bonus, whereas a poor one reduced it.

The company had introduced both the discretionary and the SAYE scheme in response to the Conservatives' 1970s legislation, although both had been revised to take account of subsequent legislative change. Some 400 senior staff participated in the discretionary scheme at the invitation of the board. The SAYE scheme was open to all employees with over three years' service who worked more than twenty hours a week. Overall, the company believed that just under half its employees were eligible to participate and that in practice around 10 per cent did. Given the structure of employment in the company, the eligibility rules certainly excluded large numbers of employees. This was especially so at Breadline, where, it was estimated, only 200 of the 900 employees on the retail side were eligible.

Management Objectives

The schemes were introduced on the initiative of the holdings board, and the prime responsibility for running them rested with the company secretariat, assisted by the personnel and public relations departments. The role of the company chairman was considered important in introducing the schemes. The unions were consulted about them, but there was no bargaining as such. The union attitude was characterized as 'shoulder shrugging', and such little opposition as there was came from full-time officers rather than convenors. There was no opposition to the introduction of the scheme from within management.

The company's managerial philosophy was seen as rooted in 'old-time paternalism which expresses a fairly high degree of concern for the people who work in the business'. This style had been tempered in recent years by the impact of market constraints, and a number of redundancies were implemented in the 1980s. Employee share ownership fitted into the overall philosophy in being an attempt to fulfil the chairman's philosophy of 'employees, shareholders, and customers in essence being one and the same person – to make us all capitalists' or, as another senior manager summed up the chairman's philosophy, 'shareholders invest money, employees invest lives'. The objectives of the SAYE scheme were expressed by the industrial relations director as 'trying to create the concept of a commonwealth':

Commonality of interest in so far as is possible, not necessarily commonality of objectives, because all the fundamental issues that exist between employer and employee are still present, but it narrows the areas of conflict very considerably if people can appreciate what each side of the coin represents.

In specific terms the schemes were intended to achieve all the objectives listed in our original questionnaire except that the objectives of attracting and retaining key staff and creating a sense of business awareness were confined to middle and senior management through the discretionary scheme.

Although it may appear that the aim of creating a 'concept of commonwealth' might have been better realized by operating an ADST scheme, which would have allowed much greater numbers to participate, the company chose the SAYE scheme primarily because it was much easier to institute in the first instance. This was particularly so with the company in a state of flux through acquisitions and disposals which created a danger of long- standing employees being upset that newcomers received the same benefits. None the less the introduction of an ADST scheme was under active consideration.

The head office respondent felt the scheme met the objectives only partially. There was a reluctance by many employees to put up their own money. It was, however, felt that for the employee shareholders the scheme created strong bonds with the company and increased employees' interest in its performance. This was particularly so when the company was engaged in an attempted merger with another company.

The company was able to provide some data relating to its SAYE scheme. These are presented in two tables, Table 29 covering the original scheme introduced in 1974, Table 30 the revised scheme introduced in 1981. The number of subscribers fluctuated quite widely each year, sometimes falling by half between years, as in 1979–80. The total number had never reached that achieved in the initial year, when, despite nearly 3 million shares being allocated, the offer had had to be scaled down. In total over the thirteen years of the scheme more than 10 million shares had been allocated.

In the case of those subscribers whose initial savings period had ended, it can be seen that some 75 per cent opted for shares, although the figure dipped by 10 per cent in 1976 and 1977. Very few people opted for cash, but the drop-out rate could be as high as a third, as in 1977. This figure covers both people leaving the company and those failing to maintain their savings contract. The evidence from the case study suggests more the former.

Those participating in the scheme have, taking the experience of

Table 29 Goodbake SAYE scheme, 1974-80

	1974	1975	1976	1977	1978	1979	1980
Number of actual subscribers	1,210	450	330	302	401	546	268
Share price five years later as a percentage of option price	467	165	231	175	173	221	344
Subscribers' decision after five years:							
Buy shares	463	205	136	128	204	262	146
Leave in building society for a further two years, then buy shares	440	137	83	68	93	n.a.	n.a.
Percentage of subscribers opting for co-shares	75	76	66	65	74	n.a.	n.a.
Take cash	0	14	11	10	16	n.a.	n.a.
Lapsed	307	94	100	96	88	n.a.	n.a.

n.a. Not available

Table 30 Goodbake SAYE scheme, 1981-86

Year	No. of actual subscribers
1981	376
1982	582
1983	609
1984	1,025*
1985	559
1986	981

*There were two offers in this year. The figure is the combined total.

1974–80, made substantial capital gains. Those in the original scheme stood to make a gain of 467 per cent on their original price per share, and the average gain over the subsequent six-year period totalled over 200 per cent.

Managerial respondents were asked what they saw as the objectives of the SAYE share option scheme. The objectives were expressed in terms of allowing employees to participate in the ownership of the company and through having a financial stake to make employee shareholders more company-oriented in their thinking. It was hoped that employees would give a broader commitment to the company on the need for change. There was also a desire that employees should receive a share of the wealth they helped to create through capital appreciation and dividends, not just wages.

The schemes in practice

These objectives were all expressed in grandiose, often ideological terms. As such it was hard to measure progress in meeting the objectives. We discuss our findings from the survey of employees later: here we examine the views of the managerial respondents as to whether or not the set objectives had been met.

At Breadline it was felt that the scheme was not effective. However, a distinction was drawn between the response of managers, who participated and bought shares, and workers, who rarely participated and, if they did, sold their shares quickly. Managerial respondents did not feel that the scheme had influenced a number of indicators such as employee recruitment, retention, or motivation, although there was perhaps an increased sense of business awareness among some participants, but others needed to have their substantial capital gains drawn to their attention.

At Scotcake management judged the success of the scheme by the continued growth of the number of participants (although on the basis of figures provided there were still sharp fluctuations in this). None the less it was recognized that many participants regarded it as a savings scheme in which the employees could not lose, although it was recognized that non-participators might see it as a bit of a gamble. Again the existence of the scheme was not felt to have influenced our various indicators of good industrial relations, but, taken in combination with the range of other employee benefits on offer, it contributed to the creation of a spirit of loyalty to 'our' company. However, as in both cases the participators were in a distinct minority, the scheme's ability to influence factors such as absenteeism, productivity, and motivation is limited.

One senior manager argued that the achievement of commitment to the company was a very long-term process which would 'drip through'. It was thus not measurable, and the process could be neither proved nor disproved. This manager believed in the scheme 'like an act of faith', even if it took generations to come to fruition.

Turning from generalities to specifics, we find that the existence of the scheme was not held to have had any concrete results, except perhaps the creation of a sense of business awareness among participants. Indeed, it was suggested that rather than create committed employees the scheme served to reinforce the loyalty and motivation of those already committed to the company.

TRADE UNION RESPONSES AND ATTITUDES

At Goodbake the SAYE scheme had been introduced with minimal trade union opposition. The industrial relations director drew a distinction between full-time officials and members. 'One or two unions didn't like it, but their members did.' The scheme had not become a subject of bargaining – the extension of the scheme to part-time employees had come as a result of pressure from part-time workers rather than unions, through the company's consultative mechanisms. The SAYE scheme did not impinge on pay negotiations, as 'it is too well bedded now into the framework of the company for anybody to really turn it into an issue of any kind'.

On the other hand the unions had been closely involved in negotiations over added-value schemes. One such scheme, proposed initially in 1974, was developed in negotiations for six years before being withdrawn in the face of union opposition. The existing productivity scheme was negotiated, and the unions sought to consolidate the bonus paid into basic pay. Conscious of the wage drift this caused, Goodbake had now separated the bonus scheme from basic pay negotiations despite union opposition.

Within the case study, contrasting states of union organization existed. Scotcake was well organized and local union representatives were involved closely in company pay negotiations and in a range of participatory mechanisms. Breadline was only partly unionised, and the involvement of the local representatives was much less.

Despite this difference in background, none of the union representatives interviewed had any firm views about employee share ownership. In neither company had the topic been discussed by any union, and consequently no attempt had been made to raise the issue either in negotiations or in consultative meetings. Only one of the union representatives interviewed was personally a participant, but only for 'greed for gold', not out of any deep loyalty to the company. All representatives were unaware whether their union had any official policy on employee share ownership, and most took the view that the decision to participate in the scheme should be left to individuals without any recommendation from the union. Only the white-collar union representative had members asking advice about the scheme. They were referred to the personnel department.

On the other hand union representatives were favourably disposed towards cash-based schemes, but more so at Breadline, which did not already have a bonus scheme. Union representatives had raised the issue with management, but without success. In the factory some representatives were wary lest a regular cash bonus detract from annual pay negotiations. They preferred money in basic pay, not as a variable element at management's discretion.

In sum, the attitude of these representatives towards profit-sharing and employee share ownership was the same 'bored hostility' that was felt to characterize overall trade union policy (IDS, 1986: 9). Unions were not involved with the scheme in any way, but did not think that its existence affected relationships between the members and their union at all. The scheme was summed up as a low-key thing which had been on the go a long time without generating a lot of interest, or as one senior shop steward put it, 'It's best to let sleeping dogs lie.'

THE EMPLOYEE SURVEY

As in all our case studies, the sample was divided into a scheme participant group and a non-participant group. As Scotcake all 119 known participants were sent a questionnaire, as were 100 non-participants. Ten employees, five in each category, were interviewed. The overall response rate to the questionnaire was 35 per cent, but there was a wide variation between the two categories of respondent, 46 per cent for participants but only 22 per cent for non-participants. At Breadline all fifteen known participants were surveyed, of whom fourteen replied, plus a further forty-seven non-participants, of whom thirty-two replied, giving an overall response rate in that company of 74 per cent. Again, an equal number of participating and non-participating employees were interviewed.

Participants: a profile

At Breadline participants were likely to be managerial or other headquarters-based staff, monthly paid, relatively long serving employees, not trade union members, and unlikely to be earning less than £100 a week. Participants were evenly split by gender, and those involved in other employee participation schemes were no more likely to be members of the SAYE scheme.

At Scotcake a rather different picture emerged. While nearly all the managerial and other white-collared staff in the sample were participants, so too were 63 per cent of the manual workers. Thus over half the participants were weekly-paid, and over a quarter earned less than £100 per week or its monthly equivalent. The average savings contract was slightly different in each workplace, £26 at Breadline, £31 at Scotcake. Trade union membership appeared not to be a barrier to participation, as 69 per cent of the participants were trade unionists, although 89 per cent of the non-union members in the sample did participate.

In both case studies there was a marked increase in numbers participating after 1980, when schemes benefited from fiscal concessions. The number of participants more than doubled in both cases. Only one person who had completed a five-year savings period elected to take her savings in cash. The vast majority bought shares, but some saved on for a further two years before making their decision.

Advocates of employee share ownership might desire participants to hold on to their shares to demonstrate their commitment to and confidence in the company. Of those who had saved long enough to acquire shares, around half in each case study still owned all their shares. The figure was slightly higher at Breadline, and as many as a quarter of the Scotcake share owners had disposed of all their shares. This behaviour, however, was not untypical of general shareholder behaviour and, given the substantial capital gains on offer, there is no reason why employee shareholders should not take advantage of the situation. Interview evidence suggests that participants cashed in their shares for a variety of personal reasons – buying a house, a car, visiting relatives abroad – and loyalty to the company did not influence these personal financial decisions.

Respondents were invited to express their opinions on a number of potential reasons for participating in the scheme. They were asked to state reasons which were important, which were unimportant, and potential reasons which were not considered. The results for both parts of the case study are presented in Figures 2 and 3. The rank order of important factors between the two parts of the case study were very similar, except that respondents at Breadline laid greater emphasis on the potential personal benefits than their counterparts at Scotcake. For both components the emphasis was very much on personal benefits – easy, risk-free saving, but with potentially substantial financial rewards, although managerial respondents were less concerned about easy saving. Interview evidence confirmed this view. While some interviewees felt that the scheme helped people to be more involved with the business, and that this was good for the business, others were quite emphatic that such considerations were not important and that they joined because of the financial gain. Motivators related to commitment to the company were much less important, and indeed for a substantial minority were quite unimportant or not considered. Evidence from the interviews suggests that this was because participators already felt committed to the company by virtue of their position, length of service, or the overall employment package on offer, in which the SAYE share option scheme was only an element. The opportunity for company share ownership may have reinforced that commitment, but it did not create it. 'It really depends on yourself – if you are conscientious and want to work. It hasn't changed me or my outlook.' Moreover, the hoped-for unity between employee and shareholder was not generated decisively. One participating respondent felt divided loyalties, as from a shareholder's point of view he could see the case for rationalization, but such decisions might jeopardize his employment as a worker. Another was conscious that there were many other shareholders and that the company was going to act in their best interests.

Non-participation

If we turn to the reasons for non-participation we can see from Table 31 that the predominant reason was not being able to afford it. This was particularly so at Breadline, where all the non-participants were weekly-paid and three-quarters of them earned less than £99 per week. As one respondent put it, 'If basic was much better, people could afford to participate in profit-sharing. Every penny is needed for housekeeping from basic pay.' That low pay

175

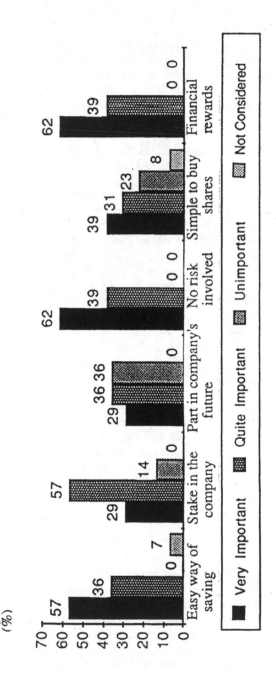

Figure 2 Motives for participation in SAYE: Breadline

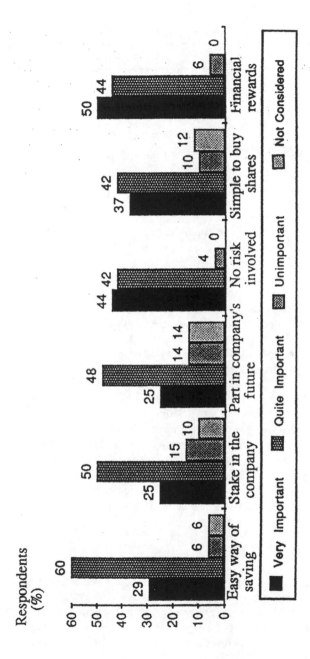

Figure 3 Motives for participation in SAYE: Scotcake

Table 31 Non-participants' reasons for not participating (%)

Reason	Breadline	Scotcake
Can't afford it	57	46
Don't know enough about it	32	18
Shareholding is not for me	11	18
Don't want savings tied to job	11	9
Too risky	11	5
Too long to commit savings	4	5
Number	28	22

Respondents could indicate more than one response.

need not be a barrier is shown by the participation of a substantial proportion of those earning less than £99 at Scotcake. None the less, even here it was the main reason for non-participation given by nearly half the respondents. There was a significant difference between the case studies in the lack of knowledge category. This was a problem at Breadline, especially in its retail outlets. Moreover a further three respondents gave total lack of knowledge as an additional reason for non-participation. The trade union criticism of schemes, that they tied savings to employment and therefore jeopardized both savings and employment, did not seem to be a significant reason for non-participation. However, at Breadline trade union representatives were concerned about the financial viability of the company and related it to non-participation. 'This is what puts people off. This place is losing money! Who is going to put money into a place that is losing money?' These sentiments were echoed in interviews with employees. Here, however, being part of a larger PLC was seen as a positive advantage. 'If my money was tied up in Breadline there would be a problem. But it is safe in Goodbake.'

EMPLOYEE ATTITUDES

The objectives set by management at Goodbake for the SAYE share option scheme very much concerned attitudinal change. As such any attempt to measure the impact of the scheme in terms of concrete measures might be premature. But if the scheme was having any impact on attitudes in terms of commitment and loyalty to the company, then the responses to our questions about the company, trade unions, ownership and control, and employer–employee relationships ought to be instructive.

If we turn first to respondents' view of their company overall we can see from Table 32 that there was a marked difference between the two locations of Goodbake, and between scheme participants and non-participants within both. Employees at Scotcake were more enthusiastic about their company's overall performance than their colleagues at Breadline. In both components, scheme participants expressed more positive views than non-participants.

Table 32 View of company as an employer overall (%)

Rating	Breadline			Scotcake		
	All	P	NP	All	P	NP
Very good	20	36	13	47	55	29
Moderately good	28	43	22	36	31	48
Average	30	21	34	16	13	24
Rather poor	17	0	25	1	2	0
Very poor	4	0	6	0	0	0
Number	46	14	32	76	55	21

P SAYE share option scheme participant.
NP Non participant.

Interviews at Breadline revealed a clear dichotomy between the company's image of being a friendly, family participative employer and the view of non-participants that such was not the case. Questionnaire responses from Breadline revealed a clear difference of opinion between participants and non-participants. However, this difference almost exactly paralleled that between management and manual respondents. By contrast, at Scotcake the difference in opinion between participants and non-participants was less marked, and manual employees' views were more closely in line with the workplace average. Most interviewees spoke of the company in terms such as caring, friendly, and good, although the managerial respondents were more fulsome in their praise, in relation both to other employees at Scotcake and to their managerial colleagues at Breadline.

While Scotcake employees rated their company higher overall

than their colleagues at Breadline, both sets of respondents had very similar views about management–employee relations. In both units more respondents felt that management and employees had common aims and objectives in their own company compared to the situation in Britain as a whole. But the difference was not as great at Breadline (17 per cent, cf. 22 per cent) as in Scotcake (9 per cent, cf. 21 per cent). Moreover, many fewer employees at Scotcake felt that management and employees were basically on opposite sides (13 per cent) compared to 39 per cent believing it for Britain as a whole. The corresponding figures at Breadline were 22 per cent and 28 per cent.

These figures confirmed the impression that Scotcake employees viewed their employer more favourably than their colleagues at Breadline. At Breadline the marked variation in view between scheme participants and non-participants was again reflected in the responses to this question. No participants considered that common aims existed in Britain generally, whereas 31 per cent believed it to be the case in their own company. On the other hand more non-participants (29 per cent) believed this of Britain generally than in their own company (17 per cent). Again these views paralleled those of management and manual workers. At Scotcake participants saw relationships in their own company as less conflictual than in Britain as a whole, but no non-participant considered that common aims and objectives existed in their own company, although 22 per cent felt it to be the case in the country as a whole. Like their counterparts at Breadline, management respondents saw their own company in a much more favourable light, but manual workers saw relationships as very much mixed.

The differences in opinion between Scotcake and Breadline and between participants and non-participants are continued when we examined specific indicators. With the exception of the more evenly balanced management openness, Scotcake received higher ratings on all our other indicators, particularly on pay, job security, and employee participation. Significantly, however, employee participation in decision-making was given the lowest ratings in both units, especially by manual workers. Within both sub-units, participants rated the company higher on every measure compared to non-participants. At Breadline these variations could again be interpreted in terms of the vast majority of participants being managers, and managers at Breadline having a higher rating of the company compared to supervisors and particularly to manual workers. In both units the views of trade unionists largely equated with those of manual workers, as most union members were to be found among this category of worker.

This marked difference in opinion between mangers and manual workers at Breadline was not apparent at Scotcake. While managers here rated the company a little higher on each indicator, manual workers had similar views to the sample as a whole, with the exception of pay, which they felt was a little below average. This manual employee dissatisfaction with pay at Scotcake was reinforced when we considered the responses to the question on pay differentials. Seventy-seven per cent of manual workers found them too high, in contrast to the 69 per cent of managers who found them about right. Again, at both units more non-participants found differentials too high compared to participants.

The picture we have built up so far is that employees at Scotcake viewed their company more favourably than their counterparts at Breadline, but within each unit the SAYE share option scheme participants tended to view their company more favourably than non-participants. Within Breadline this difference can be interpreted as reflecting a difference in views between managers and other employees, especially manual workers, as the vast majority of participants were also managers. The situation at Scotcake, as we have seen, was more complex.

Further evidence for this interpretation comes from responses to a set of questions about ownership and control and management–employee relationships. In both units more non-participants believed that 'profits should belong to employees, not shareholders', that 'employees with shares should elect managers', and that 'employees should own the companies they work for', but in only one instance was there a majority of participants in favour of any of these propositions. On the other hand in both cases more participants believed that 'employees should share losses as well as profits', but again in neither case was this a majority view, even among participants. At Breadline the managerial/manual worker divide was again apparent. Managers were overwhelmingly against the first three propositions and in favour of the latter, whereas manual employees marginally favoured the first three but were against sharing losses as well as profits. The managerial/manual employee polarity was also evident at Scotcake, except that managers here were actually slightly against employees sharing losses and manual employees were against both employees with shares electing managers and employees owning the company they work for.

Breadline non-participants strongly believed that they were treated as numbers and that they had no opportunity to use their real ability at work. They were less inclined to believe that management had their employees' welfare at heart or that management knew best. Again these differences paralleled the management/manual worker divide. At Scotcake participants and non-participants alike concurred on many of the issues, except that substantially more non-participants felt that they were treated as numbers rather than participants. Four-fifths of both categories disagreed with the statement 'management knows best ...' and while just under half the non-participants believed they had no opportunity to use their real abilities at work, so too did nearly a third of participants. The latter point can be attributed to a differentiation between managers, who *all* believed that they were able to use their real abilities, compared to only 48 per cent of manual workers.

Respondents were invited to indicate their agreement or disagreement with a number of statements reflecting attitudes to work and to employee share ownership. The responses of Scotcake employees reflected the existence of the company incentive bonus scheme as well as the share ownership scheme. Here on a number of indicators there was no real difference between participants and non-participants. Non-participants, however, were more dissatisfied with the financial aspect of the schemes, such as the risk of losing part of earnings, the unpredictability of the bonus, and the strong desire to have more say in fixing the profit share. These dissatisfactions almost certainly referred to the productivity bonus share, as probably did the strong view of non-participants that they were more likely to notice if their colleagues were not pulling their weight. Interview evidence indicated support for the productivity bonus scheme and its positive impact on motivation. Just under half the participants were more likely not to want to change job, but this was not decisive *vis-à-vis* non-participants or a sizeable minority of participants. Participants were much more likely to feel that they were able to be involved more in the way the company was run compared with non-participants, but surprisingly as many participants disagreed with that view as agreed with it.

At Breadline there was less dissatisfaction with the financial aspect of schemes, essentially because respondents were referring to the SAYE scheme only. Again, while more participants than non-participants felt better able to participate in the company, two-thirds of participants did not. Nor were participants better aware of management problems, more likely to notice colleagues not pulling their weight, nor did the existence of the scheme inhibit them from moving job. In fact throughout both companies very few positive views were expressed about respondents' experience of profit-sharing. Only in the factory did a majority of respondents believe that if they worked hard they could share in the results, but this view was held equally strongly by both participants and non-participants.

CONCLUSION

Goodbake management was looking for attitudinal change from the employee share ownership scheme. From the outset the scheme had severe limitations in achieving this, in two ways. First, the service qualification rules, especially those concerning part-timers, excluded about half of all employees, but a substantially higher proportion in the retail-oriented parts of Breadline. Second, only a minority of employees actually participated, and in Breadline in particular this minority of fifteen employees were overwhelmingly managers. Thus, as we have seen, the views attributed to participants equated with those attributed to managers. There was evidence that it was the commitment to the company flowing from managerial status and position (combined with salaries and financial commitments which permitted contributions to the scheme to be made) which led to participation, rather than participation leading to commitment.

At Scotcake the situation was more complex. It was still only a minority who participated, and, while managers predominated, a fair proportion of manual, lower-paid trade unionists participated. Yet the evidence on attitudes was mixed. Generally employees of Scotcake had a more favourable view of their company than their colleagues at Breadline, and this would not necessarily reflect the participant/non-participant division. But on some attitudinal questions there was no sharp distinction between participants and non-participants. It may be argued that the impact of the scheme was 'dripping through', but the case by and large remained not proven. Moreover even here, where there was evidence that participants had different views, it was not clear whether it was because they were participants, or whether holding such views motivated them to participate. Even if the direction was that participation did lead to changed attitudes, we must remember that less than 10 per cent of employees participated and therefore the potential for their changed attitude to permeate and influence the work force as a whole must have been limited.

Nor was there evidence that the goal of wider share ownership *per se* was necessarily achieved through the scheme, as substantial proportions of holdings had been sold off. At Breadline exactly half those who had completed a five-year savings period and had bought shares still held all of them, but at Scotcake the proportion had fallen to 40 per cent. Overall, a quarter in each case had disposed of all their shares. On the other hand some thirty respondents owned shares in other companies, and two-thirds of them had been bought after becoming a participant in the Goodbake SAYE share option scheme. Some respondents, however, held shares in other companies without participating in the company scheme, and there was evidence from the interviews of a number of employees participating in the government's privatization share issues of the time and that this represented the bulk of their other shareholding.

10

Norbrew: financial participation and organizational change

Norbrew has operated in the north of England for 180 years, where successive generations of family interests have helped to maintain its image as a closely knit, somewhat paternalistic enterprise which in common with other brewing concerns has faced a diversity of new challenges in recent years. These include a declining market for beer-drinking, exacerbated by poor summer sales and heightened product competition; the closure of traditional outlets such as working men's clubs, coupled with changing customer profiles and preferences, has also been an issue of concern. In addition, the company's consumer base in the north has been adversely affected by the impact of the recession.

To meet these diverse challenges, Norbrew has responded through diversification of product, chiefly by a series of vertically integrated moves into the off-licensing and residential hotel trades, supported by initial steps into the broadly defined 'leisure industry'. This expansion in activities is demonstrated by the change of name in 1985 from Northern Breweries to the Norbrew Group. Recent organizational restructuring reflects these developments by the establishment of four operating divisions, two of which control the group's brewing activities, a hotel division, and a division dealing with distribution through the company's trade and retail outlets. Other initiatives have included attempts to penetrate beer markets in less economically vulnerable regions of the country through acquisitions of breweries and licensed premises.

Changing consumer tastes and profiles have induced the company to introduce and step up lager production and to provide a wider, 'quality-centred' range of services, accompanied by aggressive sales campaigns in part intended to shift the company image away from its 'traditional' representation and in part to combat the intense competition taking place within the declining beer market by entering increasingly into the highly competitive take-home and supermarket 'own label' markets. Competition has also led to increased cost-consciousness, expressed in modernization plans and in the introduction of technologically advanced conditioning and packaging lines.

Management strategy has also been directed to employee developmental and attitudinal aspects of organizational change, expressed in training programmes which emphasize the need for adaptability, co-operation, and efficiency, buttressed by participative initiatives aimed to locate these themes within an organizational philosophy in which unity of interest between employees and managers is given considerable prominence. The profoundly unitarist character of senior management carries conviction in that these major developments and the accompanying organizational restructuring have involved no enforced redundancies, and in the region as a whole today Norbrew employs more people within the group than ten years ago, an outcome of which the company is especially proud. This is in marked contrast to other brewing concerns, which have undertaken considerable staff reductions during the same period. (See Cressey *et al.*, 1985: chapter 7.)

The company appears to have been successful in its attempts to diversify operations and maintain its market share, with turnover and profits continuing to advance through the 1980s. Turnover for 1985 amounted to some £145 million, with pre-tax profits at a record £15 million, an increase of £1.7 million over the previous year. The success of the company and particularly the attraction of its chain of hotels and licensed premises has made it a target for acquisition, with a number of take-over attempts rumoured and some actually materializing during the past couple of years, so far without success. One effect of these intermittent events has been sharp share-price fluctuations (along an upward trend) during the same period.

THE WORK FORCE

With such a broadly based range of commercial activities, it was decided to concentrate our research attention upon the company's traditional area of activity, brewing, and hence upon the group's brewing division head office, based in a large northern town. The division employs some 1,700 staff (out of a group total of 6,000), including approximately 1,000 part-time employees, chiefly employed in the public houses, of which there are approximately 550 operated by the group (public-house staff were not included in the study). The division is managed by its eight divisional directors, reporting to the main board. At the brewery (which also contains the group head office) employees are either hourly-paid (about 400) or monthly-paid staff (about 270), the bulk of these two groups being full-time employees.

The hourly-paid work force

The majority of the hourly-paid work force are unskilled, there being about sixty tradesmen, mainly located in the services and distribution departments. Hourly-paid employees are predominantly male. Union recognition was granted as recently as 1979, the recognized union being the TGWU. Membership density for these employees is now about 70 per cent and is unlikely to increase beyond that. Pay consists of a time rate supplemented by output-related bonus payments in some departments, overtime and shift premiums. The union side during pay negotiations is represented by shop stewards in association with elected representatives drawn from the Brewery Council. Senior brewery management lead the employer's side of negotiations.

Relations with the union were described by senior management as very good and far better than in the brewing industry generally, with no obvious areas of conflict and no history of disruptions. The quality of Norbrew management and its willingness to participate with employees, coupled to (and associated with) the absence of 'militant' shop stewards were offered as the main reasons for this state of affairs.

The salaried work force

White-collar staff number about 270, including forty part-time employees. The proportions of female employees are significantly higher than for hourly-paid employees, though the women staff members tend to be concentrated in the lower grade occupations. White-collar unions are not recognized by the company, on the grounds that staff do not want to be in a union, a sentiment generally echoed by both management and clerical respondents during the course of the interview sessions. Senior management emphasized, however, that should sufficient staff express a desire for union representation, there would be no objection or resistance by management.

Staff are paid by monthly salary through a grading system which allocates staff to one of thirteen grades (A–M). The first six grades (A–F) are negotiated between a management team consisting of the personnel director, managing director, and a number of other senior managers and a staff salaries committee comprising six elected members of the Brewery Council (see below). Extra payment is made to negotiated grades for overtime, and shift allowances are paid where appropriate. Overtime payments are not made to middle management or higher grades. In addition to negotiated basic salaries, merit pay can be added to individual salaries at management discretion in grades C–M.

Though salaried staff have a grading system, no formal job evaluation is involved, and any regrading is at the discretion of management. If a job changes, the decision as to whether the incumbent should move on to a new grade is made by the head of department or, for senior positions, by the managing director.

PARTICIPATION WITHIN THE BREWERY DIVISION

Though there has been a long history of participation at Norbrew through consultation and communication, it is only in recent years and under the present management that attempts have been made to invigorate and give substance to the procedures, as evidenced by the establishment of the Brewery Council and introduction of employee share ownership schemes. These initiatives in turn can be traced to the developments within the company and industry outlined above, in which market productive pressures have served to structure the direction and form of employee relations towards flexible and co-operative working arrangements.

The apex of this participative pyramid is represented by the Brewery Council, chaired by the managing director, with membership comprising nominated senior management members (twelve) and twenty-four members elected on a departmental constituency basis. Established as a divisional problem-solving and advisory forum, meetings of the council are held every two months, with a written agenda and minutes. Both the staff and brewery (hourly-paid) negotiating committees are drawn from the Brewery Council.

Consultation procedures are provided by five occupational groups, each with its own committee and chaired by a senior management member of the occupational group. These committees meet on a monthly basis, and are less formal in status and practice than the Brewery Council, with no agenda or minutes. Often these committees deal with the everyday affairs common to most joint consultative arrangements. Members are elected from all employees within the occupational groups and need not necessarily be union members. Briefing groups are an additional participative approach conducted by departmental heads, and sessions are also expected to be held on a monthly basis, though some departments are more committed to regular briefing than others. Finally, the chairman and group managing director regularly address the work force three times a year, using the local theatre for what is known as the 'Royalty' or, less reverently perhaps, the 'Gloom and Doom' show. These presentations consist largely of a 'state of the nation' appraisal of company performance, looking back to past achievements and forward to new developments and challenges. Though the audience is invited to contribute through question and comment at the end of the session, there is rarely a response from the assembled employees.

There was also an attempt by the company to introduce quality circles, which ran for two or three years but received little support and were eventually withdrawn. They have now been superseded by a 'Programme for Change', a year-long programme designed to integrate the activities of all management, to make it more responsive and adaptable to change, and to foster more open relations between different functional groups. The programme involves a residential week, in which problems are identified and assessed in order of importance. Based on the identified problem areas, participants are then required to prepare remedial projects during the course of the year for presentation to colleagues. This programme is still continuing.

The final strand in the company's participative network involves the allocation of shares through the operation of two schemes, an all-employee share ownership programme (ADST) and an option scheme in which employees are invited to participate. The group-based ADST scheme provides for part of the company's annual profits to be allocated among full-time employees who have served a minimum two years with the company. The scheme was inaugurated in 1979, with Inland Revenue approval.

Allocations of shares are made from the company's annual pre-tax profits to employees according to a value-added formula in which total employment costs are calculated as a ratio of value added during the same period. The lower the ratio of employment costs, the higher the allocation of shares to employees, to a maximum of 5 per cent of annual pre-tax profits. The minimum level of profits required to trigger the scheme is £5 million, a figure exceeded easily in every year since its introduction. The company can, however, suspend the scheme at the discretion of the directors, and it can also provide for a higher allocation of profits to the scheme (subject to the 5 per cent maximum) in times of exceptional group performance. Each member is allowed up to a maximum of 10 per cent of pay to purchase shares in any one year, with allocations being determined in accordance with P60 earnings (rather than basic pay).

The 1985 profit-share calculation is shown in Table 33. According to the scheme rules, when the value-added ratio falls between 56.3 per cent and 56.6 per cent, the percentage of profits to be allocated to employees is 3.5 per cent. Pre-tax profits for 1985 (excluding profits on disposals of property, investments, and profits of related companies) were £14.5 million. The scheme therefore provides to employees 3.5 per cent of £14.5 million = £508,000, to enable employees to acquire ordinary shares in the company. This amount compares with £378,000 allocated to the scheme in 1984. Allocated shares are held by the trustees for a minimum period of

Table 33 1985 share distribution to Norbrew employees (£000)

Total employment costs	26,389
Total added value	46,654
Value-added ratio	$\dfrac{26,389 \times 100}{46,654}$
	$= 56 \cdot 56\%$

two years, after which there is a tapering tax liability, with no income tax payable if the shares are held for a minimum five years. While shares are held by the trustees, members are sent copies of annual reports and accounts, notices of meetings, and any other information distributed to ordinary shareholders. Members are not able to attend shareholder meetings but can instruct the trustees how to vote on their behalf.

At present, there are just over 6,000 employees within the group, of whom 3,325 are part-time and ineligible to participate in the scheme. In the first two years of the scheme (1979 and 1980) there were 1,487 participants, to whom 213,162 shares were released by the trustees at the conclusion of their retention periods. The number of members has since increased considerably.

The share option scheme, introduced in 1981 follows the standard 'approved' model outlined earlier and is designed to allow eligible employees to save a regular amount out of their earnings for a five-year period through a SAYE scheme with a building society. Though originally open only to full-time employees, since March 1986 the scheme has also allowed for participation by part-time employees, following representations on their behalf by elected members of the Brewery Council. The minimum savings amount is £10 per month, with a maximum of £100 per month.

Senior management objectives for participation and employee share ownership

As mentioned earlier, share ownership schemes at Norbrew cannot be dissociated from other strands of participation encouraged by the company's management. In the words of one senior manager, 'It has little to do with motivation, but part of a general move to increase participation with the company', a sentiment echoed by a colleague, who commented that 'profit-sharing is part of our belief', which, prompted by the 1978 legislation, 'seemed to be the right thing to do at the time'. It was not so much aimed at securing any one defined objective, but was rather part of a package of participative practices which comprised an embracing philosophy of involving 'more people in the ownership of the company for which they work and therefore to inspire their loyalty and commitment'.

Using the classification of managerial aims developed in Chapter 5, the Norbrew philosophy can be more closely identified with employee attitudinal or motivational objectives than with more specific defensive or incentive motives. However, these broad objectives also blend consistently with developing managerial priorities stimulated by changing market and competitive circumstances. It is not surprising, therefore that this approach has gathered momentum over the past few years, during which the company 'has tried very hard to move away from the old rather dictatorial, paternalistic management style towards trying to involve everybody, i.e. working together' (managing director). This represents an evolution in management approach which can be directly associated with the changing demands of the brewing industry, where attention to profitability has become a key feature of management policy and where employee commitment, flexibility, and increased responsibility under conditions of an uncertain environment have become prominent factors in seeking appropriate levels of company performance required for survival:

> All employees are expected to do a good job, but we want them to be interested in the profitability of the company because the success of the company and its remaining independence is reflected in its performance. The more profitable we are the better. Therefore, all employees at all levels should have an eye to try to maximize profitability. [Director]

Share ownership also facilitates transmission of exhortatory messages in which traditional concepts of reward-based motivation combine subtly with unitarist sympathies and implications of external competitive threat:

> Another point of contact ... refers to us and them, but in this case we are talking about us (company) versus the competition (when for example, comparing share prices). People have to appreciate that we are not our own little world: we are governed by two things. One is the customer and there is a follow-on from that in what the competitors are doing for those customers that we enjoy or those customers that we wish to attract. [Director]

Expressions of communal interest between employees and managers may be approached from other, more oblique directions, as on the occasion when one senior manager commented to the researcher that the schemes may 'get the employees to understand that their interests are not the same as shareholders. For example, if there is a take-over in the air, employees might have a different perspective to shareholders.'

Perceived effect of share ownership on individual employees

In the absence of defined objectives, seeking specific consequences from the introduction of share ownership becomes difficult if not irrelevant. If specific aims were laid down one might attempt to examine a range of performance indicators showing heightened individual commitment as expressed through factors such as reduced labour turnover and absenteeism through to increased flexibility or improved work performance. Also, there might be expectations over collective behavioural consequences as manifested in the manner and form of negotiations over pay and other conditions of employment. As might be anticipated in view of the above comments, no specific examples of individual employee change were actively sought by the company, nor were they looked for by any of the managers interviewed, who tended to concentrate on the responses expressed by employees with regard to their position as shareholders:

> There are encouraging signs coming out of it. I remember last year when we were subject to much take-over speculation, a number of employees coming to me saying, 'Should we sell our shares? We don't want to do anything that might harm the company.' Now that's great, but I wonder what percentage of people who have shares and have profited from profit-sharing really feel that. I couldn't quantify it. [Managing director]

Some executives appeared to be guided by their own general frames of reference and orientations to ownership when assessing the relevance of share ownership, though again without pointing to specific benefits: 'The fact that employees do share in the company's success *must* have some influence.' However, others considered that the incentive element should be given greater priority, as 'seventy per cent of employees see shares as something they get, whether they work hard or not. We need to put more play into it; it's not used as a motivational part of the management of the company.' Though this faint suspicion of 'getting something for nothing' through share provision by the company was not a commonly voiced sentiment, other senior managers were aware and concerned that, in direct motivational terms, the schemes have little to offer and can become, in the words of one senior director, 'just a nice perk', which can be sold off after a few years in order to allow beneficiaries to make 'a bit of money'. Moreover, as we shall see

193

below, in collective terms there has been little evidence of any discernible change in negotiating practice or behaviour, which has generally been of a high standard, acceptable to senior management.

Perceived effect of share ownership on collective relations

The foregoing section indicates that senior management tended to concentrate upon share ownership as an articulation of a diffuse participative philosophy, aimed at drawing employees together into a coherent unit, unified in its overall objectives of maintaining profitability and market share. Our interviews with representatives responsible for negotiating with management over terms and conditions of employment also provided an opportunity to identify and assess any effects that share ownership was having on collective relations between management and employees.

A total of twelve interviews with employees were conducted; six interviewees were drawn from middle management and clerical occupations and six from the manual work force. None of the white-collar representatives interviewed was a union member and neither were any of them likely to join a union in the foreseeable future, sharing, as they did, the general view that as the company provided sufficient opportunity for employee involvement in its affairs there was no need for white-collar union representation. Five of the six had served or currently served on the Brewery Council and had been involved in pay discussions with management. Similarly, five of the six manual representatives served on the Brewery Council, all were union members, and negotiated with management over pay and conditions in their capacity as union representatives.

For both groups of representatives discussions over the share schemes in the context of negotiations were rather restricted, primarily because the schemes were seen as a management gratuity and also because, despite the growth in profitability, employee negotiators felt uncomfortable in discussions over *profits* as a basis of negotiation, for these were perceived as specialized management territory, in contradistinction to the more visible and openly justifiable principles of comparability and cost-of-living increases with which workplace negotiators felt much more at ease: 'We talked about profit, but they lose us with the figures, so much spent on this plant, so much there – you haven't a clue where it's gone ... they can do whatever they want with figures.'

All the manual employees interviewed had been involved in some way in negotiations with management, and all were adamant that the schemes made no impact upon their negotiations, mainly because the share schemes were viewed as a separate issue from pay which management, unilaterally, had decided to offer: 'The way we looked at it, the company was offering, and we looked upon it as being available.' White-collar representatives offered similar views: when asked whether the share schemes had formed part of a pay claim, directly or indirectly, one response was that 'It's not even been a factor, really. It's not negotiable; something that management give.' Moreover, there was a common suspicion that on negotiated pay, the company was not paying as well as other concerns in the same industry, or even the going rate for the area, and hence in those terms there was legitimate scope for disagreement between employees and management, not-withstanding substantial management efforts towards employee integration through consultative procedures and the introduction of the share schemes. A central priority, therefore was seen as the attainment of a 'decent' basic wage, which if forthcoming, would lead to higher share allocations and greater disposable income for contributing to the share option scheme, described in the words of one participant as 'a hell of a scheme. I save £5 a week. Nothing else can beat it, but if they gave us a decent wage I could afford £25 a week to put into it.' A colleague expressed his concern in similar terms: 'We need a decent living wage, where you are dependent on nothing ... not on the market ... a loaf of bread costs the same . you must have a decent living wage ... anything on top of that is a bonus.'

For these reasons, negotiations over pay seemed unaffected by the introduction of the schemes. Against a background of well structured and amicable relations, high local unemployment, and a degree of insecurity engendered by repeated take-over rumours in a rapidly changing industry, it would have been surprising to find anything else. That is not to say that attempts at negotiation had not been made, either formally during the course of pay discussions or at the Brewery Council, where the subject of access for part-time staff to the share-option scheme was initially (and successfully) raised. Intermittent attempts to include the same staff in the all-employee scheme had also been tentatively considered, thus far without success. The only other area to be approached had been attempts to discuss the subject of changing the system of share allocations from its total earnings base, though again efforts in this direction had been made only occasionally and pursued with little apparent conviction.

As a negotiating topic share ownership commanded little attention. The corollary, borne out by the survey findings, is that union members may tend not to consider share-scheme benefits as part of the total remuneration package, which must, therefore, be acceptable on its own merits. The impression created by interviewed participants was that in this sense pay at Norbrew was not considered satisfactory, despite the extra 3.5 per cent added to earnings by the all-employee share scheme, the inference being that negotiations over pay would not include reference to share allocations as part of the remuneration package, and its relative absence from pay discussions would tend to confirm this. Furthermore, annual pay negotiations during the year did enter into a stalemate, only to be resolved through a work force ballot, in which recommendations for industrial action to support the union's claim were rejected by the majority of the work force. This divorce of the share scheme from pay negotiations and the 'realities' of economic life were regretted by one senior manager in his comment that:

> The difficult time is the annual wage negotiations, when the union take the lead, and they do the negotiation, and that leads to inflammatory feelings being spread by small sections of the work force, which is so much against my interests and the interests of everyone else that I find it frustrating.

In other words, managerial efforts to structure a stable environment of communal endeavour might be challenged, albeit temporarily, through work force representative appeals to the equity of the reward system, though the extent to which such challenges would be endorsed by their constituents is open to question and considered in greater depth in the next section.

EMPLOYEE PERCEPTIONS OF NORBREW

Questionnaires were distributed to 500 employees based at the main Norbrew site. Only eligible employees (full-time, with a minimum of two years' service) were included in the survey. A total of 108 completed questionnaires were returned, representing a response rate of 21.6 per cent. Two main factors help explain this comparatively modest response rate: first, questionnaires were sent to employees' domestic residences, and not all employees recognized the survey as relating to their work situation. Second, the detailed questionnaires were distributed early in September, when many employees were still on holiday.

Ninety-nine (92 per cent) respondents were male, reflecting the predominantly manual nature of many of the jobs at Norbrew, which are occupied by men, and also the higher proportion of part-time female staff at the company who would not be eligible for membership of the all-employee share scheme nor, hence, to participate in the survey. Classifying employees according to general occupational status provides the following groupings of responses: management, 19 per cent; technical staff, 12 per cent; clerical, 9 per cent; supervisory, 8 per cent; manual, 52 per cent. Forty per cent of replies (N=43) were from trade union members, principally manual members of the TGWU, the only union recognized by the company for collective bargaining purposes. The mean age of respondents was forty-five, with an average seventeen years of service with the company.

As the share ownership schemes form part of a wider participative programme aimed at creating a climate of community and of shared values, an appropriate starting point for our analysis would be an overall evaluation of Norbrew as an employer as provided by the survey returns, and on this point the rating given by all respondents and by manual employees alone was high (see Table 34). This favourable response is further supported by responses to questions asking employees' opinions of workplace relations in Britain generally and in Norbrew especially. Whilst only 2 per cent of respondents considered that in Britain 'management and employees basically have common aims and objectives', 21 per cent replied that in Norbrew such conditions did exist. Similarly, one-third of respondents answered that in Britain generally management and employees were on opposing sides, but for Norbrew only 12 per cent expressed this view. Though higher proportions of manual employees did tend to take a more oppositional view of workplace relations at the company, the numbers were still considerably lower than for their perspective of industry generally.

However, when we examine employee views on specific areas pertinent to their interests the picture becomes rather more complex and blurred. This can be demonstrated, for example, by reference to the statement that 'most management have the welfare of their

Table 34 General employee rating of Norbrew as an employer (%)

Rating	All respondents	Manual employees only
Very good	40	33
Moderately good	34	42
Average	23	22
Rather poor	1	0
Very poor	2	4
(Number	108	55)

employees at heart', to which nearly half the respondents were in agreement but nearly half were in disagreement. When examining manual respondent replies alone the balance swayed markedly to disagreement with the statement (62 per cent, as compared with 35 per cent in agreement). With this in mind we have attempted to evaluate employees' perceptions of management effectiveness towards them in accordance with a range of different criteria: employee security, management capability, pay, employee participation. For each of these criteria, employees tended to interpret the effectiveness of management in contrasting ways, with potentially important implications both for the share ownership schemes and for managerial objectives.

Job security

The picture with regard to employee perceptions of security was highly positive, and it may well be that favourable interpretations over this aspect help to explain the generous overall rating given to Norbrew. As Table 35 shows, a large majority of respondents rated the company above average on this issue, which in the insecure employment climate of recession-hit northern England, and an industry undergoing considerable rationalization, represents a factor of some significance.

Management ability

A majority of respondents disagreed with the statement that management should be left to make decisions on the basis of their superior knowledge. When questioned on the levels of skill which

Table 35 Employee views of Norbrew relative to other employers

Rating	Pay	Management openness	Management skill	% chances to get on	Job security	Employee participation
Well above average	–	6	8	5	30	5
About average	10	26	9	10	42	17
Average	35	34	54	43	22	37
Below average	36	17	17	29	3	16
Well below average	11	15	9	13	3	25
No reply	7	2	3	–	–	

management brought to their position, a similar picture emerged in which the majority of respondents considered their managers to possess 'average' managerial skills, but 26 per cent rated their managers as below average, and only 17 per cent as above average. These trends were reinforced when manual workers alone were considered (34 per cent below average, compared to 10 per cent above).

Pay

As Table 35 above demonstrates, pay levels at Norbrew were not regarded highly by respondents, with about half indicating that pay was below average. Another dimension to this issue may be explored by examining perceptions of equity of pay distribution between management and employees, which may also be an important contribution to overall employee satisfaction. When asked about differentials between management and workers at the company, 49 per cent of all respondents, and 60 per cent of manual employees, claimed that the differentials were too high. Taken together, these replies provided some confirmation of interview claims that employees, especially manual employees, were not wholly satisfied with their pay levels. This had added importance in the context of the share ownership schemes in that ADST allocations increase with earnings and propensity for SAYE involvement may well be indirectly linked in the same direction.

EMPLOYEE PERCEPTIONS OF PARTICIPATION

From their replies it is evident that most employees are aware of the range of participatory procedures used at Norbrew, but interpretations of their effectiveness were rather more elusive. Thus a quarter of all respondents rated Norbrew as 'well below average' in encouraging employee participation in decisions. When manual workers alone are included, the figure rises to 36 per cent, contrasting with the 6 per cent who rated the company 'well above average' on this issue. (A comment attached to a completed questionnaire provides a stark demonstration of the views of one employee: 'Committees, schemes, groups, organization, communication; all a complete waste of time with this company. From eight till five day in and day out, utter mayhem, blind leading the blind'!) Management openness, a reflection of managerial communication practice, was not rated highly either, with over a quarter of manual employees stating that management were 'well below average', a view endorsed by 15 per cent of all respondents. This pattern receives emphasis from replies to a question in which respondents were invited to agree or disagree with a number of statements. With the statement 'Management tend to treat people like me as numbers' nearly *half* of all employees, and over two-thirds of manual employees were in agreement, whilst similar proportions were in disagreement with the proposition that 'In the end management know best and employees should let them make the decisions'. These replies, from respondents who included a high proportion of SAYE participants, may conceivably understate the general view of participation practised at the company, and it may well be that this view, particularly that of manual employees, is perhaps not as sympathetic towards management's participatory initiatives as might have been expected from the range of available procedures and the efforts made by senior management to promote them.

The survey findings tended to indicate that while employees had an overall positive orientation to the company, with regard to pay and participation areas of ambivalence were evident, and these areas became rather more focused when examining the views offered by interviewed representatives of their financial participation schemes. Thus, whilst most of the white-collar representatives interviewed regarded the share schemes as an opportunity to 'share in company profits', none had massive expectations from the scheme, either with regard to its participative potential or as a means of generating substantial amounts of additional income. Even so, comments such as share ownership 'making you part of the company' and permitting employees to 'work for themselves' were not infrequent, as were vague allusions to 'making people interested in how the company is doing'. However, greater cohesive impact was probably achieved through the direct manifestations of the participative style of management encouraged and stimulated from the top. Hence one woman's attachment to the company was more attributable to 'the people you work with' than a consequence of the share schemes, and neither 'would stop me leaving, if I found better pay elsewhere'. Another employee expressed her feelings in a similar fashion: 'Management and employees work together anyway – it's that kind of company. There's not the division ... We are not on first-name terms, obviously, but we are kept fully briefed.'

Though the response to receiving the shares was enthusiastic, it tended towards the pragmatic: 'To my mind, it's a bonus. It's something we didn't get when I started,' was one comment, echoed by a colleague but with rather more emphasis: 'It's one more thing that employees are entitled to.' And, as we have seen evaluation of participation in the share schemes as a management gratuity extended also to its absence from discussions over pay, in which the white-collar interviewees had been involved as members of the Brewery Council.

The 'bonus' interpretation received additional reinforcement when examining the outcome of share allocations; many considered that their colleagues had sold shares during a period when prices were high, a point emphasized by one participant in her comment that 'I know a lot of people had good holidays this year on their shares,' whilst another simply considered the shares to be a 'bonus ... an addition'. A colleague expressed regret that she had not participated initially in the option scheme, as she could have 'made a killing' by selling shares at the time of a take-over bid, and, whilst some employees retained their shares so as 'to protect the company' or to help prevent 'selling our own jobs', many did take advantage of the high price and sold their allocations.

The instrumental orientation to share provision as a material bonus carries with it a danger that share ownership programmes may become divisive rather than cohesive in effect, and certain manifestations of this development were demonstrated:

> Staff are badly done to in relation to brewery workers. The [share ownership] scheme is based on P60 [total earnings rather than basic pay] and therefore brewery workers have bonuses and premium included. Staff only have salaries. We argued at the time that this gives unfair advantage to brewery workers but we were told that P60 is the best way of determination.

Similar comments were pressed on behalf of part-time employees, who were excluded from the all-employee share scheme but, following representations at the Brewery Council, are now eligible to participate in the option scheme if they wish. These opportunities did not apply to the all-employee ADST scheme.

The views of manual employed representatives on share ownership schemes also contained elements both of the cohesiveness which the company was trying to foster and of the divisiveness which might derive from a bonus-operated remuneration policy. As with the clerical workers the interviewed employees were appreciative of the efforts that senior management was making to develop a cohesive environment at the company. Moreover, they tended to identify the share schemes as part of this strategy.

> When you get the certificate, I am not just a wage-earner, I am part and parcel ... I have my little bit of say in the company, no matter how little it is ... it does encourage us to be a little bit more involved and to make the company more profitable.

Even the more sceptical employees could be influenced: 'It swayed me to the company a bit, I must admit ... It shows they have a little bit of respect for you. At least, that's the feeling you get.' Moreover, some employees were clearly persuaded that an identifiable link existed between *their* efforts and the share bonus: 'If we do our job properly, the profits are going to increase all the time ...'

Those employees participating in the SAYE scheme were also ready to show their enthusiasm for an approach which could not fail to provide financial benefits to participants, provided employees pulled their weight: 'Tremendous ... This is the sort of thing the company needed,' was one enthusiastic response, motivated strongly, it would appear, by the prospect of the eventual monetary returns by which it was 'impossible to lose', though other benefits such as helping individuals to save money or increasing employee involvement with the company were also contemplated:

It gives a little more incentive to pull your weight; there's more interest in the company. If you see a guy slacking, you are going to think twice about letting him get away with it. It has that effect. The guys who bang the kegs around, you say, look, that's my profits going down the drain. You tend to tell them.

The majority of the employees interviewed were quite prepared to dispose of their shares, and many had already done so in order to finance a holiday or other expenditure at a time when the share price was soaring. These disposals could also be associated with developing business acumen ('I got rid of them fast, made a killing, but I couldn't sell all the shares on account of capital gains'). According to the interviewees, many of their colleagues had taken similar action in disposing of shares and taking advantage of the high price but often for reasons tied in with the allegedly low wages paid by the company: 'I sold my shares. I would have liked to have kept them, but can't afford it. Married man, two kids. Management can afford to hang on to them. The majority would have sold on the shop floor.' In contrast, there were some indications of belief that the take-over speculation which had inflated the share price could, in the longer term, have led to difficulties for the employees, who should, therefore, act more toward protecting their own longer-term interests by retaining their share allocations: 'If we can keep the shares, it might help us to stay independent.'

Notwithstanding these assertions of support for both scheme and company, the more apparent sentiment was that the shares were a bonus, to be taken advantage of as circumstances permitted. This in itself is somewhat paradoxical, for whilst senior management were generally seeking to extract non-specific attitudinal advantage from the schemes, employee representatives were inclined to view them as a direct bonus granted by management as a supplement to the agreed remuneration structure, but to which employee access was an entitlement. Furthermore, it was a bonus that offered some employees more benefit than others, owing to the direct relationship established for the ADST scheme between share allocations and *total* earnings: 'In transport we have the opportunity to earn more – the sky's the limit if the product is there to go out and demand is there to be met.'

As we saw earlier with the fixed-salary clerical workers, this approach clearly does not command universal appeal among all employees and especially not those whose work provides no immediate opportunity for achieving performance-related earnings

203

increases: 'I think that people would prefer it if we had it across-the-board, with everyone having a fair share.' Moreover, it was not just between manual employees that 'inequitable' comparisons were drawn, for strong indications were expressed that management would be the ultimate beneficiaries of the ADST scheme through its higher earnings and also the SAYE scheme owing to higher levels of disposable income:

> I was in a Brewery Council meeting last year and one of the directors asked if we could put our own money into the scheme. If you had a couple of thousand spare ... could you put that in with the SAYE? It must be nice to have a couple thousand to put into it.

The majority of additional comments which survey respondents were invited to append to their completed questionnaire were directed adversely to this earnings-related requirement of the ADST scheme, though none was as forceful as the interview comment which indicated sufficient antagonism as to put the general objectives of the scheme as laid down by management in some jeopardy:

> To me that is the company image. Work as a team, work with Norbrew, then you are split down the middle straight away ... it's them and us ... it always will be here. I think the rest is just a front, a good image for the company.

The preceding analysis suggests that whilst Norbrew employees inclined to favour the company in general terms, there were specific areas such as pay with which employees might be less satisfied. It also appeared that these areas of concern might be more pronounced among manual than among white-collar workers and, second, that they might introduce a negative element to the generally positive orientations expressed toward share ownership and, where appropriate, as with the SAYE scheme, might adversely influence participation in it. Furthermore, there were strong indications that both white-collar and especially manual respondents tended to relate to share ownership in bonus-incentive terms, significantly differently from the attitudinal aspirations held for them by management, which could potentially have long-term detrimental effects in terms of group rivalry, organizational morale, or loss of interest. It is to these issues that we now turn in our evaluation of the share ownership schemes.

PARTICIPATION IN THE SAYE SCHEME

With the introduction of the present SAYE scheme in 1981 there had been an immediate response, with 330 SAYE accounts started. Subsequent years showed a marked deceleration in the rate of take-up of new accounts until the figures were boosted by the introduction of part-time employee eligibility in 1986. By March 1987 the cumulative number of SAYE accounts stood at 954, representing approximately a fifth of the eligible group work force.

Manual and non-manual attitudes

A higher proportion of employees participating in the SAYE scheme responded to the survey than was found in the general employee population, indicating that participants had tended to respond to the request to complete the questionnaire, the overall response rate for SAYE membership being 59 per cent. Participation by occupational group is shown in Table 36. Whilst the occupation groups in some cases were too small to provide accurate estimates of the proportions of representation, the table confirms that manual employee participation was at a lower rate than white-collar. It is of interest, also, that managerial participation appears somewhat lower than for other white-collar groups, possibly because managerial replies covered a broader spread of participating and non-participating employees, whilst other groups tended to be self-selecting towards participants. However, the general impression that manual participation was at a lower level is clear and receives additional support from another survey finding, which shows that 49 per cent of *waged* respondents participated in SAYE, compared with 75 per cent of *salaried* respondents. Disaggregation of these figures revealed additional valuable information (Table 37). For both weekly and monthly salaried employees, participation was highest towards the high-pay end of the spectrum, falling away in the middle ranges and for the weekly-paid employees at the lowest paid levels. The one surprise is the 100 per cent participation rate by employees at the lower levels of the salaried pay range. This might be explained through participation by young people who wished to save regularly, or possibly through 'second income' employees, who were able to save from a joint income.

Table 36 Occupational participation in SAYE

Category	No. of employees	No. SAYE	% SAYE participation
Management	20	14	70
Technical staff	12	7	58
Clerical	9	8	89
Supervisory	8	7	88
Manual	54	25	46
No reply	5	0	
Number	108	61	59

Table 37 Level of pay and SAYE participation

Level of pay	% participation	No.
Weekly wage:		
£99	43	14
£100–£129	53	32
£130–£159	33	6
£160–£199	67	3
Mean	49	55
Monthly salary:		
£400	100	9
£400–£516	63	16
£517–£636	62	13
£637–£796	100	4
£797–£1,200	100	3
£1,200+	50	2
Mean	75	47

Details of share retentions also provided useful information, it generally being believed at the company that white-collar staff were more likely to retain their shares than manual employees, owing to closer identification with the company by the former, or because the latter were more likely to require cash. Owing to the considerable increase in share price which had taken place during the intervening period, when the price rose from £1.30 to £3.75, the overwhelming majority of SAYE participants had decided to purchase shares in the company at the option price of £1.17. The forty-three respondents who had completed their five-year saving agreement were asked what proportion of shares in the company they still owned. The details are shown in Table 38.

Table 38 Proportion of share retentions*

| Category | No. of employees retaining shares | | | |
	All	Most	No.	% with all/ most retention
Management	2	4	9	67
Technical staff	5	–	6	83
Clerical	4	–	4	100
Supervisory	6	–	6	100
Manual	6	3	16	56
Number of employees:	43			

*The first opportunity to dispose of shares occurred at the end of March 1986, when the five-year savings period terminated. The questionnaire was distributed early in September the same year.

Again, an interesting pattern emerges. Lowest retention rates are, as anticipated, to be found among manual employees, but with high rates for supervisory, clerical, and technical staff. A possible explanation is that these are staff who feel most committed to the continuing independence of the organization and try to demonstrate their commitment through purchasing and retaining their share allocations. Surprisingly, perhaps, only two out of nine managers still retained all their shares. An explanation for this comparatively high disposal rate may be that managers, sensitive to the historically high price of their shares, divested themselves of them to take advantage of the financial opportunity so presented by the attractive share price.

Bearing in mind the general nature of managerial objectives laid down for the scheme, it is important to explore the motives that employees might have had for participating or not in the SAYE programme. It will be recalled that the manual representatives interviewed considered that participation in the scheme was strongly influenced by pay level in that, the higher the pay, the greater the propensity to participate and, also, the higher the contribution which could be made to the savings scheme. Our analysis above appears to confirm that higher-paid employees, white-collar and manual, are more likely to participate. Table 39 examines the SAYE contributions of participants, from which a trend emerges in which the majority of employees contributed to the lower range of the SAYE scheme, a pattern which is also consistent with pay levels, where the majority of low-earning manual participants were contributing at the lower rates, whilst white-collar participation was more broadly distributed. The full details are shown in Table 40.

Table 39 Pattern of contributions to SAYE

Monthly savings contribution (£)	No. contributing
10–20	31
21–40	13
41–60	6
61–80	6
81–100	5

Table 40 SAYE contribution patterns and levels of pay

Savings	Earnings (waged)			
	Less than £99	£100–£129	£130–£159	£160–£199
10–20	5	10	–	–
21–40	–	6	1	1
41–60	1	–	1	–
61–80	–	–	–	–
81–100	–	–	–	–

Savings	Earnings (monthly salary)					
	Less than £400	£400–£516	£517–£636	£637–£796	£797–£1,200	£1,200+
10–20	3	7	1	1	2	–
21–40	3	1	1	–	–	–
41–60	–	–	2	1	–	1
61–80	1	2	2	1	–	–
81–100	1	–	2	1	1	–

A further opportunity to assess the reasons for SAYE participation was taken when employees were asked to consider those features of the scheme which had most attracted them. The most highly rated advantages were spread widely, though, as Fig. 4 indicates, there was a definite inclination towards material benefits offered by the possibility of financial reward at little risk as the main attraction rather than more general concepts of ownership and involvement.

The main reason for *not* participating in the SAYE scheme, offered by more than half the non-participating respondents, was

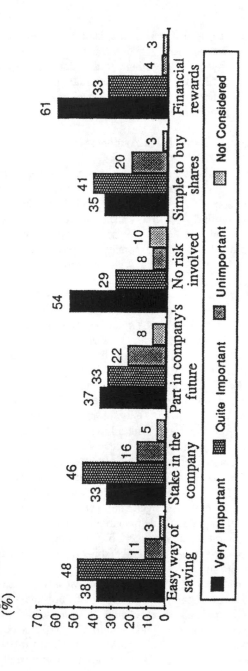

Figure 4 Motives for participation in SAYE: Norbrew

that they could not afford it, but comparison of replies indicates virtually no difference in response between manual and white-collar employees in pointing to this factor, suggesting therefore that the higher participation rate of white-collar employees may be attributable, as we have indicated, to factors additional to financial considerations.

Effects of age, service and union membership

It appears from the above analysis that manual workers are to a degree more estranged from the company than white-collar employees on specific issues, whilst their general overall orientations are similarly positively inclined. It is arguable that managerial commitment to employee security has been a major factor in contributing to this generally positive rating, whilst perceptions of low pay coupled with indications that formal participation policy has not been followed at all levels have contributed toward the less positive specific orientations identified in questionnaire responses. It is feasible that these factors could have influenced manual employees in the decision whether to join the share option scheme or not. It is also possible that other factors, such as age, length of service, or union membership might also have influenced participation. Although our findings indicated that neither age nor length of service exerted a significant effect, we did find it more common among mature employees with a middle-range length of service of eleven to twenty years. Union membership appears to have been associated with a lower rate of participation in option schemes than among the employee sample generally, but as the bulk of union membership was concentrated in manual occupations, for which there was a lower rate of participation, this is not unexpected. Comparing participation rates between union members and manual employees generally, we find that whereas 46 per cent of manual respondents claimed to participate in SAYE, the proportion for union members was 35 per cent, leading to a tentative conclusion that union membership might be associated with a lower propensity to SAYE participation.

Finally, we wished to examine the nature of any relationship between SAYE participation and expressed attitudes to the company. It will be recalled from Table 34 that the majority of respondents rated Norbrew a 'good employer' and this positive evaluation was followed by SAYE participants and non-participants alike, with a slight tendency for *non-participants* to rate Norbrew more highly. We might explain this apparent anomaly by examining the motives behind SAYE participation, which, as previously stated, appeared oriented more towards financial opportunism than symbolic expressions of identification with the company or its policies.

When evaluating the company on specific areas, a similar picture of employee opinion emerges: on areas of pay, participation, security, and management openness, SAYE participants failed to show any more significant appreciation of the company than their non-participating colleagues.

An important conclusion from these findings is that, in the short term at least, SAYE participation was unlikely to alter employees' general and specific orientations to the company, for, had there been a significant 'ownership' effect we might have expected SAYE participants to express more positive appreciation of the company than non-participants. However, there is no evidence of this. Conversely, it might have been expected that employees willing to participate in SAYE could be distinguished from non-participants by more integrative tendencies which would be revealed in their survey replies. Again, this appears not to have been the case.

Perhaps, in summary, we might conclude that white-collar employees had a higher propensity than manual employees to participate in SAYE option schemes; that their contribution levels tended to be higher; and that pay levels might be a significant contributory factor in the participation decision. Participants were typically fairly long-serving middle-aged employees who tended to identify the scheme as an appropriate savings device. The extent to which orientations to the company influenced the participation decision is questionable, but especially favourable inclinations appeared not to be a common factor, and employee perceptions seemed not to undergo any major change as a consequence of scheme involvement.

THE ALL-EMPLOYEE SHARE SCHEME (ADST)

Save As You Earn, through its optional status, is of course selective in its attraction to employees who are free to choose whether to direct a portion of their savings (and if so, what level of savings) into a scheme which secures financial benefit with minimal risk. A proportion of employees did participate, though more would have done so if, in their view, they could have afforded it. There appears to have been little difference in attitude to the company between scheme participants and non-participants, and, similarly, little association between participation and attitudes to the company other than the instrumental tendency noted earlier. As we have seen, however, the company had also introduced a share trust to which it contributed shares on behalf of all eligible employees for whom no direct outlay was involved. This provided further opportunity to enquire into the effects this approach to financial participation might have on work force opinion, for whilst voluntary SAYE participation may be regarded as a *reflection* of employee attitude (and indeed *may* reinforce such attitudes), management expectations of the ADST scheme would be more to help *promote* a climate of unity and common endeavour. We have seen earlier that a number of employees interviewed, whilst appreciating the establishment of the trust, point regretfully to a perceived discriminating bias towards the higher-paid, a perception which might serve to offset any attitudinal advantages accruing from the scheme's introduction. Relying largely upon the work force survey, our intention now is to assess the direction and strength of work force opinion towards share allocations.

When asked their impression of the all-employee share scheme, the general reaction was strongly positive, with 78 per cent of all respondents claiming to be very much in favour. Seventy-three per cent of manual employees alone expressed this view, and no one was opposed to it. A number of statements concerning possible effects of the scheme were presented, and as Fig. 5 indicates, sizeable proportions of respondents claimed to have been positively influenced by its introduction, though the *majority* appear to have remained unaffected by the share ownership experience.

Particularly prominent is the finding that 61 per cent of respondents (60 per cent of manual employees) concurred with the statement that 'If I work hard I know I can share in the results', indicating a perception of direct association between personal effort and share allocation, relevant especially in this instance to white-collar workers, who otherwise had fewer opportunities than manual employees to influence directly their earnings levels. An interpretation of this is that employees tended to regard their share holdings in bonus, reward–effort terms – an interpretation that is supported by the finding that *two-thirds* of all respondents and *three-quarters* of manual employees reported that, to them, the scheme was 'just another kind of bonus'.

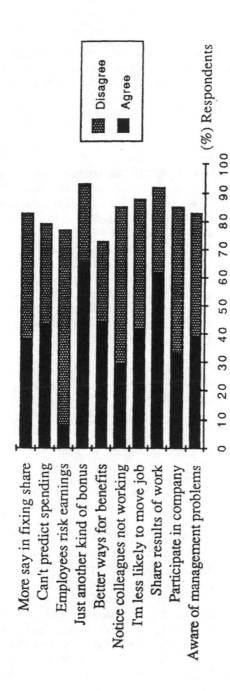

Figure 5 Employees' views on the ADST scheme: Norbrew

A sizeable minority of respondents (31 per cent) disagreed with the proposed 'work-hard/receive bonus' incentive effect of the ADST, many indicating that the scheme was relatively insensitive to individual employee efforts, a feature identified by one craftsman in the following way: 'The value of shares in the market place has an effect on the profit share I receive. The size of my share is very little incentive to work harder, stay longer, encourage efficiency, etc.' A white-collar administrator offered a similar view: 'No attempt is made to link individual effort with group profits/profits share.' This view tended to be associated less with SAYE participants than with non- participants, 44 per cent of whom disagreed with the statement 'If I work hard I can share in the results', compared with 24 per cent of participants. Similarly, non-participants were considerably more inclined than participants to view ADST shares 'as just another kind of bonus'.

Significant proportions (44 per cent of all employees, 56 per cent of manual) also agreed that there were better ways of improving benefits, a finding illustrated by the above comments and reinforced by the numerous critical remarks from individuals on the perceived discriminating nature of the scheme:

> The profit share scheme is worked out on your P60. As some departments are on more overtime and bonus, a worker on flat-time loses out. [Labourer]

> Regards profit shares. Everybody should get the same, not based on previous years earnings, i.e. £1,000 profit for 1,000 workers = £1 each. [Craftsman]

A warehouse manager was of similar opinion: 'I would prefer the profit-sharing to be based on a person's basic wage or salary. Overtime and bonus should not enter the total for calculating a person's share ...' However, compared with participants, far more non-SAYE participants agreed with the statement that there were better ways of improving benefits than through the share allocation (65 per cent to 31 per cent), again suggesting that employees who participated in SAYE tended to take a more favourable, incentive-oriented approach to the all-employee share scheme than non-participants, a point reinforced by the finding that 81 per cent of SAYE participants were very much in favour of the ADST schemes, compared with 72 per cent of non-participants.

With regard to ADST share disposals, a pattern emerged

showing that, whilst relatively few respondents had sold all their shares, more manual employees (15 per cent) compared with the total population (8 per cent) had done so. Only 3 per cent of SAYE participants had disposed of all their shares, compared with 18 per cent of non-participants. A similar pattern emerges with regard to total share retentions.

A picture is beginning to emerge that suggests different orientations and behavioural patterns among different groups towards the ADST share ownership scheme. Manual employees were least likely to retain a large proportion of their share allowance, which would be consistent with their assessment of disposal income at Norbrew, whilst SAYE participants tended to retain higher proportions of their shareholdings. They were also extremely well disposed to the ADST scheme. It appears, therefore, that whilst divergence of view between SAYE participants and non-participants towards the *company* were not readily apparent, the former group did tend to look upon aspects of the ADST scheme rather more positively than non-participants, and particularly appeared to see the scheme as providing an additional benefit in return for their inputs to the company. Perhaps it should be recalled at this stage that SAYE participation was more likely to be associated with white-collar employees, who could not otherwise influence their earnings, and with higher-paid employees, who also received bigger share allowances from the ADST scheme. In other words, the greater the benefit that employees could potentially derive from share ownership schemes the higher their appreciation of them becomes, though it also appears that this appreciation does not necessarily extend to greater understanding of managerial problems, or to loyalty to the company, where opinions of all the groups were broadly similar.

An additional feature of the ADST scheme was that very few employees tended to see their share distribution (3.5 per cent in 1985) as an integral part of pay, nearly half of all survey respondents commenting that their allocation 'makes little difference to pay' and slightly more than half seeing it as nothing more than a 'welcome addition'. These figures showed no great variance between manual employees or SAYE participants. The lack of emphasis on share ownership as part of pay, coupled with interviewees' perceptions of modest pay levels, is reflected in the minor role allotted to the schemes in the process of collective bargaining.

215

CONCLUSION

Norbrew presents us with an interesting example of a company attempting to come to terms with changing conditions. Part of the adjustment process included an adaptation of management style in which earlier paternalistic, even authoritarian traditions were giving way to an integrated approach based on participation, communication, and shared responsibility. The emergent management style was essentially pragmatic in nature and reactive to external stimuli, such as changes in the law, and its participatory intent oriented more to engaging employees' moral attachment than providing a direct financial incentive. In this sense, measurement of the impact of participation and especially of the share ownership schemes is problematic.

According to some narrow criteria of success the outcome of these initiatives is questionable, and indeed is questioned, by some line managers concerned at the lack of direct incentive in the share ownership philosophy. Similarly, 'success' might also be questioned in the attitudes of employees towards the schemes, who by relating to them in opportunistic, bonus-oriented ways resulted in their marginalization in terms of employees' central interests in securing adequate and increasing levels of pay. Or the schemes are seen as divisive in offering greater financial rewards to the higher-paid both through their propensity to participate in the option scheme and through the rewards which accrued to higher-paid participants in both ADST and SAYE programmes. The fact that many of the four-fifths of Norbrew employees who did not participate in the SAYE scheme were in the ranks of the lower-paid could well be a reflection of this divide. Furthermore, both schemes were largely identified by respondents as potential financial supplements offered by management with little apparent reference to the shared ownership/moral attachment paradigm anticipated by the schemes' instigators.

However, it is notoriously difficult to pin labels on employee orientations, and there was substantial evidence to indicate that many employees were positively inclined to the company generally and greeted its participative efforts with overall approval, even if passively expressing dissatisfaction with some aspects of their application. Furthermore, there is little doubt that in behavioural terms relations between Norbrew and its employees displayed little in terms of aggression, instability, or mutual suspicion. Though the contribution made by financial participation to this passive scheme was not quantifiable, it was unlikely to have been negative during a period when participants had enjoyed the compounded benefits of profitable group performance and a rising share price.

11

Thistle: high technology and share ownership

Over a number of years Thistle has expanded to become one of Britain's largest and most successful electronics manufacturers. Under the chairmanship of the son and subsequently the grandson of the founder, the Thistle group now competes in the defence, offshore, and hi-tech sectors as well as the domestic electrical goods markets. However, the company's development has not been without incident, the most significant being in 1975, when what is now described by management as a 'cash-flow' crisis forced Thistle to go to the Labour government for help. After the necessary injection of government cash a new chief executive was appointed. The government retained an active interest in the group through the National Enterprise Board, holding 50 per cent of stock when Thistle went public in 1978.

The National Enterprise Board retained its interest until 1980, when despite trade union and Labour opposition the Thatcher government ordered the government shares to be sold as one of the first stages in the privatization campaign. Although the vast majority of the shares were sold to 'a large number of institutions and pension funds', as part of its commitment to employee share ownership the government allocated 4 per cent for employees, 2 per cent to be purchased and 2 per cent to be 'gifted' on a one-for-one basis. These shares formed the basis of the 'bonus' scheme which has since been superseded by a voluntary SAYE scheme.

In response to increasing specialization within the electronics and defence industries, in 1985 the Thistle Group was restructured into new five trading groups, each specializing in an area of electronics production. During the first half of the 1980s the number of group employees has grown steadily from 18,000 in 1982 to 22,000 in 1986. Much of the increase was made up of

Table 41 Group profits (£ million)

	1982	1983	1984	1985	1986
Turnover	306·9	372·2	451·7	567·9	595·8
Profits before tax	23·8	31·5	38·8	46·0	41·1
Total profits	20·6	29·8	22·3	30·1	28·0

white-collar, highly qualified engineers, with the proportion of staff employees increasing from 58 per cent in 1985 to 61 per cent in 1986, a trend which seems likely to continue in the near future.

Table 41 shows that turnover almost doubled between 1982 and 1986, compared with less dramatic rises in employment and profitability, reflecting the volatile state of the markets in which Thistle operates. Increasing research and development costs, coupled with greater productivity, have led to the industry becoming more capital-intensive. However, the crisis in the world semiconductor industry, the slump in the oil industry, and the fall in Ministry of Defence overseas procurement have all adversely affected the profitability of individual group members, and the trend towards increasing turnover, without a comparable increase in profitability, may act as a warning signal, given the company's earlier experience of a cash-flow crisis. Generally, though, the future of the group seems secure, with healthy order books and a 'wide spread of leading-edge activities' both in the mature electronics industries and in the future-based technologies.

THISTLE OPERATIONS

Our study is based in a large factory belonging to the Scottish member of the Thistle group. Founded during the Second World War to manufacture electronic components for guns, Thistle Operations has remained within the defence industry and now produces a range of surveillance, tracking, and display systems. Thistle Operations was established by the 1985 restructuring and has member factories in several locations in Scotland. Subsidiaries in the US, and licensing and partnership agreements in Japan, India, the Middle and Far East, and throughout NATO account for over 30 per cent of turnover.

In common with the group, a strong emphasis on research and development has led to a large proportion of Thistle Operations

Table 42 Thistle Operations: employees by occupation

Scientists and technologists	869
Technicians	1,595
Skilled	440
Administrative and professional	1,335
Apprentices	336
Others	1,899
Total	6,474
Degree holders	738
HNC/HND	847

employees being highly skilled technical staff (see Table 42). This strong technological orientation makes Thistle one of the area's major employers of skilled engineers and of Scottish university engineering graduates. Several closures in the area have resulted in a pool of skilled labour from which Thistle is continually able to recruit, according to its requirements for hi-tech production, research, and development. Moreover, Thistle is an important source of training, as the number of apprentices currently employed suggests.

A three-tier management structure operates at Thistle. Group management, based in the north of England, is responsible for overall policy formation, while Thistle Operations management, based in Scotland, has responsibility for divisional operations. The managing director of Thistle Operations also sits on the executive committee (although not the main board) of the Thistle group. Plant-level management is responsible for the day-to-day decision-making in each factory.

Industrial relations background

Although Thistle is a high-tech company, its traditional engineering origins are reflected in the presence of a closed shop for both staff and hourly-paid employees. The AEU and Technical and Salaried Staffs' Association (TASS) represent 80 per cent of the work force, although several other unions, most notably the EETPU and GMBATU, also maintain a presence.

The main negotiating body within the division is the Works Council, made up of the senior shop stewards from the various factories in the Thistle Operations group together with similar numbers of management. Although the majority of the stewards are members of the AEU the Expanded Works Council also includes representatives of the other, smaller unions. The Works Council represents the hourly paid employees in the annual round of pay bargaining with Thistle Operations group management. The white-collar staff at Thistle are represented in the main by the AEU and TASS, and the main bargaining committee, the white-collar equivalent of the JSSC, is the Joint Office Committee. Other group committees include the Pensions Committee and the Participation Committee, which is discussed in greater detail below.

As the trade union structure would suggest, industrial relations at Thistle are typical of a traditional engineering establishment, though differences emerge because of the high proportion of staff employees. Industrial relations within the Thistle group have been relatively strike-free: during the last twenty-five years there has been only one major dispute, when a seven-week strike resulted from a breakdown in pay negotiations after the removal of the previous Labour government's incomes policy. Both personnel management and trade union representatives claimed that recent legislation has led to an improvement in the quality of the 'opposite side's' ability to negotiate reasonably. Management suggested that the new legislation regulating trade unions had made them 'easier to deal with' while one trade union representative reported that health and safety legislation had 'professionalized' personnel management.

Being based in the largest factory in the group, many of the senior stewards also represented their members on the Works Council, and therefore at group level. Trade union representatives' views on management both at group and at plant level were that they were 'firm but fair'. As one senior shop steward commented:

> They are seen throughout the whole area as a progressive management in the sense that they have tried to advance their conditions and in the same breath they are not seen as pushovers. They are tough managers. If they make a decision you know that you are going to have a fight on your hands if you want to change it.

Employee participation

During its forty years of production in Scotland Thistle had

221

developed into a high-tech company with all the training, flexibility, and skill requirements typical of a modern electronics company. However, Thistle did not project the popular image of 'Silicon Glen' small-unit production in a non-union setting. Conversely, Thistle was highly unionized and had developed within a traditional engineering industrial relations framework. Not surprisingly, then, employee participation was considered by trade unions and management alike to take place solely along trade union channels.

However, this was not only a product of the company's engineering past: after the 1974 cash injection, as part of a strategy to encourage planning agreements, the Department of Trade and Industry, then under the guidance of Tony Benn, had required that a formal structure of employee participation be set up. This took the form of a three-tiered management/union Participation Committee which still met four or five times annually. An annual two-day conference was also held between management and trade unions.

Although the Participation Committee was still in operation, the annual conferences had been abandoned when Scottish union representatives had refused to attend, much to the disappointment of management. According to the TASS convenor, who was a delegate, the unions felt that it had become a 'jamboree' and preferred not to attend. Interview material suggests that the unions felt that much of the information presented by management, such as annual company reports, was 'out of date before it was published'. In the opinion of many trade union delegates the resultant discussions left little room for productive debate. Thus the commitment of both sides, but particularly the unions, to traditional collective bargaining arrangements had been reinforced.

Nine representatives elected from the trade unions joined a potentially equivalent number of managers for discussions to form the Participation Committee, although the management team seldom reached that number. The committee met at least once every quarter, when they discussed trade results and contract bidding, and spin-off manpower planning meetings often resulted. As one member of the committee described it, 'The main participation meeting tends to concentrate on company results and the company's future activities ... The idea is to get us, without interfering with their management, to know the pitfalls and the problems.' Perhaps the continued existence of this committee can be partially explained by its origins in the crisis of the 1970s, when the employees of Thistle Operations were not informed about the problems the company faced until the crisis had become public. The JSSC convenor explained:

> It [the Participation Committee] was set up after the financial crisis under the remit of a communication vehicle where we could ask the company and they could use it from their side, the main philosophy being that the company would never have serious problems without us [the unions] knowing about it. We had read about the crisis in the papers. We were on holiday at the time and I picked up a paper, 'Thistle Are Closing!' What a shock ... So this committee was set up.

Day-to-day problems were not dealt with by the Participation Committee. These, claimed one member, were dealt with 'through the normal industrial relations set-up'. The Committee was seen both by management and by the trade unions to be a means of communication, of informing trade union representatives about company performance and prospects, but not as means of involving employees in decisions about long-term company policies, their planning and development. In the words of the TASS convenor:

> It has been a useful forum as a means of communication; we are certainly more aware now of corporate strategy and management intentions ... It has also given us a forum where we can speak directly to senior company people, including the managing director of Thistle and the managing director of the group, directly about things that concern us, of things that we want to take issue with. It is not a negotiating forum in any sense and it's not participative in the sense that there is any real dialogue or discussion prior to decisions being made – it's a channel of communication.

However, the Participation Committee was not seen as being completely free of contention, and one trade union representative claimed that both the trade unions and management used the committee to 'square the line with wage settlements' prior to pay discussions. This arrangement appeared to be accepted by both sides, but, as the quotation above demonstrates, such matters did not constitute a major area of the committee's business.

Employee participation at Thistle was therefore formally independent and separate from other industrial relations and negotiating processes in that it was a communications network

223

rather than a joint decision-making process, yet it was paradoxically inseparable from these processes in that it was trade union-based. Trade unions and management both approached employee participation in terms of 'participating in the company's information system' but not to any extent in the company decision-making. The other, perhaps more substantive, strand of employee participation was recognized as being through the trade unions via traditional collective bargaining arrangements. As one trade union member said of the committee, 'At the end of the day they make it clear that they are managing the company and we respond in criticism or whatever, but they manage the company and we accept that.'

FINANCIAL PARTICIPATION: STRUCTURE AND ORIGINS

In July 1980, acting on government instructions, the NEB put its 50 per cent holding in Thistle on to the market. Four per cent of these shares were made available to Thistle employees, 2 per cent to be offered for purchase, with the remaining 2 per cent to be used to match those bought by employees on a one-for-one basis. In October 1981 the company also initiated an SAYE scheme which has offered options annually ever since.

The original bonus scheme offered options on just two occasions. The first offer, of 853,332 NEB shares, attracted 3,355 (around one in five) employees, and the second option offered the remaining 318,412 shares in April 1982. The bonus shares were subject to Inland Revenue approval, deferment, and tax relief in much the same way as ADST schemes although the Thistle shares were not a 'profit share' in the usual sense. Perhaps because of the unique nature of the bonus scheme, the company had some problems in securing Inland Revenue approval. As one manager described it the Revenue were so slow that company representatives had to go in person to Bootle on Merseyside and solicit approval. As he expanded:

> If something is not right, the Revenue write you a letter, and when you answer it they get out a file and deal with it. They have a stack of papers; yours is on top, and there is a query; a letter goes off, and that file goes down to the bottom, and it doesn't get dealt with until it comes back to the top.

Following their initial approval of the scheme, the manager felt that the Revenue had been involved with the scheme 'only in an obstructive way'. Any changes which the company wished to make had had to go through a prolonged, laborious process. For instance, the rules laid down by the Revenue for the SAYE scheme had stated that in the event of withdrawal from the company for whatever reason e.g. redundancy, retirement, dismissal, or voluntary severance – the company must apply one uniform policy – either all leavers could exercise their options, or none at all. The company could choose either alternative but could not discriminate between reasons for leaving. Thistle had chosen not to allow leavers to exercise their options but felt that it was unfair not to discriminate between voluntary and involuntary leavers. By chance Thistle had found out that the Inland Revenue had changed the guidelines (the Inland Revenue did not inform them) and proceeded to try to change its own scheme:

> Most changes of a significant nature have to have shareholders' approval and Revenue approval. That was one that needed the approval of the option holders, the approval of the shareholders, and the approval of the Revenue. The option holders agreed, the shareholders agreed, and then the Revenue said no. [Eventually Thistle did get Revenue approval.]

Obviously Thistle had the resources necessary to complete the processes involved in gaining Revenue approval, initially for the schemes themselves and subsequently for any changes they might want to make. Yet Thistle's difficulties may help to explain the relative scarcity of Inland Revenue-approved employee share ownership schemes in smaller companies. Also, the complexities involved in changing aspects of existing schemes will have implications for employee consultation about schemes both before and after implementation, particularly as few schemes (and in this Thistle is an exception) are consulted over before approval (see Chapter 4).

Thistle management looked around for ideas for administering its schemes and, using an idea borrowed from BP, developed the idea of the 'co-ordinator network' where middle managers, not usually involved in personnel or industrial relations issues, were made responsible for publicizing and administering the schemes, and for giving guidance and advice to employees. These co-ordinators were to be unpaid and 'user-friendly', and the network appears to have been reasonably successful in that it was still in operation. Our discussion draws on interviews with the two original co-ordinators at the Thistle plant – one with a legal, commercial background, the other in quality assurance – who still administer the scheme in their areas.

EMPLOYEES, UNIONS AND THE NEB OFFER

In spite of the enticement of free shares and tax relief on their sale after the prescribed interval, only 3,500 (around 17 per cent) of Thistle Group employees and a similar proportion of Thistle Operations employees took up the NEB offer and bought shares. A number of possible reasons emerged from the interview programme.

As the first in a series of privatizations the Thistle offer was made to employees, most of whom had little or no knowledge of share ownership. As one employee explained, '...shares were like computers in those days. I knew nothing about them in those days, before all these other share schemes came out. Shares were things that frightened people off because we didn't know anything about them.' In discussing the progress of the SAYE scheme later an examination will be undertaken of the extent to which subsequent popular privatizations combined with regular SAYE scheme offers have increased the levels of knowledge and awareness of share ownership amongst employees.

The company had recently emerged from a 'partnership' with the NEB which had risen out of the 1975 crisis. The bonus scheme did not have the safeguards of the SAYE scheme in that, once employees were committed to buying shares, they could not withdraw if the share price fell. As one employee described it, 'We started talking about Thistle shares on the back of a crisis ... we're talking about investment in a company which was bouncing all over the place a few years ago.' So, at that time, confidence in the company had yet to be re-established in the wake of the financial troubles of the 1970s. Furthermore, many employees did not have the disposable cash available, as, even with the one-for-one offer, employees still had to buy shares outright. Although one of the major banks offered loans on favourable terms many employees did not want to get into debt in order to finance what they considered a risky venture.

The trade unions opposed the scheme and advised their members not to participate. They had campaigned against the sale of the NEB shares and could not be seen to be sanctioning the sale of shares to Thistle employees. As a senior steward described it:

> Our trade union stance was seen to be: Well, we were not standing in everybody's way, but we weren't touting company shares around. Therefore we took this stance that employees should be discouraged, not in a terribly hard way. We were saying, 'If it's a head-or-tails decision, don't buy them.'

The trade unions had reacted in this way both for ideological and for practical reasons. Apart from their opposition to the sale of government shares in principle, the unions refused to participate in the bonus scheme as trustees through the Participation Committee as they 'did not want to become custodians of other people's money'. Also, trade union representatives were influenced by the 'all the eggs in one basket' argument, as the current JSSC convenor explained,

> Looking at it in cold blood, it was a good deal, so in my opinion people either were sensitive to expose themselves too much or they couldn't afford to. It all came to a thousand pounds – a thousand pounds that you could either lose or have tied up for a very long time.

On a personal level the trade union representatives interviewed expressed their doubts about share ownership in general:

> To look at an up-to-date example, look at what happened at Guinness. It's just not the sort of thing I would be comfortable with. I'm being two-faced because I'm handing my money over to a building society which goes into the market for me, so I'm getting the benefits without the exposure, but I certainly would not consider the direct buying of shares. I'm talking about a take-home pay of £100–£150 per week – there is not much left over to gamble with.

Yet employees who did participate in the bonus schemes had subsequently made a substantial profit. In the words of one financial manager:

> It [the scheme] seemed like a licence to print money, if all went well ... I am only surprised that more people did not take it up.

Looking at the bodies involved, I was really surprised about how few there were from the shop floor. Maybe I shouldn't have been, because the unions had been a bit hostile initially – I think probably still are – to the whole concept – probably through lack of knowledge and through political bias, perhaps.

The possible reasons behind the different levels in staff/shop-floor take-up of the SAYE and bonus schemes are discussed at a later stage. However, several of the employees interviewed did express their regret at having taken the union's advice, given the financial success of the scheme, and this does present the unions with a dilemma. Should a scheme which unions have advised their members not to join fail, owing to ailing company fortunes, few employees will congratulate their unions on their foresight, yet if a scheme is financially successful, as in the case of Thistle, union members may feel that they have lost out by taking their union's advice.

After refusing to negotiate over the original bonus schemes the trade unions never became involved with either type of scheme, although they did not actively oppose their members' involvement. This resulted in the employee share ownership schemes becoming the exception in terms of employee participation, for as we discussed earlier, both the company and the trade unions accepted that in every other case employee participation was approached through the trade unions. The implications for the future development of employee share ownership at Thistle are taken up below.

AFTER THE NEB: THE SAYE SCHEME

The bonus scheme never became a fully fledged ADST profit-sharing scheme once the NEB allocation of shares had been sold. The administrator suggested that the bonus scheme was 'Basically a government scheme – it was their shares that they were actually dealing with.' It seems clear that the company had instituted the bonus schemes under pressure from the government and was not committed to maintaining this type of scheme. Again in the words of the current scheme administrator,

I don't think they particularly wanted to repeat the bonus scheme in a similar format. They were government shares through the

NEB. Whoever was around at the time decided that it would be better if employees paid some money towards the shares.

Instead the company turned to a voluntary SAYE scheme, which, according to the scheme administrator, was relatively easy to run and almost paid for itself in options exercised by employees as their schemes matured. The only on-going administrative problem was that the holiday, sick-pay, etc., arrangements of hourly paid participants made adjustments necessary to their SAYE contributions, while on the other hand salaried employees' monthly income was constant and not affected by these variable factors.

Management objectives: 'Greed keeps them enthusiastic'

Management interview material at both plant and head-office level at Thistle suggested that the SAYE scheme was operated primarily as a service to employees and that, although any 'spin-off' benefits like increased commitment would be welcomed, they were not expected. As the scheme administrator explained:

> When we fill in surveys with questions like 'Do you think the operation of the scheme has improved ties between employees and the company?' we always say no because we don't think it does, really. We don't think it has any significant effect on people, what we produce. I think it certainly gives them a better feeling, be it only from greed. They have a closer tie with the company and maybe they look at the share price in the paper once every six months.

It appears, therefore, that Thistle management did not expect noticeable improvements in productivity or turnover as a direct result of the employee share ownership scheme. Rather it was seen as part of a 'package' of conditions of employment which together might be necessary to attract and retain key staff but which on its own could not be expected to be very effective.

Employee take-up

Since the first SAYE offer, in October 1981, employees had been invited to join once each year and, in spite of fluctuating share

229

Table 43 Thistle SAYE scheme: share prices, number of employees participating and number of new participants

Date	Invitation	Subscription price*	No. of participants	No. of new participants
26 October 1981	1	45p	1,130	
9 February 1983	2	84p	849	582
2 February 1984	3	114p	1,038	675
31 January 1985	4	152p	1,901	1,102
31 January 1986	5	132p	1,404	612
30 January 1987	6	90p	2,818	1,562

*Share prices under the company's SAYE scheme are at a 10% discount on the market price.
Note: subscription prices have been adjusted to take account of a two-for-one capitalization issue on 28 February 1982 and a five-for-one subdivision on 17 September 1984.

prices, interest in the scheme had remained steady, with around 20 per cent of all Thistle Group employees opting to join. Around the same proportion of employees in our Thistle Operations plant participated. By October 1986 there were 3,139 employee shareholders in the Thistle Group, holding a total of 6,040,173 shares (1.3 per cent of the total) between them. This suggests that, six years after the NEB allocation of 4 per cent of total stock to employees, less than half the allocation was employee-owned. As Table 43 shows, there had been fluctuations in the number of employees joining the scheme each year, although the level of new employee participation appears to have been increasing. The high figure of new entrants for the year 1987 is due in part to the low price of shares, to employees who had completed the first option rejoining, and to employees dropping out of previous, less lucrative schemes in order to join this more promising one. The high figure of 1,901 participants for the 1985 option puzzled scheme organizers, as the price of shares was exceptionally high for that offer and therefore less likely to make a profit for the participant. The scheme administrator suggested that:

> Since the advertising on TV for British Telecom, British Gas, etc., there has been an increase in people applying for the share ownership scheme. In 1984 we had the British Telecom privatization, adverts on television, everybody became more

230

aware, and in the scheme we had after that, in 1985, we had 1,900 people wanting to join, whereas the year before it was only 1,100.

In spite of its initial popularity 575 employees had since withdrawn from the 1985 scheme. Both management and employees agreed that the main reason was that subsequent schemes offered greater financial benefits – for instance, the last option price of 90p was 62p lower that the 1985 offer. As one employee remarked:

This year is better than the last two years. That is another thing that I've thought about. One of the guys, he cashed in his last two schemes in order to put all his money into this one. He started when the shares were at £1.50; now he can get them for 90p.

Table 44 SAYE participation: staff/hourly-paid breakdown

Date of scheme	1981 No.	%	1983 No.	%	1984 No.	%	1985 No.	%	1986* No.	%
Staff	950	84	707	83	944	91	1,668	88	1,207	86
Hourly paid	180	16	142	17	125	9	233	12	197	14
Total	1,130	100	849	100	1,069	100	1,901	100	1,404	100

*Figures not available for 1987.

Although the overall rate of participation was increasing, throughout the operation of the SAYE scheme the participation of hourly-paid employees had been consistently lower than for that of staff. Factors such as relative levels of disposable income, knowledge and understanding of share ownership, working versus middle-class ideologies, and trade union attitudes may have combined to produce particular patterns of participation in voluntary schemes. We have already considered one manager's view that trade union opposition to the SAYE scheme at Thistle might have affected hourly-paid participation, and another Thistle Group head office manager suggested that 'It takes a bit more convincing for them' (the hourly-paid) 'to see the light, whereas people who are monthly paid, salaried staff seem to be more greedy. They realise the avarice aspect more quickly than the hourly-paid do.'

EMPLOYEE ATTITUDES

In order to examine employee attitudes to share ownership more closely at Thistle, management and trade union interviews were supplemented by a series of interviews with employees and by a questionnaire programmes. In December 1986, 300 questionnaires were distributed to a random sample of the Thistle plant's 2,000 employees, 50 per cent to scheme participants and 50 per cent to non-participants. The sample was selected using Thistle pay-roll computing facilities, and questionnaires were distributed to employees at the plant. This was followed by a series of in-depth interviews with employees.

Of the 300 questionnaires distributed, 180 were returned using the Freepost envelopes provided, a high response rate of 60 per cent. However, the responses were skewed towards scheme participation and towards non-manual grades. While only one in five of the factory employees was in the SAYE scheme, 50 per cent of the initial sample and 53 per cent of those responding were participants. Of the 180 respondents only 55 (31 per cent) were in manual grades, a much lower level than for the factory as a whole.

Thistle was seen by most respondents (75 per cent), whether they were scheme participants or not, as being an above-average company to work for. Disaggregated into different aspects of their work situation, the responses were as shown in Table 45. In terms of pay and job security, employees appeared to be satisfied. This is likely to have been in part a reflection of the depressed condition of employment in the district and of the company's success in securing valuable contracts. Interview material also suggested that many Thistle employees believed that the 'government would never let us close', an attitude which was partially born out of memories of the 1974 government rescue and of a recognition of the devastating effects which closure would have on the area.

In contrast, the respondents were generally less positive about their opportunities for promotion ('chances to get on'), management/employee communications ('management openness'), and employee participation. Thirty-eight per cent of the respondents indicated that they were not happy about the career structures and processes at Thistle, and this was reinforced by comments in the questionnaires. One young member of the technical staff complained:

Table 45 Employees' views of Thistle relative to other employers (%)

Rating	Pay	Management openness	Management skill	Chances to get on	Job security	Employee participation
Well above average	2	0	7	3	44	6
Above average	52	7	17	22	41	6
Average	39	46	52	37	14	42
Below average	4	28	16	25	1	22
Well below average	1	17	6	12	0	30

> My opinions are based on my belief that the company has no interest in me because of its size and its organisational methods, that it is still living in the age of promotion through dead man's shoes and promotion of incompetence.

All but a small minority of respondents indicated that Thistle management was average or below in terms of its 'openness' towards employees, while more that 50 per cent of all the respondents replied that Thistle was below average in the level to which employees participated in the company. One respondent commented

> This is a large company. The management are largely employees. The influential decisions are taken by directors. The trade union officials discourage their members from talking to management/directors. The personnel managers discourage directors from talking to the work force. There is therefore no direct interchange between work force and directors.

Although Thistle was a mature firm which had developed traditional engineering organizational structures and industrial relations processes, with an emphasis on trade union channels for employees participation and information dissemination, employees were aware of the very different conditions found in other hi-tech companies in the area. It is not clear from the pattern of responses (manual employees' responses were similar to those of the sample as a whole) whether employees felt that the trade unions should develop a more proactive approach to 'participation' through the Participation Committee, and other channels, or whether employees were looking to other, non-union, forms of employee participation.

In more general terms respondents indicated that relations between management and employees at Thistle were more consensual than for Britain as a whole (23 per cent believed that 'Management and employees are on opposite sides' in Britain but only 9 per cent thought so of Thistle), and this was supported by their views on trade union power, with 33 per cent replying that the unions had too much power in Britain but only 7 per cent suggesting that it was true of Thistle. Conversely, the figure for 'Too little power' were similar – 21 per cent for Britain and 23 per cent for Thistle – while in both cases a majority thought the situation was 'about right'.

The views of participants

If share ownership does influence employee attitudes or, as Thistle and other management interviewed suggest, voluntary schemes like Thistle's reinforce commitment where it already exists, the responses of participating employees could be expected to reflect those effects. However, for the most part both participants' and non-participants' responses to our questions about management/employee relations were similar, and in certain aspects some participating employees were, if anything, more critical of management than non-participants, most markedly for 'employee participation'. This may have been indicative of a greater interest in and awareness of the company's performance but may also suggest that Thistle employees did not consider the opportunity to participate, or participation in their share ownership scheme, to be participation in the company. This leads to the key question why employees were interested in participating in the SAYE scheme. Consistent with the impression developed through interview material, Thistle employees appeared to be primarily interested in the SAYE scheme for financial reasons, as shown in Fig. 6.

Participating employees were asked to rank their motives for joining the SAYE scheme in order of importance. The reasons indicated can be divided into 'soft' and 'hard' groups, the 'A stake in the company' and 'Participation in the company's future' being 'soft', attitude-related variables and 'Easy way of saving', 'No risk involved', and 'Financial rewards' being 'hard', financially based motivators. 'An easy way of buying shares' is less easily defined, as the motivation for the purchase could fall into either of the above categories. Although the multiple choices possible in the question may have led to an exaggeration of the importance placed on each variable, the 'hard', financially based variables appeared to be most popular. Most (fifty-six) respondents felt that the absence of risk was very important – a significant finding, given that only the SAYE scheme gave the participant a choice between cash or shares – but the other financially based variables were also popular. Forty respondents felt that 'participation in the company's future, and thirty-two that 'gaining a stake in the company', was either not important in their decision to participate, or had not been considered at all. Responses to 'an easy way of buying shares' tended to be more disparate.

The responses of participants suggested that while the 'hard' variables were all judged to be important motivators for

235

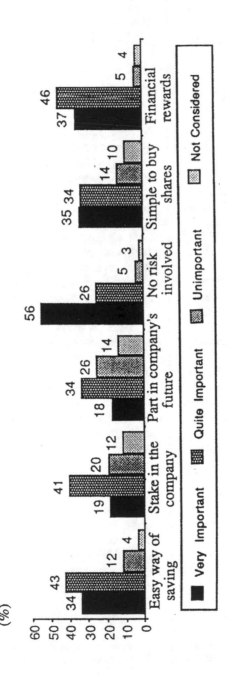

Figure 6 Motives for participation in SAYE: Thistle

participation, views were much more widely scattered for the 'soft' variables. However, substantial, if smaller, proportions of participants did indicate that the 'soft' variables had influenced their decision, and this would support the 'SAYE as a reinforcer' theory discussed earlier.

The views of non-participants

Non-participants were asked to give their reasons for not joining the SAYE scheme, and again financial variables appear to have been most influential, as illustrated in Fig. 7. 'Can't afford to participate' was the most commonly stated reason, with 'Didn't know enough about it' following. The latter may have resulted from the relatively low level of publicity given to previous schemes, and the most recent scheme, which had been much more widely publicised, appeared to have remedied this lack of knowledge to some extent. Few respondents thought the scheme 'Too risky', which is not surprising, given the structure of SAYE schemes; few felt that the minimum five years were too long to save, and a similarly small number felt that 'shareholding was not for them'. Only two respondents indicated that they had not participated for political or ideological reasons, again suggesting that the decision to participate or not seems to be made on pragmatic rather than ideological grounds.

Three-quarters of the non-participating respondents indicated that they did not intend to participate in the SAYE scheme in the future, perhaps suggesting that the scheme had been successful in attracting the majority of employees willing to consider joining an SAYE scheme. This scheme may therefore have been reaching saturation level in terms of the proportion of employees participating.

As Fig. 8 demonstrates, in our sample no significant difference emerged between hourly paid and salaried staff participation in the SAYE scheme; indeed, at some levels of pay a smaller proportion of salaried than hourly paid employees were participating in the scheme. As the company could not provide separate statistics for the factory featured in this study, a higher proportion of weekly employees may have been participating here than for the company as a whole. However, as discussed earlier, hourly-paid participation in the scheme for the whole company was much lower than for staff, and the trend for both groups was towards higher levels of

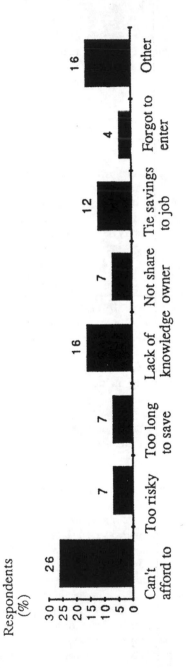

Figure 7 Reasons for non-participation in SAVE: Thistle

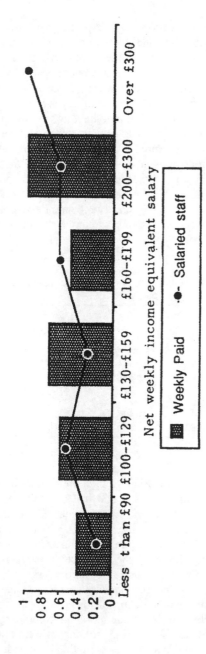

Figure 8 Percentage participating in SAYE: staff and weekly-paid, Thistle

participation at higher pay levels. One explanation of this takes the amount of disposable income available to each group into consideration; however, if pay levels, and therefore arguably disposable income, are a powerful determinant of participation, one would expect to find larger proportions of respondents in the lower pay categories indicating that they could not afford to enter the scheme. Table 46 shows that, although the numbers involved were limited, there was some evidence to suggest that at both the highest and the lowest wage levels more respondents 'couldn't afford to' participate. This pattern may have been influenced by factors such as competing priorities for disposable income and the possibility that many 'low' earners were female clerical employees perceived as providing 'second' sources of family income. Levels of income did not appear to govern the responses to any of the questions why respondents did not participate.

Table 46 Employees' reasons for non-participation in SAYE: couldn't afford to participate

	Yes		No	
Pay level	No.	%	No.	%
Very low	9	50	9	50
Low	5	33	10	67
Average	5	19	21	81
High	3	27	8	73
Very high	4	40	6	60
Total	26	33	54	67

Finally, participants were asked to give their views both on the scheme itself and on the effects it had had on their approach to work. The findings are shown in Fig. 9. Again the statements fall into two general categories: those dealing with employees' attitudes to work and to the company, and those dealing with pay and financial rewards. Many of the responses re-emphasized the points raised in our discussion of motivators for scheme participation. Relatively few respondents agreed that the scheme had made them more aware of the problems faced by management, that it had enabled them to participate more in the company, or that they were more likely to notice if their colleagues were not pulling their weight. More popular responses were that participants 'can't

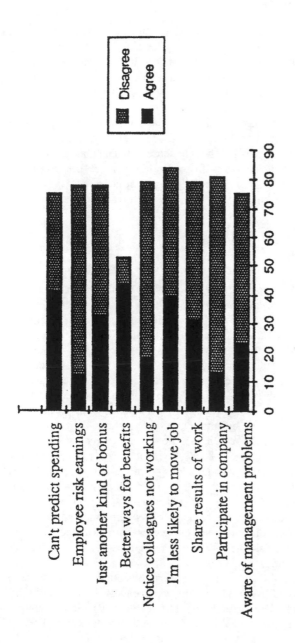

Figure 9 Employees' views on the SAYE scheme: Thistle

plan spending' (as they could not predict the final bonus'); that there were better ways of improving benefits, and that participants were less likely to move to another job (the 'golden handcuff'?). Understandably, few respondents agreed that the scheme was 'too risky', given the option of shares or cash plus bonus offered by the SAYE scheme.

Only ten respondents had joined the scheme in 1981 and were therefore already in a position to decide in what way to take up their option. Six employees had bought shares, two had taken cash, and two had left their money with the building society for two more years. Given the greater financial gains possible from taking shares, it seems surprising that any of the participants chose the cash options.

CONCLUSION

At Thistle Operations employee share ownership had developed in ways which were at once a product of the company's recent history and development and which were also a result not directly of management and trade union strategies but of general attitudes to employee participation and share ownership. In the SAYE scheme Thistle management recognized a means of providing an inexpensive service for employees in an industry where there was still a demand for skilled labour, yet which did not entail a 'profit-sharing element', and which was voluntary, demanding some financial commitment by employees participating. The rewards for management were indirect, in that the scheme was envisaged as one element in a package of employment incentives, while for employees the scheme, although long-term, made saving easier and could potentially yield a substantial profit. Although interview and questionnaire evidence suggested that the scheme might to some extent reinforce employee commitment where it already existed, both management and employees agreed that it was the financial elements in the scheme which made it attractive, and in this the scheme was currently successful.

Personal, political, and ideological objections to the scheme were expressed by trade union representatives but rarely by respondents to the questionnaire, although the skew in our sample towards participants would have lowered the probability of finding substantial numbers of 'conscientious objectors'. The decision to participate or not was most commonly made on financial grounds.

This is not to say that attitudinal factors were not involved in the decision; however, the evidence here suggested that they were incidental, both for management and for employees.

12

Financial participation in practice: an overview

In this chapter we draw together the findings from the various case studies and use the comparative information to address some of the questions raised in Chapter 6. Each case study on its own tells a specific story: taken together, the case studies allow a perspective to emerge, in which the particular environment and characteristics of the individual company are reduced in scale, and the differences and similarities across companies are more in evidence. We follow the structure set by Chapter 6, looking in turn at management objectives, trade union responses and consequences for collective relationships, and individual employee reaction.

MANAGEMENT OBJECTIVES

From the survey evidence reported earlier (Chapter 4) we formed the initial impression that companies commonly run more than one scheme of financial participation, and that the scheme(s) they operate are usually regarded by management as having multiple objectives. While a few respondents were highly selective in relating objectives to their scheme, many others checked virtually all items on our questionnaire list, which might imply at best that they had only a very general sense of what they were trying to achieve through the schemes. However, we cannot be sure of this, since our survey did not allow us to discriminate between the objectives envisaged for different schemes, and rational managements could well have exercised a choice to provide a complementary coverage of the whole range of aims.

Some schemes are discretionary or selective in employee coverage, which suggests that they may be chosen for quite specific reasons e.g. to attract or retain key groups of staff. More than one scheme may be needed if different groups of staff, with different needs and characteristics, are to be brought within the fold of participation.

The case studies indicate in fair measure the variety of objectives associated with the introduction of financial participation schemes and the diversity of management strategies delineated in Chapter 5. At one extreme we had Thistle, which operated two schemes, one which was really not of its choosing (and therefore did not represent a true managerial selection from the menu), and another (SAYE) which was operated mainly 'as a service to employees' without any positive benefits being expected or looked for by management. The most that could be said in this case was that the SAYE scheme formed part of the package of employment conditions offered by the company, and at the margin this might be a factor in the attraction or retention of employees.

But Thistle was by no means alone in not having explicit objectives: indeed, our case studies suggest strongly that this is the norm, although Thistle was exceptional in the view it took. At Fairbrush the objectives reflected a unitarist mode of thought, but with a strong and apparently pervasive ethical overtone, in that it was seen as a moral obligation that employees should share in profits, and no other objectives were specified. Goodbake and Norbrew were more able to see their schemes in relation to particular objectives, but nevertheless represented their SAYE and ADST schemes respectively in much more general terms. Thus Goodbake emphasized the 'concept of commonwealth', an attempt to narrow the area of conflict within a pluralist framework, while Norbrew viewed its scheme as part of a broad package of employee involvement concerned to enhance employee commitment and loyalty. Bossguide, finally, operated two discretionary schemes outside the Inland Revenue guidelines for taxation benefits, and regarded them as covering the whole range of objectives for adopting financial participation. But even here the sense that emerges is that the specific schemes evolved from a policy which was firmly rooted in a unitarist framework: that policy did, however, establish an explicit link between the profit and share ownership schemes and employee commitment to profitability – and that is as near to a specific objective as any of our case studies displays.

With the partial exception of Goodbake, there was a strong sense of unitary thinking, in which share ownership (and probably to a

245

lesser extent profit-sharing) was seen as reinforcing employee loyalty and commitment. In none of the cases did there appear to be any systematic attempt to measure the benefits of the schemes from the company's point of view, which is at least consistent with the lack of clear, single-targeted objectives. In Goodbake, for example, no concrete results were looked for, but in a sense there was a long-term expectation that attitudinal adjustment would 'drip through'. At Norbrew attitudes were again highlighted, but motivation to increased productivity or profitability was not a dominant feature.

Not surprisingly, in view of the analysis in Chapter 5, there was a fairly strong line of paternalism running through the case-study companies, which was allied to the unitarist philosophy. This would certainly seem to have been the case with Fairbrush, Norbrew, and Bossguide, and perhaps Goodbake, even though the latter had some pluralist tendencies; the other case (Thistle) perhaps fitted best into the sophisticated modern pattern, in which financial participation is seen as part of the range of management techniques designed to produce healthy industrial relations. However, although there appeared to be a fairly strong unitarist-paternalist line running through a majority of cases, some caution is required in the use of such labels, especially in multi-divisional, complex organizations. For, as Purcell and Gray (1986) has argued, 'the possibility must be allowed for that there is no one dominant belief system in the preferred way of dealing with employees nor any concerted attempt to develop one'.

Even where a clear policy is apparent at one level, there may be reasons why it is not followed through consistently in separate divisions with different market or operating circumstances, or at different levels in the organization. Our evidence would tend to support this view, particularly at Goodbake and its constituents. Thus although the concept of commonwealth is evidently pluralist, other views were expressed which were much more unitarist in outlook.

A different approach arises from the question how far the schemes represent a bandwagon effect (cf. Chapter 6, pp. 117–18). With the exception of Thistle, the evidence of our case studies is that this was not at all the case, though we recognise that they may not be typical. The roots of the financial participation schemes were in some cases long established, and in general there was little evidence of the pursuit by management of a temporarily fashionable or tax-beneficial opportunity. There was, conversely, support for the idea that financial participation was generally in line with the overall management style and strategy. What was observable, however, was that companies did not necessarily have what might be regarded as the most appropriate scheme for their purposes. Goodbake probably had the 'wrong' scheme (SAYE) for their purpose of 'commonwealth' (which would seem to imply a commonwealth of 'primary' employees from which certain categories would be excluded) but chose their scheme for its ease of introduction. A similar consideration applied to Bossguide, which had difficulties fitting into 'approved' scheme formats and went its own way.

UNION REACTIONS

The most significant conclusion from the case-study evidence on union representative reaction to financial participation was the virtual absence of any substantial response. The cases ranged from the closed-shop extreme in Thistle, where the trade unions were strongly established in a quite typical engineering industry structure, to the non-union case at Bossguide. The strongest reaction came at Thistle, where the unions were opposed to the sale of shares generated by the government's initiative, and refused to participate as trustees. But this was an unusual case in a number of ways, and the initial (government) scheme was of a different genre from most of the others we encountered in the study as a whole. Opposition may well have been as much a politically motivated demonstration of dislike as an aversion to financial participation as a matter of policy or trade union principle. The later SAYE scheme, in contrast, appears to have been received more neutrally, with the unions recognizing that they were in a 'no win' situation. If the share scheme proved to be profitable for those who participated, active union opposition which inhibited members from joining in the scheme might rebound on the union itself. If they supported it, they would appear to have had little opportunity to influence the scheme, which would tend to be viewed as a management initiative. Thus, so long as the scheme did not get in the way of union–member relations, the best ploy for the union might be to maintain a neutral stance. This appeared also to have been the case at Goodbake, where only one of the union representatives interviewed was a participant, but in general the unions were content to leave individuals to make up their own minds. However, it was notable in the Breadline case, where there was no cash-based bonus scheme like that at Scotcake, that there had been union pressure to introduce such a scheme, if without success. This might suggest that, where the form of financial involvement is in a cash-equivalent form more closely related to the usual wage-reward concept, unions will be more likely to show a positive interest.

Nor was it clear that there was a strong sense, among union representatives, of their official union policy on profit-sharing and share ownership schemes, though there were certainly traces, as at Thistle, of union concern about employees having all their eggs in one basket – both wage expectations and share values being dependent on a single company. But there was no evidence in our cases of a strong line against financial participation being passed down from union headquarters to workplace representatives: not surprisingly, perhaps, in view of the relative paucity of clear union orientation on this issue.

The general sense of union representative reaction, then, is not dissimilar from that of the union movement as a whole: neutrality at best, a bored hostility at worst, but even the latter not taking on a high profile such as to make the operation of any scheme difficult for management. Views on financial participation did not seem to determine perceptions of management, which could range from respect for generally firm, even tough, but fair management to gloom and alarm about management's ability to maintain a viable concern. At Fairbrush, for example, the efforts to develop participation, quite genuinely, were not matched by employee or union approval, and management was not regarded as either particularly competent or particularly participative. It is just as though the arrangements for financial participation were on a different plane from that on which the unions normally operate – the plane which links unions with management, on the one hand, and union leadership with the rank and file on the other. Financial participation schemes in general (though perhaps not the cash-based bonus scheme) did not appear to be perceived as cutting across this plane, and were therefore of little concern to the unions. However, confirmation of that view will also depend on the extent to which profit-sharing and share ownership schemes interact with more general industrial relations processes, to which we now turn.

INTERACTION WITH OTHER INDUSTRIAL RELATIONS
PRACTICES AND PROCEDURES

The overwhelming evidence of our case studies was that financial participation schemes are operated quite independently of the normal run of industrial relations. In Chapter 6, introducing the case studies, we identified three areas where some interaction effect might have been observed: negotiation, consultation, and communications.

So far as collective bargaining is concerned, the conclusion is almost entirely negative. In no case was the introduction of the scheme the subject of bargaining, and although the union representatives may have been at best neutral and occasionally antagonistic or unsympathetic, it seems generally to have been accepted that it was for management to decide to introduce a scheme and to select the kind of scheme it wanted. The unions stayed aloof from the process.

Once the scheme was in operation there was likewise comparatively little evidence of interaction, at first sight. At Thistle, for example, the share and SAYE schemes were formally separate from other industrial relations procedures, and the administration was in the hands of managers who were not personnel or industrial relations specialists. In the Norbrew case there was little acknowledged effect on discussions in the Brewery Council. Closer inspection, however, suggests that there may have been some slender link. Bossguide, operating without unions or staff association, determined pay on a performance rating basis but conceded that, although the profit-sharing bonus was independent in theory, the practical exercise of management discretion involved consideration of the whole management employment package offered to employees, including the profit-share component. Some traces of a similar disposition may be detected at Norbrew, where work-force opinion appeared to be that the company did not pay the going local rate for the types of job concerned, and just conceivably this might have reflected a company view of the total remuneration package. At least the danger of such an effect was picked up at Scotcake, where the cash bonus was seen as possibly detracting from the annual pay negotiations, which were expected to concentrate on basic pay increases, and where there was a fear that aspects of pay might become non-negotiable (as indeed had happened as a result of management separating the bonus scheme from basic pay negotiations despite union opposition). Thus although formally there is an absence of linkage between financial participation schemes and pay bargaining, at an informal level the association is at least understood, and the prospect of a profit share or capital gain may be a factor underlying normal wage negotiations. On the whole, however, the conclusion must be that collective bargaining does not touch directly on the profit-sharing and share ownership territory to any significant degree.

When we turn to consultation, we should not be surprised to find that the case-study companies in general had a strong commitment to consultative machinery, even though it did not always produce the expected results, as was particularly true of Fairbrush. Despite this, however, there was little sign that the regular machinery had any significant involvement with financial participation. Nevertheless, the Norbrew case illustrated changes in the coverage of the SAYE scheme as a result of representations made through the negotiating machinery. These led to the scheme being extended to part-time employees. And there was a further attempt to achieve change in the basis of calculation, which the white-collar staff thought was unfavourable to them – again through the same machinery, but this time without effect. And again, at Goodbake, the extension of the scheme to part-timers was derived through consultative processes from the initiatives of the part-timers themselves, not through the union. However, it seems to be the rule that financial participation does not have much, if anything, in the way of routines for involving employees: it is the company's scheme, and to a large extent it is managerial discretion that rules the day. At Goodbake, for example, the SAYE scheme could have been raised through consultative mechanisms but rarely featured. In the words of a personnel director, 'The SAYE scheme ... is almost exempt from participation. There is no consultation over the share price. It doesn't fall into the general participative philosophy.'

On the third front, communications, the evidence suggests that a wide variety of methods are used to convey information about the schemes. Although none of our case study companies had videos, a number of companies in which we conducted a second-stage interview had adopted this technique. In-house magazines or newspapers, either at company or at divisional level, would feature the schemes. Scotcake included reference to its company scheme in the weekly Factory Brief at appropriate times and made use of factory notice boards. Oral briefing through briefing groups and the like appeared quite commonly, particularly in some of the smaller, more closely knit kinds of organization (e.g. financial services, advertising, publishing), such as Bossguide, where small size and an integrative approach allowed considerable openness. However, the emphasis here again tended very much to be management communicating to employees, with little formal response from less senior employees, further emphasizing the general conclusion that the thrust derived from higher levels of management.

The conclusion must be that whether or not profit-sharing and share ownership schemes are formally separate from the normal industrial relations procedures, as at the Thistle group, they are well insulated in practice. The regular machinery for negotiation and consultation is collective, and it may be significant that financial participation, as a voluntary option for employees, is kept apart. Management discretion is quite fundamental to profit-sharing and share ownership schemes, within a set of rules which is essentially determined by management (often within legal provisions). It may then reflect a strategic decision by managements to keep it that way, rather than incorporate it into the collective machinery – a strategy which has been made easy to sustain, given the unions' general tendency to regard such schemes with indifference and mild hostility.

This separation is all the more surprising since virtually all the wage bargaining in the case-study companies was conducted on a company or workplace level, which ought in principle to make it easier to integrate financial participation into a well developed company strategy for pay as a whole. Although as we have seen there is some suggestion that managements may take all the elements of remuneration into account in determining or negotiating a competitive wage or salary, the processes of determination emerge as quite distinct. Only in one case (Norbrew) did a senior manager express regret over the separation because this separation was seen as underlining the divisiveness which the participation scheme was designed to reduce; whilst at Scotcake, although the unions had never tried to negotiate, there were signs that management would have been prepared to re-examine the eligibility conditions, if challenged.

EMPLOYEE MOTIVATION AND ATTITUDES

As earlier explained, in each of the case-study companies arrangements were made to distribute questionnaires to the whole or part of the employees of the company or workplace, whether or not they were participants as individuals in any of the available profit-sharing or share ownership schemes. In all, we received back just over 500 usable questionnaires, which have in part already been analysed in each of the case studies. Apart from their relevance to the companies, however, the data as a whole provide a basis for some further analysis, though there are some important limitations.

First, we are dealing with different types of scheme, and in some cases more that one scheme. We can largely control for this by focusing on the four cases which had SAYE schemes. Most of the remainder of this chapter is based on these four cases, but at the end some briefer comments are made on the evidence of other types of scheme.

Second, the companies or workplace covered were of different size, and this may well have an effect on attitudes (either to the scheme or to industrial relations matters in general) quite independently of the presence of a scheme or an individual's involvement in it.

Third, the response rates varied both across company cases and between participants and non-participants. For SAYE schemes, for example, only a minority of employees were participants, but their response rate was considerably higher than that of non-participants. As a result, our returns for just over 400 employees in SAYE companies show a ratio of about 1.27:1 in favour of respondents.

Fourth, the response rates from different classes of employee also varied. We distinguish between management, technical staff, clerical, supervisory, and manual workers. Ideally we would have wished to have been able to weight the responses, but the necessary information was not available, and in any case there may have been differences of classification across companies.

Despite these considerable limitations, it is worthwhile examining some selected aspects of the responses, mainly for the four SAYE cases, particularly to see the differences in response between participants in schemes and non-participants. As we shall see, the conclusions in some cases require attention to be drawn to the employee classification groups represented in the responses.

Before looking at more specific aspects, we provide an introduction to the characteristics of the sample SAYE population, summarized in Table 47. Among our respondents, males were three times more likely to be participants than females, but this was no different from the male–female ratio among non-participants. The

Table 47 Characteristics of participants and non-participants in the case-study employee sample (N = 413 max.)*

Characteristics	Participants	Non-participants
Male	169	133
Female	57	44
Trade union member	127	119
Non-trade union member	98	60
Manual	89	91
Non-manual	133	88
Owned shares outside company	79	21
No shares outside company	143	153

*Totals for each group do not always add up to 413 owing to missing data.

participation rate among trade union members was just over 50 per cent, compared with about 62 per cent among non-union members. Among manual worker respondents the sample was evenly split between participants and non-participants, but, for non-manual workers, participants outnumbered non-participants by a ratio of 1.5:1. A minority of respondents held shares outside their companies, but a much higher proportion of participants owned other shares (35 per cent, compared with 12 per cent of non-participants). However, in both groups a majority had bought outside shares *after* their own company scheme had been brought into operation (many of them, admittedly, shares in privatized companies), so involvement in the company scheme was in no sense conditional on prior knowledge or prior ownership of shares. Thus those who were SAYE participants in our survey were more likely to be male, a majority were trade union members, and non-manuals were more prominent than manual workers. Only a small minority were share owners before the company scheme was introduced.

In addition we know the average age of the whole sample was forty-one, and the average length of service just over thirteen years. SAYE participants saved an average of £31.86 per month.

Motivation

From Fig. 10, over 90 per cent of participants rated the possible financial gains as very or quite important, and over 80 per cent expressed similar views on the virtual absence of risk and the fact

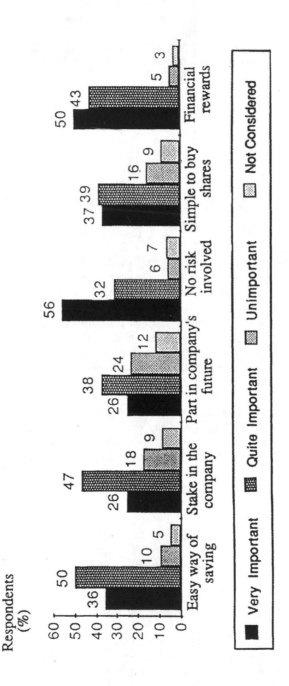

Figure 10 Motives for participation in SAVE: all cases

that it constituted an easy way to save. Progressively lower ratings were given to the fact that it was an easy way of buying shares (76 per cent), a means of gaining a stake in the company (73 per cent), and a way of being more involved in the company's future (64 per cent). Thus the financial aspects appeared to dominate the share-owning or participative aspects of SAYE. It is worth noting that apart from the first two reasons, the 'very important' class drops to a range between just over a third down to a quarter. Equally notable is the fact that the last three reasons, including the 'participative reasons', were regarded as quite or totally unimportant or not considered by at least 25 per cent of respondents.

Among non-participants the biggest response (44 per cent) related to their inability to afford involvement, and a further 20 per cent indicated that they did not know enough about it. Positive objections to involvement on specific grounds such as risk or an aversion to shareholding accounted for no more than 11 per cent of responses.

Thus it would appear that financial factors act both as a spur to involvement and, in other cases, as a barrier to participation; while non-financial factors, though not unimportant, play a secondary role. In response to a further question about future participation, only a quarter of non-participants indicated they would be likely to do so in future. The evidence on inability to afford involvement appears consistent with the pattern of participation by current pay levels, as shown in Table 48. Below £100 per week the participation rate of our respondents was 40 per cent, but each successive band of pay above this produced a rising participation rate (except for a marginal dip in the £130–£150 per week band).

Table 48 Percentage of respondents participating in SAYE scheme, by pay band

Weekly pay	Participants
Under £100	40·2
£100–£129	56·5
£130–£159	54·3
£160–£199	70·5
£200–£300	75·5
£300+	83·3

Attitudes

As reported in the individual case studies, our survey covered a range of topics designed to reveal employee attitudes which we believed might be of relevance to an understanding of the issues. In particular, we were interested in the extent to which SAYE participants and non-participants shared the same set of values and attitudes. Of course, care has to be taken in the interpretation of any such results. Evident differences in attitudes which emerged might be 'caused' by involvement in the schemes, but it is equally possible that such differences were there from the outset, and that attitude differences act as a kind of filter to determine whether an individual will join the scheme or not. As we shall see, however, perhaps the most striking conclusion was that, although there were attitudinal differences in many cases, they tended to be moderate. First, let us consider the evidence.

Table 49 sets out the rankings of respondents on various aspects of their own companies, and distinguishes between the views of SAYE participants and non-participants. There are two areas in which companies score very well indeed: as an employer overall and on job security. (In a period dominated by employment insecurity, any employer who manages to achieve security of jobs may well tend to be rated well by his employees.) There was little to choose between the views of participants and non-participants except for a marginal tendency for participants to rate the company higher overall. On pay, the companies were fairly evenly distributed about the average, but participants again gave a marginally higher rating. All the other company attributes had 'negative' values (i.e. the distribution about the average leant towards the 'below' or 'well below' mark). Significantly, perhaps, this included management openness, opportunities for employee participation in decisions, and chances to get on – all being features which might be expected to be rated favourably in participative companies. Nor was there very much difference between SAYE participants and non-participants, except that, overall, the former tended to give a slightly more favourable view.

The conclusion from this table must be that even where the company affords opportunities for financial participation it is not necessarily seen as being open or participative in other dimensions. Furthermore, although there were differences between participants and non-participants, they were small, for the most part, though in the expected direction: that is, participants had a marginally more

Table 49 SAYE participants and non-participants: views of company (%)

	View of company									
	Very good/ well above average		Moderately good/ a little above average		Average		Rather poor/ a little below average		Very poor/ well below average	
	P	NP	P	NP	P	NP	P	NP	P	NP
Overall as employer	39	31	38	38	21	22	2	6	0	2
Pay	3	1	35	29	41	41	17	20	4	9
Management openness	3	4	16	13	45	35	23	32	13	16
Management skill	6	8	17	15	57	45	14	19	5	13
Chances to get on	4	2	18	17	38	41	26	27	13	13
Job security	27	34	42	34	26	26	3	2	2	5
Employee participation in decisions	3	3	14	7	36	39	18	24	29	27

favourable view of the company on most scores. But these differences were submerged by the striking differences in the attitudes of *all* employees to specific characteristics, such as job security, which scores well, or employee participation in decisions, which scores badly.

Ownership and control

What, then, of the attitudes to ownership and control? Table 50 summarizes the views of participants and non-participants on four statements touching on this issue. In all four statements a majority of both participants and non-participants were in disagreement: thus majority support was given to the right of shareholders to profits; and there was *no* majority support for the principle that share-owning employees should elect managers, or for that of employees owning the company they work for, or that employees should share losses as well as profits.

The most striking result in Table 50 is that relating to loss-sharing, for although there was a majority against for both participants and non-participants, the margin for the former is relatively narrow; and as many as 41 per cent of participants seemed to accept the loss-sharing principle. Equally interesting is the fact that one-third of non-participants also took this view, perhaps suggesting that, while they were not at risk, they thought it proper that those who stood to gain in profitable periods should also share the losses.

Management–employee relations

When we turn to attitudes to management–employee relations in general, the results of which are shown in Table 51, there was again evidence of comparatively minor differences between participants and non-participants. By far the strongest line of argument for both groups was in relation to the principle that 'a good management consults its work force'. Non-participants were significantly more likely to agree with the view that they were 'treated as numbers'. Both groups revealed a strong majority against the idea that workers should never strike for reasons of loyalty, and almost as strongly against the view that 'management knows best'. On the 'welfare' and 'use of abilities' items there was little to choose between the groups, but the participants took a slightly more favourable view of both management and opportunity.

The main conclusions here may again be negative ones. Participation in SAYE is not significantly associated with a set of

Table 50 Views of SAYE share option scheme participants and non-participants towards ownership and control issues compared: all SAYE schemes (%)

Statement	Agree		Disagree		No opinion	
	P	NP	P	NP	P	NP
Profits should belong to employees not shareholders	27	39	62	46	11	16
Employees with shares should elect managers	21	28	70	59	9	14
Employees should own the companies they work for	24	25	59	57	17	18
Employees should share losses as well as profits	41	33	49	56	10	11

P SAYE share option scheme participant (N = 219).
NP Non-participant (N = 174).

values and attitudes which produce a rosy view of the company and its management. It does not dramatically affect the sense of the legitimacy of strike action, nor does it diminish the value placed on management consultation. And although participants were less likely than non-participants to feel as if they were treated as numbers, there were as many participants who disagreed with the statement as agreed with it.

Experience of profit-sharing and share ownership

A very important part of our purpose in the case study was to develop a better understanding of views on financial participation schemes themselves. We approached this question by obtaining reactions from participants and non-participants alike to a series of statements relating to the effects of financial participation. Not surprisingly, non-participants were more likely to have no opinion on many of the points: on average, one-third of non-participants, compared with about one-sixth of participants. Further, an

Table 51 Views of SAYE share option scheme participants and non-participants towards various general statements of management–employee relations compared: all SAYE schemes (%)

Statement	Agree P	Agree NP	Disagree P	Disagree NP	No opinion P	No opinion NP
In the end management knows best and employees should let them make the decisions	32	21	64	71	7	8
Workers should never strike, for reasons of loyalty to the company and management	19	14	72	76	9	10
A good management always consults its work force	89	91	9	7	1	2
Management tends to treat people like me as numbers	48	59	48	35	4	6
Most managers have their employees' welfare at heart	39	35	47	56	14	9
People like me have no opportunity to use their real abilities at work	32	33	60	53	8	14

P SAYE share option scheme participant (max. N = 226).
NP Non-participant (max. N = 177).

important *caveat* needs to be added. Some of the statements to which employees were asked to respond were more relevant to schemes such as the cash-based bonus or ADST type, rather than SAYE, and where SAYE was run in conjunction with another scheme the responses clearly cannot be related solely to SAYE involvement. Despite these difficulties, the results seem worth reporting.

The statements implicitly reflected commonly held views about the advantages and disadvantages of profit-sharing or employee share ownership, and it is therefore worth while examining each in turn, with reference to Table 52. As in the Bossguide case study, we group these in sets, covering incentive issues, other motivational and behavioural matter, awareness, and employee influence.

Incentives

Hard work will lead to a share in results. A majority of both groups agreed with this view, and significantly more participants were positive on this effect.

There are better ways of improving benefits. A strong majority opinion on both groups supported this view, though over a third had no opinion.

Just another kind of bonus. Participants were fairly evenly split on this, whereas non-participants were more likely to agree than disagree. The implication would seem to be that roughly half of participants see it as a bonus but the remainder regard it as something more.

Employees risk losing some earnings. Participants overwhelmingly disagreed with this statement on a 5:1 ratio, while non-participants also disagreed, but on a more modest 2:1 ratio. Since this relates to SAYE participants, where the risks of loss were minimal, the results are not surprising, but cannot be readily carried over to other types of scheme.

Bonus cannot be predicted. There was majority agreement in both groups on this statement, but over one-third of participants disagreed.

Other motivational factors

Less likelihood of moving to another job. The balance between agreement and disagreement was fairly even for both groups. Briefly, for every participant who felt he was less likely to move, there was another who felt the opposite.

More likely to notice colleagues not pulling their weight. Surprisingly, perhaps, nearly 60 per cent of participants disagreed with this statement, substantially more than the nearly 40 per cent of non-participants.

Awareness

Scheme generates greater awareness of management problems. Most respondents disagreed with this view, but, surprisingly, participants were more vehement in their disagreement, nearly half expressing a contrary view.

Employee influence

Scheme produces greater participation in the company. Again, this view was rejected on balance by both groups, and more strongly by participants. Sixty per cent of participants disagreed with the statement, more than twice as many as agreed.

Employees should have more say in fixing the profit share. Participants were inclined to reject this view, but non-participants were strongly in favour of more employee say.

To summarize this collection of attitudes is far from simple. In general, participants and non-participants tended to share common majority views, but the size of the majority differed from one statement to another. The only real exception was on the involvement of employees in fixing the profit share, with non-participants being much more positive about the desirability of involvement.

For participants, there are two ways of assessing these results. First, there is the *majority opinion*, which accepts that hard work will produce a share in the results: a paradoxical result, in that few managements were looking for this kind of direct incentive effect. However, other aspects of the 'incentive' group were less favourable: in summary, the risks are small, but better ways exist of improving benefits; many regard it as just another bonus, and an unpredictable one at that. Other motivational or behavioural effects on mobility and on spotting slackness were not strongly marked. A majority did not give the awareness factor much credence, nor the ability of schemes to generate greater participation. Altogether, the results must constitute a disappointment for those who see in such schemes a new dawn in employee relations.

Secondly, however, it is worth registering that, in a number of respects, the *absolute proportion* of participants expressing an opinion may also be significant. For example, for 44 per cent the SAYE scheme had reduced the likelihood of a change of job, for 33 per cent it had increased awareness of management problems, and for 27 per cent it had enabled a greater sense of participation. Forty-four per cent regarded the scheme as more than just another

Table 52 Views of SAYE share option scheme participants and non-participants towards various statements about experience of profit-sharing compared: all SAYE schemes (%)

Statement	Agree		Disagree		No opinion	
	P	NP	P	NP	P	NP
If I work hard I know I can share in the results	53	40	37	32	10	28
There are better ways of improving benefits	43	44	23	18	34	38
Just another kind of bonus	47	43	44	27	9	31
Employees risk losing part of their earnings	14	23	71	41	15	35
As you cannot predict the bonus you cannot plan spending	46	46	36	22	18	33
It has made me less likely to move to another job	44	30	46	36	11	33
I am more likely to notice if my colleagues are not pulling their weight	28	32	58	38	14	31
Made me more aware of the problems which management faces	33	27	47	34	20	30
Enabled me to participate more in the way the company works	27	21	60	42	13	38
Employees should have more say in fixing the profit share	29	45	50	24	21	30

P SAYE share option scheme participant (max. N = 215).
NP Non-participant (max. N = 136).

bonus. What is significant about these results is that for some substantial fraction of employees covered there are positive results, as measured by the attitudes expressed, and that may well be a significant benefit to the company, even if these views are not held by a majority. In other words, even where the overall effect on employee attitudes is less than might have been hoped, there were some areas where there did appear to be a positive effect on opinion and behaviour at the margin.

Trade union power

A further test of opinion relates to trade union power. By hypothesis, we might predict that scheme participants would be more individualist and less supportive of the collective strength of a trade union. How far do the responses bear this out? And to what extent do participants' views differ as between trade unions in general and trade unions operating in their own company? Table 53 reports the results. For trade unionism in Britain generally, just over a third thought that union power was about right; of the remainder, those who thought there was too much power outnumbered those who thought there was too little by nearly two to one. As predicted, the views of participants were more strongly biased in the 'too much power' direction, but even among participants there was a small bias in that direction.

The picture at company level is intriguingly different, with nearly two-thirds of all respondents expressing the view that the unions' power was about right, and over a quarter taking the view that the unions had too little power. As expected, the views of participants tended to be less supportive of the unions than non-participants. Even so, one-fifth of participants thought the union had too little power in the company situation (compared with one-third of non-participants): unsurprisingly, a high proportion of the 'too little power' school were manual workers.

It is not clear how this is to be interpreted. The image of union power in general appeared to be unfavourable; only in the case of manual workers was there a small balance on the 'too little power' side. Yet at the company level the workplace unions were seen as having inadequate power; and this was the case for SAYE participators as well as non-participants. At least so far as the own-company orientation is concerned, there was no suggestion of a strong anti-union bias among scheme participants, who, only a little less strongly than non-participants, seemed to want a more powerful union voice in company affairs.

Table 53 Views on trade union power in Britain generally and in own company compared: all SAYE schemes (%)

Opinion	Britain generally			Own company		
	All	P	NP	All	P	NP
Too much power	39	48	30	7	9	4
About right	35	32	39	64	68	57
Too little power	21	18	25	27	21	33
Don't know	4	3	5	3	1	6
Number	401	222	173	389	221	162

P SAYE share option scheme participants.
NP Non-participants.

General management–employee relationships

Finally, in this connection, we consider attitudes on the commonality or otherwise of management and employee interests, both in Britain at large and in the specific company situation. The results are shown in Table 54. For Britain at large, a third took the view that management and employees were basically on opposite sides; the distinction between participants and non-participants was very slight. Nearly 60 per cent expressed the 'mixed' view that some interests were shared, others were in conflict. Few thought aims and objectives were common to both management and employees, and participants were less likely than non-participants to adopt this unitary view. It is clear that the unitary stance was greatly outnumbered by a pure or mixed form of pluralism.

Once again, however, the company orientation produced different results. Sixty-three per cent took the mixed view – not significantly different from the 'Britain at large' evaluation. But nearly one in four thought that in the company context management and employees shared common objectives, compared with one in seven who took the pure pluralist approach. Participants were more likely to adopt the unitary view, less inclined to opt for the more pluralist view.

What happens in the company is thus seen differently from what happens in the country at large; and the company context seems to provide a closer bonding of interest than is apparent in our respondents' view of the external world of industrial relations.

Table 54 Views of management–employee relations in Britain generally and in own company compared (%)

Statement	Britain generally			Own company		
	All	P	NP	All	P	NP
Management and employees basically have common aims and objectives	8	5	12	23	26	21
Management and unions have some shared interests, but also some areas of conflict	59	60	56	63	64	62
Management and employees are basically on opposite sides	33	34	32	14	11	17
Number	319	182	133	328	187	136

P SAYE share option scheme participants.
NP Non-participants.

An evaluation of the attitudinal information

What, then, are we to make of the evidence on attitudes? The picture is clearly quite complex, and we are extremely conscious of the need to be cautious in our conclusions, since although we have a reasonably good cross-section of employees, the aggregate data used in the analysis almost certainly contains some biases arising from the sample structure.

Even accepting that qualification, however, there was little suggestion that we were observing a fundamental cleavage of attitudes as between participants and non-participants in the SAYE schemes. For the most part, where differences existed, they were modest, and they operated in the expected direction – reflecting more favourable views of the company, the scheme, and management–employee relations than in the case of non-participants; and less favourable views of union power. But the attitudinal evidence by no means suggested that participants were company lap dogs. They were critical of management openness, lack of employee participation, management skill, and limited opportunities for career advancement. They represented a strong voice in favour of greater participation in company decisions, of more attention being paid to the individual employee, and of effective consultation. Whatever their view of the trade unions at large, they hardly saw their own unions being over-powerful; more often the reverse. Yet, at the end, they perceived their own company's approach to objectives as being more harmonious than in the world at large.

Four further points seem to emerge. First, financial involvement in SAYE schemes was not seen as an effective component of employee participation in the round. There was little or no trace of a strong carry-over of attitudes from scheme involvement to a belief that it was the key to deeper participation: and there are good grounds for believing that much of the motivation for employees to join the scheme is a relatively riskless opportunity for saving and/or financial advantage. It is almost as if the employee participants saw the SAYE scheme as belonging to a different area of working life from the routine of union–management interaction in negotiation and consultation; and this is perhaps not altogether surprising in view of the quite stringent separation of financial participation schemes from normal industrial relations processes. Managements have done little to promote this interaction, and the trade unions have likewise made little effort to bring financial participation into the central arena.

Second, there was little evidence of a hard core of employees who were fundamentally opposed to the principles of profit-sharing and share ownership, though in saying that we must be mindful of the restricted coverage of non-participants. From our survey results, only about one in ten non-participants expressed positive objections, and the most important deterrents were inability to afford involvement or a lack of knowledge. Our evidence of the positive association between pay levels and scheme participation suggests that ability to afford the regular savings commitment is indeed a significant factor. But low pay was certainly not an absolute deterrent.

Third, as observed earlier, we are unable from the survey

267

evidence to say much about the cause-and-effect aspect of financial participation. How far the rather more favourable attitudes of participants to the company, the scheme, and management–union relations are attributable to the fact of involvement, and how far the existence of these more favourable attitudes disposed employees to participate in the schemes, cannot be determined satisfactorily. We can only reiterate that, for the most part, the divisions of opinion on a wide range of germane matters between participants and non-participants were marginal rather than indicative of a deep-rooted split.

Fourth, from the point of view of managements who had introduced such schemes, the evidence on the extent to which the objectives were being met was somewhat mixed. Certainly there were variations in the attitudinal indicators which would have been of interest to the managements of the workplaces covered by our enquiries. But, at an aggregative level, many of the *majority* opinions expressed would lead to the conclusion that, for the broad mass of workers, the schemes did not do a great deal for loyalty and commitment to the company. As we have seen, however, that may not be the only test, for on a number of scores the minority expressing positive views was substantial, and at the margin the advantages this brings to company management may be ample justification. Whether or not there are such advantages may again hinge on the *change* in attitudes brought about by financial involvement, as compared with the reinforcement of existing predispositions.

What is clear, from the evidence noted at the start of this section, is that, since the scheme in their company was introduced, more employees had been acquiring shares in other companies, a tendency much more prominent among participants than non-participants. Thus there could well be some kind of spill-over effect from having a company scheme of share ownership, and particularly from involvement in such a scheme, to engaging in share ownership on a broader front. We know that in recent years a larger proportion of the population has acquired shares in the privatized companies formerly under public ownership, and we may be picking up no more than a microcosmic reflection of this much wider tendency. The fuller implications must, however, be postponed until the final chapter.

OTHER TYPES OF SCHEME

In this final section we summarize some of the more important evidence on non-SAYE schemes. There is much less material here on which to work, but a number of points can usefully be made. As we indicated from the outset, there may well be different motives for the introduction of financial participation schemes. Interview data relating to cash-based or incentive schemes, for example, suggested that in some cases this type of scheme was introduced in response to straightforward pay claims which management was unwilling to concede unless extra pay could be linked to extra performance. In other cases management saw this type of scheme as a solution to the problem of putting across to employees the need to relate pay to performance. In one example this was associated with a revitalized employee briefing system, in which information on sales performance, market share, supply performance, and the company's financial position was provided monthly, to raise awareness of business performance and market trends. In such a situation the trade union was much more likely to be involved, at least indirectly, in the introduction of the scheme. The union would have much preferred a straight pay award without strings, but where management insisted the union was willing to accede. In particular, the union might be suspicious about particular features of the scheme, such as the setting of bonus or performance targets, and would then become involved in negotiation on detail. In another case the union expressed concern about the unevenness of the bonus across the plant.

Quantifying these tendencies is not easy, but the evidence implies greater union involvement in cash-based and incentive schemes, as compared with SAYE and ADST schemes. Survey evidence shows that although cash and incentive schemes were subject to bargaining in only about 10 per cent of cases, this was well above the level of union involvement in other schemes. This is perhaps not surprising, since there is a much closer connection between cash-based and traditional payment-by-results schemes in which unions are typically involved through negotiation. More generally, we can compare the objectives cited by management in introducing the scheme in cases where *only* cash-based and incentive schemes operated with objectives in all other schemes (SAYE, ADST, executive share option etc.). The results are shown in Table 55.

269

Table 55 Management objectives: cash-based/incentive and other schemes compared: percentages cited

Objectives of scheme	Cash-based/ incentive only	All other schemes
Encourages employee co-operation	65·2	71·2
Identification with company	29·3	69·8
Reward for improved performance	59·8	33·8
Develops business awareness	45·7	39·6
Encourages employee ownership	2·2	59·0
Retains key staff	21·7	32·4
Helps employee remuneration	26·1	13·7
Other	3·3	1·4
Number	92	139

Source: company survey.

Cash-based schemes were associated more strongly with rewards for improved performance, development of business awareness, and as an aid in employee remuneration. Other schemes scored more heavily on company identification, encouragement of employee ownership, the retention of key staff, and (more marginally) encouragement of employee co-operation. The data for 'all other' schemes include cases where cash-based or incentive schemes were employed alongside another scheme, so that if we were able to separate them out the differentiation might be even stronger. Even as it is, the evidence on objectives tends to bear out our hypothesis that, although there is often some lack of clarity in objectives, we can distinguish rational differences in motivation for different types of scheme.

From a different perspective, both ADST and cash-based schemes share the characteristic that they apply to all qualified employees, and so we cannot directly confront the questions concerning the attitudinal and behavioural consequences associated with participation or non-participation, as we could with SAYE schemes. However, it would be wrong to neglect the evidence we have gathered on other types of schemes through the case studies in this final commentary. For this, we turn first to an examination of other schemes involving employee share ownership before considering cash-based profit sharing.

Two schemes other than the SAYE type were found in the case-study companies. One, the Bossguide discretionary share option scheme, had much in common with SAYE (in that employees had to opt in and decide to what extent to do so), but its inclusion of almost all staff, and the drift of company policy further in that direction, brings it close to all-employee arrangements. At the same time it was in practice linked to a weighty profit-sharing bonus scheme.

The second, the ADST scheme at Norbrew, was also a companion to another scheme, in this case the company's SAYE scheme. This sort of scheme might be thought to have a potentially very different flavour from SAYE, and indeed the existence of the two types of scheme side by side was a not uncommon feature of organizations covered in our survey. ADST purports to cost the recipient employee nothing, nor does it create the division between participants and non-participants, which could have been expected to associate it more firmly with the aims of creating unity.

Our evidence on ADST, although indicating a high level of support for the principle, suggested that the unity objective may founder because of problems of equity in the distribution of the benefits. At Norbrew the problem was that share allocations were based on a total earnings rather than on basic pay, so that those excluded from overtime and bonus payments did less well. But the problems of distribution are always likely to be debatable as between the principles of equal shares per employee, benefits linked to basic pay, or benefits linked to actual pay. There is no obviously 'right' answer, and some grumbles are likely to remain among those who would fare better under a different criterion.

Apart from the distributional effects, the relative failure of ADST to make a strong participative impression at Norbrew may lie in the fact that the quite modest benefits had a low profile among the range of participative devices which had been employed in the company. As we observed, employees tended not to see the ADST scheme as primarily a participative arrangement but more frequently as just another form of bonus: 65 per cent regarded ADST in this light and only 8 per cent regarded it as involving a risk of earnings loss. In other words, it was seen by employees as motivational rather than as an avenue of employee involvement. Furthermore, the evidence reviewed in Chapter 10 indicated that those who elected to join the SAYE scheme were more inclined to take a favourable attitude to the incentive aspect of the all-employee ADST scheme. This is not, of course, to suggest that the

271

financial participation schemes were necessarily ineffectual – they may well have played a part in the generally favourable attitudes of employees to their company. And in that respect the fact that there were two schemes, offering both an automatic involvement and an elective approach, may be a way by which management can satisfy different employee aspirations.

The most popular category of financial participation scheme encountered in our survey remained the cash-based profit-sharing type, despite the impulse towards ownership-based schemes provided by legislation. Our survey yielded the expected tendency for such schemes to be oriented towards the incentive rewards end of the objectives spectrum, with less emphasis on attitudinal goals such as identification, though not with the clarity of distinction that would be expected were strongly defined management strategies typically to be found at work (see Chapter 5).

Among our case studies two examples of cash-based schemes are to be found, in very contrasting circumstances. At Fairbrush a long-standing scheme was beset by the limitation of payments imposed by company profitability per employee, whereas at Bossguide success had gone with payments which could be a substantial proportion even of what were relatively high rates of pay for much of the work force. Direct comparisons are rendered of only limited value by the sheer number of contrasts between the two companies, but some useful observations can be advanced.

Although our survey and interview material suggested that cash and incentive schemes were more likely to be subject to a degree of union response, either through some form of bargaining or at least an effort at influencing the arrangement, it indicated that this remained the exception rather than the rule. In our two case studies there was no evidence of union input whatsoever, at Bossguide because there was no union, and at Fairbrush because the management denied the validity of any union input and the unions themselves felt powerless to do anything about it. This would not necessarily preclude other channels of employee participation, however, and since profit-sharing did form part of income the possibility of concern about it was present. In the event, however, the diminutive size of the payment and other attitudes minimized interest at Fairbrush, while the individualized work force at Bossguide and the apparent success of some aspects of management style ensured that any pressure in that direction was marginal. This does not mean there was no feeling that the respective schemes should not be more participative in decision-making terms, however, since this view was supported by a substantial minority at Bossguide, and by a strong majority at Fairbrush.

Without the comparison between participants and non-participants to go on, there is a major element of conjecture in evaluating the effects of these profit-sharing schemes on employee attitudes. At Fairbrush, though, all the evidence suggests that it was marginal. At Bossguide, judgement difficulties are compounded by the scheme's co-existence with the share option offers, but our assessment is that it was the level of pay and the prospects for the future, together with other aspects of management style, which predominated in determining a generally favourable assessment of the company by its employees. What seems apparent, confirming an earlier conclusion for SAYE schemes, is that profit-sharing does not necessarily link with a sense of the company as participative in other ways. In confirmation, a strong majority of Fairbrush employees disagreed that financial participation had led to greater participation in the way the company worked, and even with both schemes at Bossguide the answers on this were split, with those at the bottom of their respective hierarchies (clerical staff and consultants) tending to disagree also.

The perceived effects of profit-sharing were markedly at variance between these two examples. On the incentive front, most Fairbrush respondents did not feel that work effort was linked with shared revenues, and agreed the scheme was just another bonus and that there were preferable ways to improve benefits, but as with the SAYE replies only a minority thought part of earnings were at risk. At Bossguide, again complicated by the fact that the assessment was of more than just cash payments from profits, the perception that the results of effort could be shared was strongly positive, in marked contrast to Fairbrush, though the results produced substantial minority judgements against the value of profit-sharing on other scores, including almost half who thought it 'just another bonus'.

In both companies most employees chose not to see the profit-sharing pay-out as an essential part of pay – at Fairbrush for obvious reasons, but at Bossguide because despite the scale of payments they were too variable to be relied on. This last influence raises the interesting thought that if a combination of company profitability and individual performance is embodied in a scheme to maximize any incentive, the effect is an insecurity which creates a greater reliance on basic salary. This may have implications for the effects of profit-related pay.

On other attitudinal and motivational questions, while responses at Bossguide tended to be more positive from a managerial viewpoint than those at Fairbrush, the results from neither company indicated a strong impact of the schemes for most employees. Only minorities reported greater awareness of management problems or less likelihood of leaving the company, while even at Bossguide there was only just a majority who would be more likely to spot colleagues slacking. On these scores, then, the impact of profit-sharing seems limited at best.

The most distinct lesson to emerge from these cases of cash-based profit-sharing is probably the dependence of the scheme on the factor of company success, rather than vice versa. At Fairbrush attitudes were overcast by pessimism about the longer-term survival of the company, and profit-sharing pay-outs were at most a diluted indicator of these problems. At Bossguide, once again in contrast, management garnered much of its legitimacy from the exceptional performance of the company, and from this sprang the impact and acceptance (for the most part) of the schemes. Again lessons may be drawn for more stringent proposals to relate pay and profits, taken together with the observation about the reliance on a basic income earlier. The dependence of pay on profits places a greater onus on management effectiveness, not merely individual effort, and it may well be that, while success does yield enhanced legitimacy, a failure to live up to employee expectations will be a far more direct cause of scrutiny, anger, and depleted acceptance of managerial authority. To pursue this, it would be fascinating to have survey findings from a more successful Fairbrush or a less buoyant Bossguide, but for now the issue must be deferred.

CONCLUDING REMARKS

Two points may be made by way of conclusion. The first is that, up to the present, the benefits of most schemes are generally too small to have much prospect of making the kind of impact that management would wish. The benefits tend not to be seen by employees as an essential element of pay which would generate commitment (even for a majority at Bossguide, where profit bonus benefits were quite substantial) but are more typically regarded as 'just another kind of bonus', falling short of the objective of moving on from financial motivation to the higher plane of unity of purpose. Most employees believe that there are better ways of improving benefits – they would no doubt opt for straight increases in cash – but that would be unlikely to produce the kinds of effect management is pursuing in the development of a performance-related element in pay. The most positive responses in most cases came from those who had higher pay (and hence higher cash benefits or share allocations) or higher status (in which case they would identify more with management aspirations). The positive link with higher pay might suggest that where the bonus or share allocations are permitted to grow to a significant proportion of pay, the fulfilment of objectives beyond the level of financial motivation might be more feasible. But there is, as yet, insufficient evidence on high levels of reward to warrant a strong conclusions on that. The counterpart would be that the risks of loss-sharing would be increased, adding further to the insecurity factor attaching to bonus allocations, and that would almost certainly be an unpopular outcome.

Second, it is worth reflecting on the fact that, on the evidence reviewed, there is no specific type of scheme which appears to hold significant advantages over the others. In part this is a function of the different managerial objectives in introducing the schemes, which we have stressed will differ from case to case and ought properly to be thought out in relation to the likely effects on employee attitudes. But that still does not take us far enough: the evidence indicates that how well a scheme works is by no means a simple matter. In part it may depend on the detailed design of the scheme, in part on the way its design impacts on different groups of employees – high or low-paid, white-collar, managerial or manual, high or low overtime groups, etc. – and in part on how successful the company is in its commercial operations. In other words, there is at least an implication in the evidence that the effectiveness of a scheme in relation to its objectives will be a matter of specific circumstance at workplace or organization level, rather than an automatic outcome of rational selection of one type of scheme. There is certainly enough evidence to indicate that the objectives of management, even where quite well specified, are not being achieved across the board, and that, for example, personal financial gain is a stronger motivating factor among employees than most of the loftier objectives.

Part 4

Looking ahead

13

Future trends

The evidence reviewed in this book and in many other writings on aspects of financial participation demonstrates that there has been a considerable growth in the variety and volume of profit-sharing and employee share ownership schemes in Britain in recent years. Yet there is still a very long way to go before employees' involvement in the financial affairs of their employing organizations becomes a pervasive characteristic of employment relations. It seems likely that further pressures will be exerted, for example through the Conservative government's profit-related pay scheme, to extend the scope and further diversify the influence of financial participation schemes. At the conclusion of our work, an obvious question concerns the prospects for significant extension of this form of employee involvement within a context which combines a somewhat precarious economic outlook and a political thrust in the direction of 'people's capitalism'.

A second question involves consideration of the reasons why employee financial participation is believed in so many quarters to be 'a good thing'. Are the pressures and the favourable conditions created for expansion – for example, through tax concessions – in fact warranted by evidence from past experience? It is with this second question that we begin, drawing together some of the main threads of our previous analysis to provide a basis for reviewing future prospects.

OBJECTIVES

In the introductory chapters, developments in financial participation were set in the wider context of the evolution of employee participation. The shift in emphasis from collective, representative forms of involvement to more individually oriented types was stressed. In succeeding chapters we have attempted to assess the objectives, explicit or implied, in the introduction of these schemes, and to relate them to the benefits as perceived by those they concern: employers, employees individually and collectively, and in many cases trade unions as a representative voice. We have also noted that, as well as the objectives associated with particular schemes, there is a set of controversial economic arguments in favour of a climate in which share ownership by employees and a clear relation between pay and performance on profit are seen to be desirable for macro-economic as well as micro-economic reasons.

Our evidence indicates that employers have entered into one or more forms of financial participation for a diversity of reasons, ranging from seeking to ensure greater employee commitment and loyalty, through encouragement of wider share ownership as a desirable principle, to more mundane but highly practical considerations such as underlining the need to relate pay to performance. Our conclusion is that in general these objectives are not well specified, tending to be somewhat woolly in the way they are expressed and without a very clear understanding of the way the derived outcomes will be generated by the choice of scheme. Nor is there any significant evidence of measures being taken by managements to establish criteria on the effectiveness of the particular systems adopted. The net effect is that we encountered no cases where there was a clear system of evaluation. Assessments of what schemes were achieving were broad-brush and impressionistic, in some cases revealing differences of view within management itself.

Financial participation schemes, then, have some resemblance to an 'act of faith' on the part of management. The objectives themselves are laudable, they are consistent with recent political thinking, and legislative assistance through tax relief has reduced the cost of experimentation. These factors have encouraged some employers to enter this area of participation, while others have adapted established practices to conform with the newly available financial advantages.

Our thesis from the outset has been that different types of scheme have different potential for influence, and it is important that objectives are well specified and that the choice of scheme(s) is related to the objectives. We have detected a distinct variation in

the aims of companies pursuing a cash-based or incentive approach
and those pursuing a share-ownership strategy though there is still
an uncomfortable blurring at the edges. To understand this, we need
to search for explanations of the attitudes of management towards
participation.

It is well established that managements prefer to confine
participation to job-related as opposed to business-related decisions
(Brannen, 1983; Cressey *et al*. 1985). Financial participation, then,
proves a problem for management, particularly when it moves from
the relatively simple link between production performance and pay
to a situation where work-related income is influenced not just by
individual but by collective effort and by capital ownership as well
as income flows. If employees are to be encouraged to be aware of
business realities through the link with profits and share-price
fluctuations, this is likely to require more open discussion of
profits, how they are generated and distributed, and the
requirements for investment. This might entail employees, or more
threateningly their trade unions, questioning sensitive areas of
business-related decisions which, by and large, most companies
have sought to keep out of the collective bargaining arena. Concern
about this possibility was shown in the CBI response to the
government's Green Paper on profit-related pay:

> While the process of defining profits at corporate level and of
> providing figures to employees and, as appropriate, their trade
> union representatives, does not constitute a major problem for
> most companies, it could open the way for business decisions to
> be called into question on the grounds that they reduced the
> surplus available for the profit related pool ... Nonetheless, it
> would be unrealistic to expect that unpalatable decisions will
> always be acceptable without any cost to employee relations;
> and therefore wrong to believe that the PRP approach would
> offer only a one-way option on the commitment and motivation
> of employees. [CBI, 1986: 5]

We can, therefore, recognize the dilemma for managements
pushing down the line of more developed financial participation. So
long as it can be framed in an individual relationship with the
employee, the link with profits or with share participation in the
company may produce dividends in terms of favourable attitudes
and behaviour. But the more widespread the coverage within the
organization the more important it becomes that the scheme be seen

as part of management's 'gift' to employees, rather than as an area which can be opened up to collective consultation or even negotiation, which could have very wide implications indeed. Moreover, the most recent evidence from the 1984 Workplace Industrial Relations Survey suggests that, if anything, managements have been pulling back the margin of issues which they are willing to subject to collective bargaining, in contrast to the extension of that margin, which an all-out development of financial participation would imply (Millward and Stevens, 1986).

It is not surprising, then, that our evidence reveals considerable ambivalence on the part of managements embarking on a strategy of greater employee participation in the financial structure of the business. Although the objectives of financial participation are typically seen as an extension of employee participation more generally, and share ownership schemes are positively, if not strongly, associated with other forms of employee involvement, our evidence indicates that these schemes were essentially introduced by management *fiat*, were very rarely subject to negotiation, and seldom involved employees even in consultation before or during the implementation. Yet the dominant management objective for such schemes was to increase employee commitment and loyalty!

Two examples illustrate this ambivalence. At Scotcake, while some senior managers believed that the SAYE share option scheme was consistent with the company's overall philosophy, the personnel director believed that the scheme was 'almost exempt from participation' and went as far as to say that it did not fall into the general participative philosophy. The scheme was rarely discussed in the Factory Advisory Committee. At Thistle employee participation was highly developed, but management and unions both agreed that it operated solely through union channels, and through this the participation channels are in practice linked to negotiating channels, although formally independent. But because union representatives refused to get involved in the original bonus scheme and maintained this aloofness from the SAYE scheme, financial participation had become the only form of participation in the company which was outside established trade union/management channels.

We are driven back to the conclusion that financial participation, particularly the more advanced forms involving access to share ownership, does not sit easily alongside the more job-related forms of employee involvement. Managements in general do not appear to have worked through the mechanics by which financial participation is to produce its desired results, nor have they fully taken on board the potentially complex relationship between financial and other forms of employee involvement. That is not to say that schemes do not produce results of benefit to the company; but whether those are the benefits sought, where in the organization the benefits are obtained, and whether there are negative features, are questions that deserve fuller examination.

RESPONSES

Part of that fuller examination requires consideration of what employees, both individually and collectively, have made of management's initiatives in introducing financial participation schemes. At the collective level, as represented by the trade unions, the answer must be 'very little', but that needs to be a qualified conclusion. We have argued that management has been well aware that extension of employee participation into the financial domain carries the risk that the scope of consultation and negotiation might be extended into areas regarded as part of management's preserve, and that for this reason they have kept tight control over the schemes. Trade unions would appear to have been apathetic about these innovations, despite their non-negotiability. How long they will continue in this manner will depend on whether the existence of such non-negotiable benefits threatens their position, or gives rise to pressure from members to seek improvements. Apart from some of the cash-based and incentive schemes which have attracted union attention, a vast majority of management-initiated schemes have been accepted or at least tolerated by the unions, since they are either voluntary (such as SAYE schemes) or marginal in terms of earnings, so that they do not cut into the security of the union's role or pose a serious threat to their collective bargaining relationship with employers.

There is, however, some evidence that unions have moved from an attitude of 'bored hostility' to more active involvement. But the pressure for this has come from two other arms of government policy – privatization and the pull towards wage flexibility through profit-related pay. The first of these may be seen by the unions as a political threat, the second as eating into the central issues of basic pay, its stability in the face of recession, and the unions' role in protecting members' interests. Further developments along these lines would almost certainly increase union interest and involvement in the range of issues surrounding financial participation and pay-performance linkages, and the apathy of the past could dissolve quite rapidly.

We turn next to employee responses, which have been discussed in some detail in the case studies and in Chapter 12, and we need merely to gloss on them here. The strongest message which emerges is that, so far at least, the main impact of financial participation has been through its financial motivation rather than through a real development of a participative or unitary set of attitudes. This we might expect to be the case with cash-based and incentive schemes in any event, in which the participative theme is more muted, but the evidence is that this applies equally to schemes such as SAYE and ADST.

This conclusion carries over into a second area. Although the principles of financial participation are generally applauded, and a relatively small minority are opposed, it does not mean that favourable attitudes are necessarily extended to the company, its management performance, and its participative dimension at large. Far from it! Comparatively modest differences in attitude were observed between SAYE participants and non-participants, and ratings of the company on such matters as pay and employment security might be high in both groups. Yet the companies still rate quite poorly in terms of management openness, managerial skill, and access to employee participation. It is almost as if employees were instinctively aware that financial participation measures are often viewed by management as an add-on element to a range of other participative devices, without carrying the deeper commitment to enhanced employee involvement which a fully fledged financial participation scheme would require.

Similarly, we found there was comparatively little carry-over into the broader area of industrial relations. Financial participation, in whatever form, did not, for example, radically change attitudes towards strike action or to management infallibility. And although there was considerable evidence of employees regarding trade unions as having too much power in the country as a whole, the balance of opinion on trade union power in the company or workplace lay in the direction of too little rather than too much. The differences in attitudes between participants and non-participants in optional schemes are again quite small. In the light of our evidence that financial participation is kept well clear of collective bargaining and even formal consultative machineries, by management design, these findings are perhaps not surprising. But we suspect that at least part of the implicit motivation for the introduction of financial participation measures involves the hope of improvements in the management–employee relationship.

In summary, our evidence suggests that there is no strong link between the adoption of financial participation schemes and an acknowledgement by a majority of employees that they have become more aware of management problems or are able to engage in fuller participation. Employee responses as a whole do not seem to bear out management expectations. Having said that, we must also acknowledge that there is evidence of some differences in attitude between participants and non-participants in optional SAYE schemes, and this could reflect an important influence of such schemes at the margin. That is, although such schemes have not yet brought about a major swing in attitudes, they may well have improved the balance of employee opinion in the directions sought by management. Thus it is quite possible that companies have made important gains through such schemes, and also that, given more time, a greater shift could take place. Our evidence does not allow us to judge how far this is likely, for that would require an ability to measure progressive *changes* in attitudes over time, rather than differences at a moment of time.[1] The generally minor differences between participants and non-participants may suggest that the marginal effect is small, but we cannot say so positively.

We can only speculate on why more favourable attitudes have not followed from what are undoubtedly in many cases sincere attempts by management to extend the scope of employee involvement. One reason may be that the reward elements are too small in most cases, relative to total pay, to make much impact. So long as the benefit remains small, the typical attitude that it is 'just another bonus' is likely to prevail, and there is some evidence that higher levels of benefit do promote greater commitment. Another reason may be that managements have not fully followed through on the participative dimension of the schemes, with design and implementation being essentially non-participative, so that employees are left with the purely financial motivation. The limited degree of involvement could also be explained in terms of Espinosa and Zimbalist's (1978) view that there is an evolutionary process in the development of employee participation from the individual viewpoint. Specifically, they argue that participation tends to begin in areas close to workers' knowledge and experience and gradually spreads to more remote areas. They see a movement from social administrative and personnel problems, through technical and production problems, to economic and financial problems. Thus financial participation schemes could come into the latter category and would seem particularly remote if introduced unilaterally by management without reference to employees or their representatives.

All these explanations are in some measure consistent with our evidence but we have no adequate means of discriminating among them and we take no formal position on this. We conclude our assessment of developments to date by reiterating the desirability of disentangling the various approaches to financial participation and ensuring that goals are matched with specific scheme characteristics, rather than some form of financial participation being adopted in the hope that it will somehow fulfil a variety of loosely defined participative and co-operative objectives. Beyond that, there would appear to be a need to think through the mechanisms by which means and ends will be matched, and to consider carefully the issues of design, including distributional equity and the interface with other participative or consultative devices.

FUTURE DEVELOPMENTS

If there appears to have been some confusion at the enterprise level in the rationale for introducing (or modifying) financial participation, the lack of clarity in debate at the public policy level is probably even greater. Again, the problem is that of disentangling the multitude of objectives and relating them clearly to specific types of scheme, rather than expecting one form of scheme to produce a generalized set of economic and social benefits. As we have seen in earlier chapters, this criticism can certainly be levelled at the Conservative government in the way it has sought to link its proposals for profit-related pay and its benefits to the (unproved) benefits of increased commitment and identification through share option or allocation schemes.

In similar vein, emphasizing the doubts about anticipated benefits, Blanchflower and Oswald (1987) use 1984 Workplace Industrial Relations Survey data to examine the relationship between forms of 'income sharing' (including both profit-sharing and share ownership schemes) and company financial performance. The evidence does not suggest, *ceteris paribus*, that establishments with profit-related pay do in fact achieve superior financial performance – a conclusion which applies both to individual types of scheme and to the generality of schemes. In the context of a discussion of the links between profit-sharing and participation Cable (1987: 184) has pointed to a further problem. Following through the Weitzman analysis, he concludes that policy-makers may face a choice 'between profit-sharing alone with increased employment, and profit-sharing-cum-participation with improved productivity, but without Weitzman-type employment effects'.

Nonetheless the Conservative government is pressing ahead with the introduction of PRP, and continued reform of the earlier Finance Act schemes is expected. It is unlikely to respond to proposals that executive schemes should be restricted to companies which also operate all-employee schemes. While the government has introduced legislation enabling PRP to be set up, it will not necessarily be able to achieve the establishment of a large number of schemes. Indeed, Blanchflower and Oswald (1986) have suggested that a likely scenario is that a large number of cash and incentive schemes (and our research clearly demonstrates there are many in existence) will be converted into tax-exempt schemes, at considerable cost but very little benefit to the public. It is questionable, however, how many genuine schemes will be established. The CBI is lukewarm on the issue, on the grounds that there is little evidence that employment-enhancing effects would follow, that bureaucratic regulation would be a problem, and above all that profit figures are by no means the best measure of performance on which to base a pay–performance relationship (CBI, 1986).

The TUC is also opposed. By directly influencing a proportion of employee pay PRP would impinge on trade union negotiating rights and could convert the 'bored hostility' shown on share schemes to 'active hostility'. Any widespread introduction of PRP by unilateral management action could strike at the very basis of trade union existence and therefore be opposed vigorously. Financial participation would move from the margins to the centre of industrial relations.

ADST and SAYE schemes, however, are likely to continue, with further minor modifications, because they have, on the one hand, all-party support, and on the other, no active trade union opposition. While they may continue, our evidence does not suggest that there will be a marked upsurge in the numbers of individuals participating or that attitudes towards their employers will change markedly as a result of participation. The motivation to participate is essentially based on personal financial considerations. The bull stock market of the mid-1980s has meant substantial financial gains for early participants, and the effect of these employees realizing their gains may encourage more colleagues to take up new options. The opportunistic basis of their motives, however, could mean the situation going into reverse. If the growth of the stock market were to reverse (as it did after October 1987), many small investors would have their fingers badly burnt. Personal financial considerations could lead to people opting out of schemes or at least not converting their savings into shares. There is evidence of such a tendency already from those companies which have not performed well while the stock market overall has risen.

One trend that may well gain in significance is the move to create ESOPs in Britain. This too has all-party support, but more crucially there is a source of finance through Unity Trust and the evidence of trade union support from the early pioneers. The Conservatives may well be encouraged to overcome some of the tax and other legislative barriers to their progress.

TOWARDS PEOPLE'S CAPITALISM?

There is one final context in which the developments in profit-sharing and employee share ownership must be placed: the extent to which they contribute to the creation of a 'people's capitalism'. While there is very little evidence that this is a dominant concern among employers, it is clearly part of Conservative philosophy and has shaped the push towards privatization, the extension of employee share schemes and the introduction of Personal Equity Plans. The government claims great success in this area, judged by a number of indicators – the growth in the number of Inland Revenue-approved schemes, the uptake of privatization share issues both by employees and by the general public, and the rise in the proportion of the UK population which owns shares (Moore, 1986). John Moore summed up the government's position:

> The number of shareholders in Britain has doubled in seven years. The sensations of share ownership are now known to about six million adults, and through them to their families. The mystique of share ownership is being diminished. The opportunities are growing. Employee share schemes are mushrooming. Further chances to buy into British industry will

be offered soon as the privatisation programme continues. Personal Equity Plans will soon begin. The momentum is very strong and the process irreversible. [1986: 10]

However, a closer examination of the situation reveals that the government's claims may be based on shaky foundations.

Figures on the extent of share ownership are derived from a Treasury/Stock Exchange survey conducted by National Opinion Poll in 1987 (Treasury, 1987). This showed that 19.5 per cent of the adult population owned shares, up from 7 per cent in 1979 and 12 per cent in 1985. The government's claims to success are based on these figures. The survey reveals that 3.5 million people (40 per cent of all shareholders) hold shares only in privatized companies or the Trustee Savings Bank and that 75 per cent of all shareholders hold shares in those companies. On the other hand, only 7 per cent of adults own shares quoted on the stock exchange, but do not own privatized shares or TSB shares. In other words there is a hard core of share owners, roughly similar to the 1979 figure, and the upsurge in the number of shareholders is based entirely on the privatization share issues and the growth in employee share schemes covering 1.5 million people. The Treasury survey findings are supported by a survey conducted by Dew Rogerson for the Observer.[2] This found that only 7 per cent of the population – 2.8 million people – owned shares in companies other than those which employed them, or British Gas, British Telecom, or the TSB. By contrast the number of individual shareholders in both ICI and Shell has declined since 1979.

That this may be regarded as a flimsy basis for claims of a 'very strong and irreversible momentum' can be shown in two ways. First, the evidence from our survey suggests that the number of shares in employee hands is very limited. In over half the cases less than 1 per cent of share capital was held by employees, and only in a handful of companies did employee shareholding exceed the 10 per cent limit imposed by the Investment Protection Committees. The very existence of this limit and the desire of institutional investors to protect their interests indicates that employee share owning is unlikely to lead to any serious degree of employee-shareholder control. Similarly, the much heralded uptake of employee share ownership in the privatized companies is not significant in control terms. At the time of flotation Amersham International employees owned 3.7 per cent of the equity, British Telecom employees 4.6 per cent, Associated British Ports

289

employees 4.3 per cent, but at Jaguar only 1.3 per cent. These proportions have also declined post-flotation.

The other aspect of such a large proportion of share holding being based on the narrow band of privatization issues is the question of how long people actually hold the shares, given the opportunities that have existed in nearly every case for a quick capital gain. The evidence is presented in Table 56. The *Observer* estimated that investors receiving the minimum allocation in each case could have made a profit of £1,800 on an outlay of £1,300, if they sold at the subsequent share-price peak, but only £180 if selling at the low points. Timing was therefore of the essence. The potential capital gain on offer through the privatization issues underlines the importance of financial motivations in a similar way to our findings on employee share schemes. That many new investors have taken the gain is evidenced by the decline in the number of shareholders after the flotation, the Amersham share register falling to one tenth of its size at flotation despite the continued buoyancy of the share price. The later share issues went through a similar pattern; a decline of 25 per cent in TSB in less than six months and a drop of over 1,250,000 in the case of British Gas, so that the public stake fell from 60 per cent to 28 per cent.

Even those first-time shareholders who hold on to their shares face problems. Narrow portfolios based on the privatized companies are increasingly unwelcome to stockbrokers. Post-Big Bang dealing costs have risen for small shareholders to a minimum to £15 or £20. Some stockbrokers have imposed a minimum share purchase of £1,000, and the Consumers' Association (1987) estimates that shares must rise 6 per cent to break even in dealing costs. The government's Personal Equity Plans have also come in for a great deal of criticism. This scheme was designed to entice new investors through tax reliefs, but the evidence suggests that PEPs are being used by existing investors to gain tax advantages. Progress with PEPs has been described as a 'damp squib'.[3]

The shift towards a 'home-owning, share-owning' democracy is more tentative than government commentators would have us believe. No doubt Conservative politicians will rest assured that 56 per cent of new shareowners voted Conservative in the 1987 general election, compared to only 18 per cent Labour. But evidence suggests that the enthusiasm for privatization issues, as indeed for employee share ownership, rests on 'greed for gold' rather than on political support for people's capitalism or commitment and loyalty to an employer. The relationship is based

Table 56 Privatization issues

Company	Date of privatization	Issue price	High/ low	No. of shareholders	No. of shareholders at floatation
Amersham	1982	142	392/186	6,600	63,800
Associated British Ports	1983	112	625/129	n.a.	n.a.
British Aerospace	1981	150	608/170	130,000	260,000
British Telecom	1984	130	278/180	1·6 million	2·1 million
Britoil	1982	215	208/160	245,500	452,000
Cable & Wireless	1981	168	369/284	211,000	218,500
Enterprise Oil	1984	185	154/128	14,200	13,700
Jaguar	1984	165	578/171	43,000	125,000

Notes

1 Figures for BT may exclude the joint holders and employees in the employee share scheme.

2 High/low share prices from first dealings to 30 September 1986.

3 Issue prices are fully paid. The following sold further tranches: Associated British Ports (270p, 1983), British Aerospace (375p, 1985), Britoil (185p, 1985), Cable & Wireless (275p, 1983, and 587p, 1985).

Source: *Observer*, 26 October 1986, based on Treasury figures.

on a cash nexus, and in the context of a bull stock market it is no surprise that most new small investors did well. But stock markets are capable of collapsing, and if the relationships are as fragile as we suggest, then large numbers of disgruntled small investors may take revenge on those they hold responsible for their sudden misfortune. There is evidence that this has happened in France, where the Chirac government's privatization programme was hit by a fall in the stock market in June 1987. Further falls were forecast, putting into some doubt Chirac's ability to win the 1988 presidential election. The French case reveals that the momentum can be broken and that the process is reversible. The direction in which the British experience will move during the next few years is not clear, but the foundations of people's capitalism are built on shifting ground. Many of the claims made for the 'home-owning, share-owning democracy' and for the benefits of employee share ownership and profit-sharing are at best unproven, and certainly not to be taken as irreversible.

NOTES

1. It is precisely these *changes* which we would expect managements to be concerned with in their evaluation of schemes, but, as we have seen, there is little sign of systematic measurement and evaluation.

2. *Observer*, 18 January 1987.

3. ibid., 1 February 1987.

Appendix 1

Inland Revenue-approved profit-sharing and employee share option schemes

While the following is designed to be helpful, it should not be taken as an authoritative statement of the law. The details given here were applicable at the time of the research but have been amended by the Finance Act, 1988. The Inland Revenue produce a guidance booklet on each type of scheme and these should be consulted.

1 APPROVED DEFERRED SHARE TRUST SCHEMES

Legislative background

Finance Act, 1978 (as amended 1980, 1983, 1985, 1986).

How they work

Any company wishing to establish an ADST scheme must first establish trustees of the scheme. The company allocates a portion of its profits each year to the trustees to acquire ordinary shares, either by purchase in the market or by subscription. Companies usually have a trigger point below which no allocation is made. The trustees appropriate the shares to each participating individual, who is expected not to sell, assign, charge, or otherwise dispose of his/her shares for at least two years from the date of appropriation.

Eligibility

All full-time (over twenty-five hours per week) employees with five or more years' service must be eligible to participate. The company may invite those with less service and part-time employees to participate by writing this into the scheme's rules.

Basis of share allocation

The appropriation of shares must be on 'similar terms'. This means that a common criterion for the calculations of each participant's profit share must be established. This could be based on, say, length of service or level of pay, equally to all employees. The Inland Revenue must approve the formula. However, there is a statutory maximum annual limit of £1,250 or 10 per cent of pay, whichever is the higher, and an overall ceiling of £5,000. These limits are subject to periodic review.

Retention period

Although the shares are appropriated to each individual participant, they cannot be taken into his/her own hands unless they have been held for a minimum of two years. During this period the trustees are the legal shareholders and are entered into the members' register as such.

Taxation situation

The company

Profit set aside for a share scheme qualifies for corporation tax relief. This covers the reasonable expenses of running the scheme as well as the cost of buying the shares. If new shares are issued the effect of the scheme is to involve the company in an immediate cash drain liability; if existing shares are bought by the trustees the existing shareholders are bought out with company money on a tax-allowable basis.

The participant

No income tax on the value of the shares is payable at the time of appropriation. Provided the participant retains the shares for five years there are no income-tax liabilities on disposal. Shares sold between the end of the two-year retention period and the five-year limit are subject to PAYE on the following basis. Taxation is calculated upon the value of the shares at the time of appropriation (or the current value if less). Shares sold in the third and fourth year after appropriation are subject to income tax on 100 per cent of their value, in the fifth year at 75 per cent of their value, and thereafter are not subject to income tax. Capital gains following a sale of shares acquired through a scheme are subject to capital gains tax in the normal way. As the capital gains exemption limit (£6,600 in 1987/1988) applies, most participants would not pay any tax.

Leavers

If participants lose their jobs because of injury, disability, or redundancy, or if they reach State pensionable age, their shares may be sold immediately, no matter how long they have been held. No income tax is payable, even if the shares have been held for less than five years. Similar rules apply in the event of the participant's death. However, if employees leave for any other reason the shares cannot be sold until they have been held for two years.

Dividends

Participants receive dividends even during the two-year retention period. Basic-rate income tax is deducted from these at source, but the full tax liability depends on the participant's total income.

Voting rights

The company can make its own arrangements about voting rights attached to the shares issued. If the shares carry voting rights employee shareholders can attend and vote at members' meetings, but while the shares are still held in trust it is the trustees who exercise the voting rights. The scheme members can, however, instruct the trustees on how to vote.

Types of scheme:

(a)*Shares only*. All eligible employees receive shares without any alternative offer of cash.

(b)*Cash/shares choice*. All eligible employees are offered shares, but the company may at its discretion offer a cash bonus instead to those who decline shares.

(c)*Matching offer*. The company offers shares only to those eligible employees who also purchase shares on their own behalf. Usually this is on a one-for-one basis but it could be more.

2 SAVE AS YOU EARN SHARE OPTION SCHEMES

Legislative background

Finance Act, 1980 (as amended 1982, 1987).

How they work

The company grants participating employees options over shares and they embark on a five or seven-year savings contract involving monthly payments deducted from pay to a recognized savings institution to accumulate the capital to buy the shares. The share price is fixed at the date of granting the option (usually market value less a discount of up to 10 per cent). Once the contract has begun, the sum may not be altered, and may not be less than £10, or more that £100, a month. At the end of the five-year savings period a bonus equivalent to fourteen further monthly savings instalments is added to the sum saved. The participant can at this stage opt to leave the money in the SAYE account without additional contributions for another two years, when a further bonus equivalent to fourteen monthly savings instalments is added.

Participants should decide at the outset whether they are entering a five or a seven-year savings contract.

If a small number of payments have been missed, a period of six months' grace may be allowed at the end of the savings period for the participant to make up the missing sum and retain all bonus and option rights.

At the end of whichever savings contract has been entered into the participant may either withdraw the cash saved or use it to exercise the option in full or in part. Obviously if the market price of the shares is then above the option price the participant is extremely likely to exercise the option, but to take the cash if the share price has fallen.

Eligibility

All full-time (over twenty-five hours per week) employees with five or more years' service must be eligible to participate. The company may invite those with less service and part-time employees to participate by writing this into the scheme's rules. Once the eligibility criteria are met, the decision to participate is an individual one.

Basis of share allocation

All employees within a scheme must take part on similar terms.

Taxation situation

The company

There are no special tax advantages from this scheme.

The participant

Savings are from post-tax earnings but participants do not have to pay income tax on any bonus and any interest received under the SAYE contract; on any benefit they get from being able to buy shares at favourable prices; or on any increase in the value of the shares between the date the options were given and the date on which they were exercised. If, after exercising an option, the participant sells some or all of the shares at a profit, then he or she will be liable to pay capital gains tax. However, as the capital gains tax exemption limit (£6,600 in 1987/88) applies, most participants will not pay any tax.

Leavers

If participants lose their jobs because of injury, disability, or redundancy, or if they reach State pensionable age, or retire at any other age under the terms of their employment, they have six months to make a choice. They can keep the cash saved plus interest due, or buy shares to the extent that this sum will allow. They may not supplement the sum due to buy more shares through the option scheme. In the event of a participant's death, whoever is legally responsible for his/her affairs has twelve months to make the same choice.

Participants leaving for any other reason may, if permitted in the scheme rules, be allowed to exercise their option provided they have participated for at least three years. Leavers may be allowed to continue to pay SAYE contributions but will not be able to buy any shares when their contract matures.

Termination of the contract

Participants still in employment with the company who wish to terminate the savings contract may do so subject to the following rules:

(a) *Termination after less than one year*: money repaid but with no interest or bonus.
(b) *Termination between one and five years*: money repaid with interest at 8 per cent per annum, but no bonus.
(c) *Termination between five and seven years*: money repaid with a bonus equivalent to fourteen monthly instalments, plus interest at 8 per cent per annum on this total amount for the period over and above five years.

Dividends

The shares on which options are granted must be part of the ordinary share capital of the company establishing the scheme or of its parent company. The shares must have the same rights to dividends and bonus issues as ordinary shares. However, dividends are not paid until participants have actually bought the shares.

Voting rights

These are not exercisable until participants have actually bought the shares.

Take-overs

In the event of a take-over, company reconstruction, or voluntary winding up, participants may exercise their options (to the extent of their SAYE credits at the relevant date) within six months thereafter. If this happens within three years of signing the contract, the gain is chargeable to income tax. From 1987 it is possible for participants to exchange their existing share options for options over shares in the acquiring company.

3 DISCRETIONARY (OR EXECUTIVE) SHARE OPTION SCHEMES

Legislative background

Finance Act, 1984 (as amended 1987).

How they work

The board of the company invites employees, at its discretion, to participate in the scheme. The discretion is usually exercised only in favour of senior executives and full-time directors, but it is possible to extend it to all employees.

Selected employees are granted an option to acquire shares in the company at a price fixed at the date the option is granted. The option price must not be manifestly less than the market value of the shares at the date of granting the option. In the case of unlisted (including USM) companies the price has to be determined in agreement with the Inland Revenue. To quality for tax relief the option must be exercised between three and ten years after the date of grant. Participants have to finance the exercise of the options themselves, and may have to pay a nominal sum for the grant of the option.

299

Eligibility

Participation in the scheme is at the discretion of the board of directors of the company. Participants must be full time (twenty-five or more hours per week for directors, and twenty hours or more for employees). No person may participate who has, or within the preceding twelve months had, a material interest (defined as 10 per cent of the share capital) in the company granting the option if it is a close company.

Basis of share allocation

No option may be granted to a person under the scheme if the aggregate amount payable to exercise all the options under the scheme which he/she then holds would exceed £100,000 or four times his/her Case 1 Schedule E earnings, whichever is the greater. Companies may, subject to Inland Revenue approval, introduce performance criteria to trigger the exercise of the option.

Taxation situation

The company

There are no special tax advantages from this scheme.

The participant

There is no taxation liability on the grant of the options. When exercised options are sold, the difference between the sale price and the option price is taxed under capital gains tax, not income tax. The capital gains tax exemption limit (£6,600 in 1987/88) applies. For top-rate taxpayers remuneration through a discretionary share option scheme is therefore taxed (after deducting the exemption) at 30 per cent, not 60 per cent (1987/88 rates).

To quality for relief from income tax the option must be exercised between three and ten years of the date of grant, and there must be an interval of three years between exercises. Options can be exercised outwith these periods but would not qualify for tax relief.

Leavers

In the event of the participant's death, whoever is legally responsible for his/her affairs has twelve months (as long as this does not take the period from date of grant beyond ten years) to exercise the option free of income tax, regardless of whether three years have elapsed since the date of granting the option or since the date of last exercise of an option with tax relief. Participants losing their posts may be permitted to exercise their options but this is at the discretion of the company. It would usually be granted in cases of retirement, redundancy, and disablement, but not necessarily in cases of dismissal or resignation. Companies are able to exercise a great deal of discretion in these decisions.

Dividends

The shares on which options are granted must be fully paid-up and not redeemable shares, not subject to special restrictions, forming part of the ordinary share capital of the employing company or a company which has control over it. Dividends are not paid until participants have actually bought the shares.

Voting rights

These are not exercisable until participants have actually bought the shares.

Take-overs

In the event of a take-over, company reconstruction, or voluntary winding up, participants may exercise their options within six months. From 1987 it is possible for participants to exchange their existing share options for options over shares in the acquiring company.

4 STOCK EXCHANGE AND INVESTMENT PROTECTION COMMITTEE GUIDELINES

In addition to seeking approval from the Inland Revenue as outlined above, companies must also meet the requirements of the stock exchange and of the Investment Protection Committees of the National Association of Pension Funds Ltd (NAPF) and the British Insurance Association (BIA). The main points of these are detailed here.

Stock exchange

Quoted companies must have their schemes approved by a general meeting which must be told, *inter alia*, who is entitled to participate, the total number of shares subject to the scheme, the percentage of issued share capital this represents, and the minimum entitlement for any one participant.

Investment Protection Committees' guidelines

With ADST schemes the upper limit on the allocation of profit is 5 per cent of UK profits per annum. In any year no more than 1 per cent of the issued ordinary share capital may be subscribed for a profit-sharing scheme. The price at which shares are subscribed should be the middle market price of the shares on the dealing day prior to the appropriation of profits. In companies operating both ADST and share option schemes the 1 per cent rate applies to both schemes, but the 1 per cent limit may be 'gathered up' over a three-year period so that in any one year up to 3 per cent could be placed under option provided that the total number of options granted over a three-year period containing the year in question did not exceed 3 per cent. This applies only to option schemes: the 1 per cent rule cannot be varied for profit-sharing schemes. Thus in a company with both and ADST and an option scheme which placed 3 per cent of issued share capital under option in any one year, the trustees of the ADST scheme would have to use money allocated to them to buy shares in the market for that year and the following two.

Overall, the limit for the granting of options and the issue of new shares under any combination of schemes which includes a profit-sharing scheme is 10 per cent of the issued share capital over a ten-year period. Additionally, in the case of option schemes under the Finance Act, 1984, and unapproved schemes, no more than 5 per cent issued ordinary shares may be made available to restricted groups of employees, in aggregate, over a ten-year period. No one within two years of his/her normal retirement date should be granted an option. The option price should not be less than the middle market price at the time of the grant.

NAPF require that the documentation asking shareholders' approval should include a statement that 'The following proposals conform to the broad guidelines issued by the NAPF in November 1984' or state why not.

Appendix 2

Methodology

THE SAMPLE

A sample size of 1,000 companies stratified by industry sector and size was regarded as the minimum number necessary to obtain a coverage which was representative, reliable, and possible to administer. The 1981 Census of Production and the September 1984 Department of Employment SIC classifications were used to ensure that an adequate sample was constructed. Northern Ireland was included in spite of the lack of reliable statistics (the 1981 and 1984 figures do not include Northern Ireland), as it was felt that, as a region, it was too important to exclude. The final sample, stratified in terms of SIC, was as in Table 57.

The final pattern of responses, controlling for size and SIC, is shown in Table 58. This response pattern is roughly proportionate to the original sample and can be taken as reasonably representative of the total company population by employment. However, our final figures were skewed towards large companies in terms of numbers of establishments and away from larger companies in terms of volume of employment. This may influence our data where schemes do not occur evenly across industries and sizes of company (as in the case of Inland Revenue-approved schemes).

THE QUESTIONNAIRE

The questionnaire was designed to be completed by either personnel or finance departments. The information requested included details of size, ownership, employee profile, industrial relations and employee participation background, as well as details

Table 57 Final sample stratified by size and industrial sector (SIC)

SIC division	% employment UK September	No. of companies in sample	% sample
0 Agriculture, forest, fisheries	–	–	0
1 Energy and water supply (modified)	0·54	5	0·5
2 Extractive industries, metal manufacturing, chemicals, etc.	5·64	56	5·6
3 Engineering, metal goods, vehicles	18·29	183	18·3
4 Other manufacturing	15·04	151	15·1
5 Construction	7·02	70	7
6 Distribution, catering, repairs	30·54	305	30·5
7 Transport and communications (modified)	5·09	51	5·1
8 Banking, insurance, finance	13·42	134	13·4
9 Other services (modified)	4·44	45	4·5
Total	100	1000	100

of profit-sharing and employee share ownership schemes, their introduction, recognized aims and objectives, degree of success, and details of any failed or aborted schemes. Companies were also asked to forward company reports and any publicity materials or documents relating to their schemes. Copies of the questionnaire are available on request from the Department of Social and Economic Research University of Glasgow, Glasgow G12 8QQ.

Table 58 Respondents, stratified by size and industrial sector (SIC)

| | Size (by employment) | | | | | | | Total | |
SIC division	20–50	50–99	100–199	200–499	500–999	1,000–4,999	Over 5,000	No.	%
1 Energy			1	1	1	2	2	3	0·8
2 Extractive industries			1	4	2	9	10	26	7·3
3 Engineering, etc.	1	5	3	4	5	16	18	52	14·6
4 Other manufacturing	2	9	5	6	9	10	14	55	15·4
5 Construction	5	3	6	6	5	5		30	8·4
6 Distribution	27	30	14	11	9	5	4	100	28·1
7 Transport	4	7	4	3	2	1		21	5·9
8 Banking, etc.	9	11	3	12	2	9	2	48	13·5
9 Other services	2	2	3	8	4	1	1	21	5·9
Total (No.)	14	19	11	15	11	16	14	100	

References

Baddon, L., Hunter, L., Hyman, J., Leopold, J., and Ramsay, H. (1987) *Developments in Profit Sharing and Employee Share Ownership; Survey Report*, Glasgow University: CRIDP.

Bate, S. P., and Murphy, A. J. (1981) 'Can joint consultation become employee participation?', *Journal of Management Studies* 18 (4), 389–409.

Bell, D. W., and Hanson, C. G. (1984) *Profit Sharing and Employee Share-holding Attitude Survey*, London: Industrial Participation Association.

Benn, A. W. (1979) *Arguments for Socialism*, London: Penguin.

Blanchflower, D., and Oswald, A. J. (1986) *Profit Sharing – Can it Work?* LSE Discussion Paper 255, London: London School of Economics.

Blanchflower, D., and Oswald, A. J. (1987) *Profit Related Pay: Prose Discovered?* LSE Discussion Paper 287, London: LSE.

Blasi, J., Mehvling, P., and Whyte, W. F. (1983) 'The politics of worker ownership in the US', in Crouch, C. and Heller, F. (eds), *International Yearbook of Organizational Democracy*, I, New York: Wiley.

Brannen, P., (1983) *Authority and Participation in Industry*, London: Batsford.

Bristow, E. (1974) 'Profit-sharing, socialism and labour unrest', in K. D. Brown, (ed.) *Essays in Anti-labour History*, London: Macmillan.

Cable, J. (1987) 'Employee participation and Enterprise Performance: an Economic Analysis', (unpublished Ph.D. thesis, University of Warwick).

Confederation of British Industry (1986) *Response to the Green Paper on Profit Related Pay*, London: CBI.

Child, J. (1985) 'Managerial strategies, new technology and the labour process', in D. Knights *et al.*, *Job Redesign*, 107–41, Aldershot: Gower.

Church, R. A. (1971) 'Profit-sharing and labour relations in England in the nineteenth century', *International Review of Social History*, XVI, Part 1.

Cmnd 522 (1920) *Report on Profit Sharing and Labour Co-partnership in the United Kingdom*, London: HMSO.

Consumers' Association (1987) *Buying, Selling, and Owning Shares: an Action Kit from Which?*, Hertford: Consumers' Association.

Copeman, G., Moore, P., and Arrowsmith, C. (1984) *Shared Ownership*, Aldershot: Gower.

Copeman, G. (1986) *Employee Share Schemes*, London: Wider Share Ownership Council.

Creigh, S., Donaldson, N., and Hawthorn, E., (1981) 'A stake in the firm: employee financial involvement in Britain', *Employment Gazette*, May, 229–36.

——(1982) 'Sharing the incentive', *Employment Gazette*, April, 155–60.

307

Cressey, P., Eldridge, J., MacInnes, J., and Norris, G. (1981) *Industrial Democracy and Participation: a Scottish Survey*, Department of Employment Research Paper No. 28, London: HMSO.

Cressey, P., Eldridge, J., and MacInnes, J. (1985) *Just Managing*, Milton Keynes: Open University Press.

Daniel, W. W. and Millward, N. (1983) *Workplace Industrial Relations in Britain: the DE/PSI/SSRC Survey*, London: Heinemann.

Deaton, D. (1985) 'Management style and large scale survey evidence', *Industrial Relations Journal* 16 (2), summer, 67–71.

Dowling, M. J., Goodman, J. F. B., Gotting, D. A., and Hyman, J. D. (1981) *Employee Participation: Practice and Attitudes in North West Manufacturing Industry*, Department of Employment Research Paper No. 27, London: HMSO.

Elliott, J. (1984) *Conflict or Co-operation? The Growth of Industrial Democracy*, second edition, London: Kogan Page.

Espinosa, J. G., and Zimbalist, A. S. (1978) *Economic Democracy: Workers Participation in Chilean Industry 1970–73*, New York: Academic Press.

Estrin, S. and Wilson, N. (1986) *The Micro-economic Effects of Profit-sharing: the British Experience*, Centre for Labour Economics Discussion Paper, London: London School of Economics.

Farrow, N. (1964) 'The John Lewis Partnership', *Business*, September; reprinted in P. Derrick and J. F. Phipps (eds), *Co-ownership, Co-operation and Control*, London: Longman.

Freeman, R. and Weitzman, M. (1986) 'Bonuses and Employment in Japan', National Bureau of Economic Research, Working Paper No. 1878.

Fitzroy, F. and Kraft, K. (1986) 'Profitability and profit-sharing', *Journal of Industrial Economics* 35 (2), December, 113-30.

——(1987) 'Co-operation, productivity and profit-sharing', *Quarterly Journal of Economics* V11 (1) February.

Fox, A. (1974) *Beyond Contract: Work, Power and Trust Relations*, London: Faber.

Gospel, H., and Littler,C. (eds) (1983) *Managerial Strategies and Industrial Relations: an Historical and Comparative Study*, London: Heinemann.

George, M., and Levie, H. (1984) *Japanese Competition and the British Workplace*, London: CAITS, Polytechnic of North London;

Gummer, J. S. (1984) 'Participation, industrial relations and the law', *Topics*, July.

Hanson, C. G. (1965) 'Profit-sharing schemes in Great Britain', *Journal of Management Studies*, Vol, 2 (3), October.

Hattersley, R. (1985a) 'The "third sector": expanding co- operatives and employee share ownership', speech to Institute of Personnel Management Conference, Harrogate.

Hattersley, R. (1985b) 'Economic democracy', Speech to Crosland Society, Oxford.

Hattersley, R. (1986) 'Profit sharing', speech to Savoy Monday Luncheon Club, London.

Hattersley, R. (1987) *Choose Freedom: the Future for Democratic Socialism*, Harmondsworth: Penguin.

Heller, R. (1984) *Shares for Employees*, London: Esmée Fairbairn Charitable Trust.

Howell, D. (1977) *Personal Capital Building and Wider Participation in the Creation of Wealth*, London: Conservative Political Centre.

Hyman, J., and Schuller, T. (1984) 'Occupational pension schemes and collective bargaining', *B.J.I.R.* XXII (3).

Industrial Participation, winter 1985/6, No. 589, 17–25.

Industrial Relations Review and Report (1987) 'Cash-based profit sharing', *Industrial Relations Review and Report*, No. 386, 17 February, 5–13.

Incomes Data Services Ltd, Study 306 (1984) *Profit Sharing and Share Options*, London: Incomes Data Services Ltd.

——Top Pay Unit (1985) *Executive Share Options*, London: Incomes Data Services Ltd.

——Study 357 (1986) *Profit Sharing and Share Options*, London: Incomes Data Services Ltd.

Inland Revenue (1978) *Approved Profit Sharing Schemes*, Booklet IR36, London: Board of Inland Revenue.

——(1980) *Approved Savings-Related Share Option Schemes*, Booklet IR39, London: Board of Inland Revenue.

——(1984) *Finance Act, 1984, Approved Share Option Schemes*, Explanatory Notes, London: Board of Inland Revenue.

Klein, K., and Rosen, C. (1986) 'Employee stock ownership in the United States', in R. N. Stern and S. McCarthy (eds) *International Yearbook of Organizational Democracy*, New York: Wiley, 387–406.

Knights, D., Wilmott, H., and Collinson, D. (eds) (1985) *Job Redesign*, Aldershot: Gower.

Labour Party (1973) *Capital and Equality*, London: Labour Party.

——(1986) *Social Ownership – a Vision for the 1990s*, London: Labour Party.

Labour Research Department (1986) 'Profit-linked pay – who gains, who loses?', *Labour Research*, October.

Landon, M. (1985) *Employee Share Schemes*, London: Copeman Paterson.

Liberal Party (1928) *The Liberal Yellow Book – Britain's Industrial Future*, London: Liberal Party.

Marchington, M., and Armstrong, R. (1981) 'A case for consultation', *Employee Relations*, 3 (1), 10–16.

——(1983) 'Shop steward organisation and joint consultation', *Employee Relations*, 12 (1), 24–31.

——(1986) 'The nature of the new joint consultation', *Industrial Relations Journal*, 17 (2), summer, 158–70.

Marsh, T., and McAllister, D. (1981) 'ESOPs fables: a survey of companies with employee stock ownership plans', *Journal of Corporation Law*, 6: 3.

Meade, J. (1986) *Different Forms of Share Economy*, London: Public Policy Centre.

Meenan, F. (1986) 'Profit-sharing', *Gazette of the Incorporated Law*

309

Society of Ireland, July–August.

Meidner, R. (1978) *Employee Investment Funds: an Approach to Collective Capital Formation*, London: Allen & Unwin.

Millward, N., and Stevens, M. (1986) *British Workplace Industrial Relations, 1980–84*, Aldershot: Gower.

Minns, R., (1980) *Pension Funds and British Capitalism*, London: Heinemann.

Moore, J. (1986) *The Value of Ownership*, London: Conservative Political Centre.

Morse, G., and Williams, D. (1979) *Profit Sharing: Legal Aspects of Employee Share Schemes*, London: Sweet & Maxwell.

Owen, D. (1985) *Ownership: the Way Forward*, London: Social Democratic Party.

Partnership Research (1987) *Employee Stock Ownership Plans in the United States*, London: Partnership Research.

Pollard, S., and Turner, R. (1976) 'Profit-sharing and autocracy', *Business History* XVIII (1), January.

Poole, M. (1987) 'Who are the profit sharers?' *Personnel Management*, January, 34–6.

Purcell, J., and Sissons, K. (1983) 'Strategies and practice in the management of industrial relations', in G. S. Bain (ed.), *Industrial Relations in Britain*, Oxford: Blackwell, pp.95–120.

Purcell, J., and Gray, A. (1986) 'Corporate personnel departments and the management of industrial relations: two case studies in ambiguity', *Journal of Management Studies*, March.

Ramsay, H. (1977) 'Cycles of control', *Sociology* 11 (3).

Ramsay, H., Leopold, J. and Hyman, J. (1986) 'Profit-sharing and employee share ownership: an initial assessment', *Employee Relations* 8 (1).

Rose, M., and Jones, B. (1985) 'Managerial strategy and trade union responses in work reorganisation schemes at establishment level', in D. Knights *et al.* (eds) *Job Redesign*, New York: Basic Books, pp. 81–106.

Rosen, C. (1984) 'Employee ownership gaining popularity in the United States', appendix to D. W. Bell and C. G. Hanson *Profit Sharing and Employee Share-holding Attitude Survey*, London: IPA, 247–52.

Rosen, C., and Klein, K. (1983) 'Job-creating performance of employee-owned firms', *Monthly Labor Review*, 106, August, 15–19.

Scottish Liberal Party (1983) *Proposals for Industrial Reform*, Edinburgh: Scottish Liberal Party.

Schuller, T. (1985) *Democracy at Work*, Oxford: Oxford University Press.

Smith, G. R. (1986) 'Profit-sharing and employee share ownership in Britain', *Employment Gazette* 94 (8) September, 380–5.

Social Democratic Party (1982) *Industrial Relations 1: Industrial Democracy*, London: SDP.

——(1985) *Wider Share Ownership: Equality and Opportunity in an Enterprise Economy*, London: SDP.

Steel, D. (1986) *Sharing Profits*, Hebden Bridge: Unservile State Group.

Tannenbaum, A. S., Cooke, H., and Lahmann, J. (1984) *The Relationship of Employee Ownership to the Technological Adaptiveness and Performance of Companies*, Ann Arbor: Survey Research Center, Institute for Survey Research, University of Michigan.

Thatcher, M. (1986) 'Profit-sharing and share options', *IDS Study*, 357, March.

Thomas, D. (1986) 'Labour's smooth operators', *New Socialist*, October.

Thurley, K. (1984) 'Comparative studies of industrial democracy in an organizational perspective', in B. Wilpert and A. Sorge (eds), *International Yearbook of Organizational Democracy*, II *International Perspectives on Organizational Democracy*, Chichester: Wiley.

Thurley, K., and Wood, S. (1983) 'Business strategy and industrial relations strategy', in K. Thurley and S. Wood (eds) *Industrial Relations and Management Strategy*, Cambridge: Cambridge University Press, pp.197–224.

Trades Union Congress (1974) *Industrial Democracy*, London: TUC.

——(1986a) *Annual Report*, London: TUC.

——(1986b) *Profit Related Pay: the TUC's Response to the Green Paper*, London: TUC.

H. M. Treasury (1987) *Economic Progress Report*, No. 189, March–April.

Wadhwani, (1985) 'The Macro-economic Implications of Profit-sharing: some Empirical Evidence', Discussion Paper No. 220, London: Centre for Labour Economics, London School of Economics.

Wagner, I. (1984) *Report to the New York Stock Exchange on the Performance of Publicly held Employee Ownership Companies*, Arlington, Va.: National Center for Employee Ownership.

Weitzman, M. L. (1983) 'Some macro-economic implications of alternative compensation schemes', *Economic Journal* 93 (4), December.

——(1984) *The Share Economy*, Cambridge, Mass.: Harvard University Press.

——(1985) 'The simple macro-economics of profit-sharing', *American Economic Review* 75, 937–53.

Wider Share Ownership Council (1986) *Employee Share Schemes*, London: Wider Share Ownership Council.

Williams, D. F. (1985) *Share Schemes for Directors and Employees*, London: Butterworth.

Wright, M., and Coyne, J. (1985) *Management buy-outs*, London: Croom Helm.

311

Index

Printed in the United States
by Baker & Taylor Publisher Services